FEARLESS FUNNYMEN
THE HISTORY OF
THE RODEO CLOWN

Fearless Funnymen

THE HISTORY OF

The RODEO CLOWN

By

GAIL HUGHBANKS WOERNER

Illustrated By GAIL GANDOLFI

EAKIN PRESS ★ Austin, Texas

Published in the United States of America
By Eakin Press
A Division of Sunbelt Media, Inc.
P.O. Box 90159
Austin, TX 78709
email: eakinpub@sig.net

2 3 4 5 6 7 8 9

First Printing
Paperback Version

1-57168-282-1

Library of Congress Catologing-in-Publication Data

Woerner, Gail Hughbanks, 1936-
    Fearless funnymen : the history of the rodeo clown / by Gail Hughbanks Woerner :
illustrated by Gail Gandolfi.
    p.   cm.
    Includes bibliographical references (p.   ) and index.
    ISBN 1-57168-282-1
    1. Rodeo clowns--United States--History. 2. Rodeos--United States--History.
I. Title
GV1834.5.W65   1993
791.8'4--dc20   92-45066
                                                                CIP

Dedicated to the "old men" in my life.

You know who you are.

Contents

Preface

Growing up on the plains of northeastern Colorado in the 1940s and 1950s, I had the opportunity to live on a working ranch. My family raised cattle and farmed wheat. I had the good fortune to grow up with my parents *and* my paternal grandparents. Both families had homes just a few steps apart on the ranch. My grandfather and my dad were partners in all aspects of the ranch life.

As a girl I would sit and listen to the wonderful stories my grandmother told of earlier days—homesteading days. I spent many hours with my grandfather on horseback. We herded cattle, weaned calves, and brought them in for branding, shots, and all sorts of things necessary to their well-being.

I do not remember learning to ride a horse. I always knew how. My grandfather also taught me to break and train colts to ride and perform. He was continually entering me in local horse shows where I competed in kid classes. My grandfather and I also attended horse sales, cattle sales, and rodeos. Much of the time I spent listening to my grandfather visit with other old-time cowboys. I loved it and never tired of hearing the wonderful accounts of early life on the range.

I enjoyed rodeos better than any football game—probably because I understood rodeo rules better than I did the rules of football. Two special occasions each year were the National Western Stock Show and Rodeo in Denver in January, and Cheyenne Frontier Days in July. I looked forward to both events. I recognized most competing cowboys by name. Cy Taillon announced both events, and his voice was the voice of rodeo to me. I laughed and enjoyed the hilarity of the rodeo clowns. No matter how many times I saw their acts, their humor never got old to me.

A few years ago, as a member of the Texas Longhorn Breeders

Association of America, I was co-chairperson of the national convention held in Austin, Texas. We organized a ranch rodeo for the entertainment of our members and for various Texas Longhorn ranches that were to be represented by teams of cowboys. In addition to some 600 conventioneers, we invited over a thousand underprivileged children from the Austin area to come and enjoy the rodeo.

George Doak, retired rodeo clown, was also a member of the association. I asked him if he would put his make-up on again, don his baggy clown pants, and entertain the children at the ranch rodeo. In fact, I told him I would be his protégé and dress up in a rodeo clown costume. He said, "It's a deal."

George got two other retired rodeo clowns, Jack Long of San Antonio and Bo Damuth of Magnolia, Texas, to perform at the rodeo. George helped me with a clown face, loaned me a pair of oversized Wrangler britches, and I joined the three real rodeo clowns in the stands to welcome and entertain the children.

I had so much fun. Joking and playing with the audience left me totally exhilarated. I was fascinated with the transformation that took place while wearing the costume and clowning around. My enthusiasm spilled over into a series of questions directed to George and Jack about their rodeo clown careers.

Later, I searched libraries, book stores, used-book stores, and book and paper shows for books written on the history of rodeo and rodeo clowns. I found nothing on the history of rodeo clowns, and there were few books about the history of rodeo.

When I told George I wanted to write a book on the history of rodeo clowns, he was excited. He directed me to others and turned over all the old rodeo magazines, books, and memorabilia he had available.

Jack Long not only is a former rodeo clown, he is also a rodeo historian and a great source of information. Jack was given boxes of mementos belonging to Foghorn Clancy (one of the earliest rodeo announcers and rodeo promoters), and he allowed me to dig through those as well as stacks and stacks of *Hoofs & Horns* magazines and old *Rodeo Sports News*. Jack also spent many hours relating stories to me about early cowboys and the early days of rodeo. Another good friend, Bob McKenzie of Iliff, Colorado, also let me examine his collection of *Hoofs & Horns,* from which I gathered facts for this project.

Greg Tuza, of the Wrangler Bullfight Program, met with me in Cheyenne, during the 1987 Frontier Days, and he explained how the Wrangler Bullfight Tour evolved. He introduced me to competing bullfighters and judges, who were kind enough to give me much of their time for interviews.

I attended the Pro Rodeo Cowboy Association convention in Las Vegas in 1987, as an associate member. I talked with PRCA members of long standing, such as Montie Montana and J. W. Stoker. I also attended the rodeo clown annual meeting at the convention, conducted by spokesperson and board member Jerry Wayne Olson. Near the end of the meeting I announced my plans to write this book. I was overwhelmed with the response I was given from the seventy-five rodeo clowns in attendance. Many gave me their media packages, which they take to the convention to promote their abilities and gain jobs for the upcoming year.

I joined the Rodeo Historical Society and attended their activities held each year during the National Finals in Las Vegas. Through this organization I've met many of the rodeo greats of past years, such as Charley and Imogene Beals, Buster and June Ivory, Harry Tompkins, Bobby and Phyllis Clark, Gene and Nita Clark, Larry McKinney, Tad Lucas, Mitzi Riley, Kajun Kid, Jimmy and Alice Schumacher, Alice, Marge and Turk Greenough, to name just a few. They have all talked with me at length and shared many memories about the early days.

As a member of the Texas Special Olympics Board of Directors, I have asked retired rodeo clowns Junior Meek, Wright Howington, Jon Temple, Duane Stephens, George Doak, Clark Shultz, and current rodeo clown Allan Nelson to volunteer their time and participate at the Texas Special Olympics Summer Games for the last several years. They each autograph and hand out thousands of photographs to visiting Special Olympians.

I attended the Cowboy Clown Reunion in 1989 in Roseburg, Oregon. Mac and Katy Barry, chairmen, introduced me to seventeen retired rodeo clowns and their families and friends. We not only shared four laugh-filled days of fun, they answered my never-ending questions.

In August 1991, I attended my second Cowboy Clown Reunion in Moses Lake, Washington, hosted by Jack Saulls and the Rodeo Committee of Moses Lake. Twelve rodeo clowns and their families were in attendance. Five days of entertaining and being entertained by these wonderful funnymen of today and yesterday gave me an even deeper insight into their innate ability to be witty and clever—continually. In November of that year I attended the National Old Timer Rodeo Association Finals in Reno, Nevada. They honored the Old Timer Rodeo Clowns and introduced those attending at each performance. The rodeo clowns visited local schools, signed autographs, and visited with fans from early morning until late in the evening.

Every year Junior and Ann Meek invite me to their annual Super Bowl party, where I can be assured of cornering at least seventy-five of rodeo's past and present performers and family members. They have so much to share.

As a result of my research for this book, I have been asked to submit articles for the *Ketch Pen*, a magazine sponsored by the Rodeo Historical Society. Willard Porter, longtime rodeo historian and contributing editor to this periodical, died in April 1992. The loss of this great source of information on rodeo history resulted in my being asked.

The more information I gather about the rodeo clown, the more I find he has been admired, honored, and respected. However, at the same time he has been taken advantage of, taken for granted, and has been insulted and ignored. I find the rodeo clown to be simple and complex, funny and sad. He is indeed a hero, and yet he is a character. There is not another profession like it. No other occupation uses such diverse parts to make the whole than the rodeo clown.

Introduction

The first rodeo was never recorded. It was a spontaneous event that evolved when two or more cowboys needed to prove who was the best at cowboyin'. They rode the rough stock from ranches where they worked and with the saddles they used daily. It is doubtful that any money changed hands. The proof who was the best was reward enough. Besides, there would probably be a rematch. You could bet your boots on that.

Early rules were vague. In fact, rules were probably developed as the competitions occurred. After all, these were the very first rodeos—there was no model to follow.

Historians have argued over which rodeo was the first. Many variables must be taken into account in making this decision. Did spectators pay admission? Were prizes awarded the winners? Should a competition that did not charge admission or didn't award prizes be considered? Who can make that decision?

Prescott, Arizona, was only a few months old when the first recorded rodeo contest was staged there on July 4, 1864.[3] Then another July 4 contest, in 1869, was held in Deer Trail, Colorado.[2] Cowboys from several nearby ranches competed in a bronc-riding contest. It is recorded that the winner was an Englishman, Emilnie Gardenshire, cowboying for the Milliron Ranch.[3] A suit of clothes was the prize, and he earned the title "Champion Bronco Buster of the Plains." He won the title with a fifteen-minute ride on a horse named Montana Blizzard, belonging to the Hashknife Ranch.

In 1872 in Cheyenne, Wyoming Territory, another July 4 celebration included an exhibition of steer riding by Texas cowboys who had just come off a trail drive. A year later, Cheyenne townspeople were entertained again with a show of bronco-busting on

Sixteenth Street. In those days, bronco busting was far different from the eight-second ride we have today; the horse was generally ridden until it, or the rider, gave out.[3]

North Platte, Nebraska, marked the beginnings of both the Wild West Show and Rodeo, at that locale, July 4, 1882, as documented in the book *The Wild West*, by Don Russell. Austin, Texas, held a Texas State Fair in 1882. Cowboys who competed in a steer-roping contest vied for a silver-trimmed saddle valued at $300.[3]

The first public cowboy contest wherein cash prizes were awarded to the winners of bronc riding and steer roping was held on an open flat adjoining the courthouse in Pecos, Texas, July 4, 1883, but no admission was charged the spectators. Many consider this the first planned rodeo, as we know it today, where cash prizes were awarded to winners.

In the fall of 1887, a cowboy tournament was held in Denver, Colorado, in connection with the Denver Exposition. A local newspaper, *The Denver Republican*, pointed out: "Every cowboy who entered the arena did his best, and the untamed broncos and longhorned steers did their best to get away." [3]

Once spectators were charged a fee to watch the contest events, a new responsibility took place to keep the audience entertained. And so the need of a support crew became essential. This included the rodeo clown.

As the rodeo developed and unfolded into a production, the need for hands to keep the rodeo moving and the audience interested, involved, and amused became important. The first announcers yelled loudly or used a megaphone to carry their voices to the audience. There were no public address systems that could blare out their humor and patter to the onlookers. Visual entertainment was essential.

The first rodeo clowns were undocumented. They were cowboys who saw the need to amuse, or the cowboy a promoter asked to do something funny when a delay in the performance occurred. The delay could have been a broken chute gate, a runaway animal, or an injured cowboy. No matter what the delay, it was soon discovered the audience responded better and enjoyed the rodeo more if they were distracted by some form of entertainment while a problem was being solved.

Willard Porter, rodeo historian, wrote an article in 1984 for *The Western Horseman* about an early rodeo clown known as

Tin Horn Hank Keenen. Keenen's career in rodeo began at age seventeen, around 1912. Porter wrote that Keenen's "early events in Wild West shows and rodeos were steer wrestling, wild horse races, and some clowning." [22]

Foghorn Clancy, early rodeo announcer, wrote in his autobiography, *My Fifty Years in Rodeo* (covering the period 1897 to 1947), that "in the beginning there were no calf roping contests, no trick riding, fancy roping and no clowns." [4]

Charley Shultz homesteaded near Clayton, New Mexico. At the Fourth of July picnic in 1914, a neighbor got Charley to join him to entertain the picnic-goers. They put on old circus clown suits and pointed hats. A burro kept bucking them off. Charley learned to walk a tightwire. Charley was inspired by the laughter, and he spent most of the rest of his life as a rodeo clown.

In the book *Rodeo Road, My Life as a Pioneer Cowgirl*, Vera McGinnis told of the 1914 Salt Lake City Roundup: "The program that afternoon staged the usual events—all of them new and wonderful to me. I was completely absorbed in the action until I heard the announcer call: 'Snowball Johnson will now ride an exhibition bucking horse.' Then to my amazement—and horror—they almost dragged a little white horse with red ears onto the track. He was pulling back, lunging, biting and kicking. I couldn't believe it. He was my first relay horse. They finally got him saddled and Snowball (the Negro clown) mounted to his middle. Red Ears bucked, bawled, sun-fished and sky-dived—to the great satisfaction of the cash customers." [6]

The 1915 season of the Miller Brothers & Arlington 101 Ranch Real Wild West introduced three clowns: Bill Caress, Lorette, and Joe Lewis. Then, in 1916, the 101 Ranch Show again included Lorette, the clown.

It was not unusual for the early-day rodeo clowns to work the Wild West shows from time to time. Early-day rodeos were not held often enough to provide a continuing source of income. The Wild West shows could. Also, the shows gave clowns an opportunity to work on perfecting their routines and to travel the country.

Tin Horn Hank Keenen started out with the Wild West shows around 1912, working for the old 101 Ranch, Hinkle, and many others. He rode steers, saddle broncs, and barebacks, wrestled steers, and rode in wild-horse races before starting his clowning career. Hank married Dessie Walter and in 1924 they had a son, Carl, who traveled with them, sleeping in boxes, dresser drawers, etc. The boy was known as Little Tin Horn and learned to trick ride and rope, as well as to help in the clown acts.[13]

The first record of a clown at Cheyenne Frontier Days was 1916. According to Bob Hanesworth, "Dan Hix [I believe this name to be in error; it should have read Dix] entertained the crowds by attempting to get his mule to move by pulling and jerking on a rope fastened to the halter. In response, the mule laid down. Dan then talked nicely to him and everything was rosy again."[5]

Red Sublett joined Booger Red's traveling cowboy show at sixteen years of age. He worked and rode rough string on several Texas and Oklahoma ranches, including the 101 Ranch.[8] Red was a traveling horse trainer. In 1917 he joined Lucille Mulhall's show and rode broncs and steers. For variety and to help at the gate, he would avowedly mount anything that could be dragged, pulled or pushed into the arena—buffalo, zebras, mules, and ostriches. He hung up his rig and joined the army during World War I and saw action on the battlefields in France. When the war ended in 1918, Red returned to the rodeo arena.[7]

My father, Guy Hughbanks, remembered seeing Red Sublett and Tommy Douglas at Cheyenne Frontier Days in 1919. Red and Tommy rode a bronc facing one another and holding onto each other's arms, to balance themselves.

Red was contesting, putting on riding exhibitions and rides on rough stock, when Tex Austin, rodeo producer of that era, and Foghorn Clancy, rodeo announcer, explained to him that the paid clowns were getting the money but he was getting the laughs. That was when Red Sublett decided to become a rodeo clown.[4] Others have followed in these early rodeo clowns' footsteps. Some have tried and given it up, and some have made it a lifelong career.

Willard Porter wrote in an article, printed in the *The Daily Oklahoman,* "But in the old days, before the availability of huge, recalcitrant, crossbred Brahma bulls, clowns were just that—painted buffoons, true laugh-getters, rubes who dispensed very large amounts of trite burlesque and corn tomfoolery."[24]

What a wonderful way to make a living.

CHAPTER 1

The First Cowboy Clowns

Early rodeos were an idea in motion. Cowboys have always enjoyed having an opportunity to see who is the best at roping and riding. Early rodeo organizers were members of a community—the ranchers or the cowboys themselves. Since early rodeos had no prepared format, they usually came to life spontaneously. The Fourth of July seemed to be a logical celebration, a time when everyone could attend. Nearby ranchers usually provided the rough stock and the cattle. Various community citizens assisted in building arenas or pens to hold the stock. By the time the event took place, it seemed that most everyone had participated in some way.

The riders and ropers were quite familiar with their event; in fact, they were probably some of the area's best in their chosen competition. They spent many a workday doing similar tasks. A chance to display one's ability in front of the entire community took confidence and determination. Competitors who outrode and outroped the rest were proud of those accomplishments and enjoyed the notoriety—at least until the next contest.

Since early rodeo contests were not held on a regular basis, it was necessary for the earliest rodeo clowns to earn a day's pay in a variety of ways. Some early cowboy funnymen, such as Tommy Douglas, Red Sublett, Tin Horn Hank Keenen, and Homer Holcomb, were cowboys who competed in a variety of events and exhibitions.

Some Wild West and circus clowns made early marks in the world of rodeo. Dan Dix, the first rodeo clown at Cheyenne Frontier Days in 1916, was a circus clown in 1910. In 1911 and 1912,

1

Early rodeo clown in circus costume entertains rodeo audience.
(Photo by Dean Photo Service; submitted by Ben Johnson)

according to the Circus World Museum records, in Baraboo, Wisconsin, he was with various Wild West shows, as were Lorette, Joe Lewis, and Bill Caress.

Milt Riske, in his history of Cheyenne Frontier Days, said, "In 1918 the rodeo clown, according to a press report, was a two foot midget, Joe Hertzer. The clown was actually a part of California Frank Hafley's touring Wild West Show which closed down for a week so that Frank's fifteen year old daughter, Rainee Hafley, could make her first appearance at Frontier Days." [9] Later, Joe did clown rodeos.

Most of the early rodeo clowns, however, went unnamed as they might have clowned, worked as hands, contested, and done whatever was necessary around the rodeo. Those who stayed with it and made it their profession for life, such as Charley Shultz, Red Sublett, Tin Horn Hank Keenen, and Homer Holcomb, were well remembered. They carved for themselves, and for those who followed after them, a career that included making people laugh, working with and teaching animals all sorts of strange tricks, being out-of-doors, and gaining the opportunity to travel.

Unknown rodeo clown from early days.
(Photo by J. A. Stryker; submitted by Bill Wittliff, courtesy of University of Texas–Permian Basin Collection)

Foghorn Clancy reported an incident that happened around 1920: A farmer said to Foghorn, "Tell you what, I'll make you a little bet that none of your cowboys can ride that bull."

"I laughed at that," said Foghorn. He told the farmer, "The bull is hardly big enough for a grown cowboy to ride. You see our little clown there—Joe Hertzer? Well, I'll bet fifty dollars against the bull that Joe can ride the animal backwards."

Foghorn remembered: "The bet was made. So we put the bull in the chute and Joe got on him backwards sitting well up on the bull's neck and holding on to the surcingle which passed around the bull's withers and with his legs locked under the bull's neck. In this fashion he rode the bull without a bit of trouble. I had won the bet, but nevertheless I paid the farmer twenty-five dollars, which was about all the bull was really worth, and we kept him for the clown to ride backwards in the rodeo." [4]

Ed Wright was an early competing cowboy and performer in western pictures. His wife, a lady bronc rider, was killed while riding a bucking horse at Overland Park in Denver in 1917. Wright

Homer Holcomb, one of the first bullfighters, and Jasbo Fulkerson, the first barrelman.

(Photo submitted by Mrs. Homer Holcomb)

went to pieces. He joined the army during World War I. After the war was over, Ed started making the contests again. "I finally figured all frontier shows needed a comedian or clown ta ease the fowl tension, ta make people laugh, an' ta protect the cowboys from those fightin' Brahma bulls." He went on to say: "They paid a good clown more money fer a show than a cowboy could make if he won, so I got me a jackass, an' tried ta dress so I'd look like one myself. Well, it worked. I got contracts in Cheyenne, Pendleton, Madison Square, Calgary, Canada, Soldier's Field, Yankee Stadium, even London, Hawaiian Islands, Monte Vista, Fort Worth, an' Dallas, Texas State Fair." [36]

Homer Holcomb started his career rodeo clowning in 1919 at Spokane, Washington. Among other things, he rode a bucking horse while he carried a bunch of chickens in a suitcase, which flew open during the ride. The fowl scattered all over the arena. He also "clowned Soda Springs, Idaho, that year, at the Old Henry Stampede. It was a bedroll and camping out deal. Homer sure made a hit there, told Henry C. Horton of Soda Springs." [10]

Red Sublett carries mule in the rodeo arena of an early-day contest.
(Photographer unknown; submitted by Charley and Imogene Beals)

Red Sublett was one of the first rodeo clowns Tad Lucas could remember. Tad was an early lady bronc rider and longtime trick rider. "Red was ornery, just plain ornery," said Tad, in her quiet and uncondemning way. "He was a dirty talker and always up to something mischievous. But I liked him. He made us all laugh." An account in *Cheyenne Frontier Days, A Marker from Which to Reckon All Events,* told that "Ben Johnson won his first of two Steer Roping Championships and set a 20.4-second record, but it was clown, Red Sublett, who attracted the attention of the crowd by roping a steer by the tail." Later in the book Red was described as wearing an "oversized Stetson and angora chaps." [9]

Red Sublett clowned the Houston rodeo in 1924. Burnett, the producer, always saw to it that the two greatest rube clowns who ever worked a rodeo or circus were on hand—Bert Davis and his wife, better known as Uncle Hiram and Aunt Lucinda.

Montie Montana, trick roper for over sixty years, could recall seeing Happy Jack Hollander in 1922 in McLaughlin, South Dakota, where he clowned by doing a drunken Roman stand.

Alice Greenough, former competition and exhibition cowgirl of the 1920s, said her earliest recollection of a rodeo clown was Earl Hayner, a round-up wagon cowboy by profession, in 1924 at Red Lodge, Montana. She also remembered Overland Red Anderson, who did not continue as a rodeo clown but later raced horses.

By the mid-twenties other names started appearing on the growing list of arena funnymen. Abe Lefton, who later found his mark as a famous rodeo announcer, tried his hand at bronc riding and clowning at Salinas, California. [13] At age seventeen Glenn Randall, well-known horse trainer and rodeo contract act man, went rodeoing. He rode bareback, bulls, and clowned. He once clowned Cheyenne with Jimmy Nesbitt. [13] In 1925 Nesbitt "was contesting at a little show at Dexfield Park, Iowa, and the clown did not show up. The manager asked Jimmy to try to do it. A wig and a lot of purple paint and Jimmy was a clown." [10]

A 1925 rodeo in Lewiston, North Dakota, had the same problem—no clown. "My brother Harold and I were contesting and Harold said he would act as clown, though he had no experience," told Howard O'Neill, of the O'Neill twins. "His act went over so well the manager of other shows saw him and contracted him. We thought a twin clown act would go over big, especially as we look so much alike that few people can tell us apart. So we got our mule, Skimmilk, and trained him and started out." [10]

John Lindsey started rodeoing in 1921 by riding bulls and horses. John had a natural flair for comedy and in 1927 he began clowning. [13]

Jasbo Fulkerson also gave up bareback and bull riding in 1927 and started clowning. He thought people took rodeos too seriously. "Everybody all scrunched down in their seats pullin' on their hats like it was life and death," says Jaz. "So I figured I'd make them laugh." [14] And make them laugh he did—for twenty-five years. In the *Daily Oklahoman,* August 7, 1987, Willard Porter described Jasbo: "He was called naturally funny by his peers. He was cowboy enough to parody each event, and he had both a sense of the dramatic and ridiculous. This, of course, helped him when he roped a steer on his mule and the mule was jerked down." [24]

Monk Carden and George Moens were asked to clown the Pendleton Round-Up for the first time in 1928 by Harry Collins, president of the Round-Up. Tommy Douglas had been hired to clown that year but had broken his leg just prior to the event. Monk and George had no previous rodeo experience. They were local boys who had a burlesque acrobatic and wrestling act. The

Pendleton Round-Up cut-ups George Moens and Monk Carden.
(Photo by Waible E. Patton; submitted by Monk Carden)

Pendleton celebration was described in the book *Let 'Er Buck,* published in 1921: "Laughter strange as it may seem in the humor-loving West, was the hardest element of all to handle. It was impossible to figure out any comedy that would not be produced at the expense of the naturalness and historic quality which above all must be retained as the vital element in the show. They wisely decided they would not make any deliberate attempt to plant comedy, and that they would leave it to accidental incidents." [25]

The earliest Pendleton Round-Up was held in 1910. Sometime between 1910 and 1928 the decision-makers of the Round-Up changed their attitudes about using comedy. John A. Stryker, famous rodeo photographer and rodeo engineer in the early years, had worked with the circus and introduced some of the greatest acts under the bigtop. "He saw how clowns, only beginning to be introduced in rodeo, added to the crowd's enjoyment and served a useful purpose in the arena," wrote Ron Tyler in his book *The Rodeo of John Addison Stryker.* [26]

Early rodeo clowns would have starved to death if they had not supplemented their income in other ways. Rodeos were few

Early-day rodeo clown and Wild West performer Tiny Jack Knapp.
(Photo by J. A. Stryker; submitted by Bill Wittliff, courtesy of University of
Texas–Permian Basin Collection)

and far apart, and it took longer to prepare for each one. Sometimes cowboys spent several weeks in a town preparing for the
rodeo.

Willard Porter wrote: "Tin Horn Hank Keenen didn't start
full-time clowning until 1929, and because he was such an excel-
lent bronc rider, he made difficult acts look easy. He often strapped
a tin tub to a bronc, got inside and rode the horse out of a chute.
Records indicate he rode some of the top mounts of the era, including Kickapoo and Banjo Jake, both reputation broncs, at Belle
Fourche one year. Once, at McLaughlin County Fair (Nebraska)
the committee offered $500 to anybody who could make an eight-
jump ride on the mighty Tipperary. Not knowing quite what to
expect, Hank mounted up–and won the money." [22]

The Wild West show was a good place for up-and-coming
rodeo clowns to spend some time honing their skills. While practicing their acts they could earn a decent wage. A 1937 advertise-
ment in *Hoofs & Horns* requested: "Wanted for Wild West Rodeo–Cowboys, Cowgirls, Vaqueros, Indians and Clowns. Will Hire

calf ropers and bull doggers with or without horses. Will buy rodeo stock of all kinds. 32 Weeks' work to right people. Opening
April 1 and booked by George A. Hamid for fairs and parks. Write
Milt Hinkle." [10] Thirty-two weeks of work was mighty appealing
to many rodeo hands.

A 1946 *Hoofs & Horns* magazine gave the following mention
about one of the best who spent time with the Wild West show:
"Zeke Bowery went with Colonel Zack Miller's 101 Ranch Wild
West Show to improve his clowning and showmanship. They
toured 12 western states, and while with the show Zeke learned
to juggle, rope spin, trick ride and manipulate the Australian bull
whips. Zeke is said to be the only clown in the rodeo business
who features an Australian bull whip act in comedy which he performs with Celie (his wife). So closely at times and precise is the
act that a stiff breeze can ruin the entire performance and endan-
ger his wife." [10]

Since the earliest rodeo clowns, mules, donkeys, and horses
have been important elements in their acts. Foghorn Clancy gave
this account in his book: "Our rodeo clown was Red Sublett with
his famous trained mule, 'Spark Plug.' We had a lot of trouble getting Red, or rather getting his mule, as the animal had been attached by a Chicago booking agent who claimed a previous breach
of contract against Red. But the dynamic little Cliff Trimble, a real
showman that worked fast and was never at a loss to know what
he wanted or what he intended to do, knew just what to do and
how to do it to get the release of Red's mule for our show. It was
worth all the trouble, for Red was one of the greatest rodeo clowns
who ever lived and was then right at the top of his career." [4]

Acrobats George Moens and Monk Carden based their humor
on their physical agility. Monk said that after the trick roping ended,
"I would come down the race track spinning a rope. I actually had
a wire hoop white taped to a cotton rope attached to a swivel on a
rope." He reminisced, "I would appear like I was spinning a rope
but rolling the loop on the ground. Luckily the crowd would ap-
plaud. I would stop to take a bow—and the hoop would continue
to roll on down the track." Monk also described, "I would grab
Moens by the nose with my left hand, lead him around, then I
would hit the back of my left hand with my right hand. Moens
would go flat on his face on the ground, as if my slap had caused it.
He would jump up and kick me on the shin. I would bend over
and grab my shin—he would then kick me in the butt. I would go
on my face. Upon getting up on my knees Moens would take a run

Red Sublett and mule Spark Plug at Tex Austin's Rodeo in Chicago.
(Photo by R. R. Doubleday, National Cowboy Hall of Fame Collection)

to kick me again in the butt. I would straighten out—he would miss and land on his back on top of my back."

Occasionally some of the routine acts were enhanced by accidental events, lending to some of the most humorous events. Foghorn stated:

> Dallas State Fair, 1928, there was plenty of excitement at that rodeo. The local agency for International Trucks had given my son, Pat, a miniature truck—just a big toy about two feet in length, but complete except for the motor. The agent, myself and Pat, with his pony, stood in the center of the arena for the presentation. Just as this was finished, out of the chute came a wild bucking steer with Red Sublett, the clown, doing his trick riding stunt aboard.
>
> The truck agent lit out for the fence as fast as he could go, I grabbed Pat in my arms and ran for the fence with him. We had to leave the pony to take care of itself.
>
> The pony ran down toward the catch pen and the steer followed, bawling in a manner which told us that he was really peeved. Sublett quit the steer when it was about two-thirds of the way across the arena. Everyone in the grandstand expected

to see the steer charge and gore the pony to death. But as the steer neared the catch pen, the pony took the initiative. He charged the steer, then suddenly wheeled and let fly with both feet. The steer's ribs boomed like a drum, an expression of surprise crossed his face and he changed his mind about that pony pronto. He took himself off, leaving the pony in full possession of the field. [4]

As rodeo clowns became familiar figures at rodeos, the audience would arrive anticipating the recognizable funnyman and look forward to his hilarious routines. Wayne Ingram and Jane Pattie wrote of one of the crowd's favorites:

Jasbo first clowned Madison Square Garden in 1929, he didn't miss a year from then on. Of all the rodeos he worked he looked forward to the New York show. The first bareback bronc rider came out and had a good ride. At the horn the two pickup men moved out and spurred alongside the bucking horse, one man caught the halter shank and the rider reached for the second pickup man and pulled himself clear of the horse.

While the crowd cheered the cowboy, a disreputable derby hat sailed toward the bronc, curved, and returned to the grinning Jasbo. He capered about joyously and sent the hat sailing out once more, vigorously beckoning it back to him. Obediently the derby came spinning back to his hand, and he strutted in triumph and slapped his chest. Now inconspicuously he unpinned the black thread hanging from the girders. He made his boast and threw the derby out with a fine flair. Despite his imperious gesture, the truant continued across the arena and landed ignominiously in the dirt, and the little clown's dismay under this crushing blow was a pitiful thing to behold. [14]

Some of the early rodeos provided quite a variety in acts, as indicated by a 1933 Boston Garden program. It listed Bill Keen's Auto Hurdling Team, Jasbo Fulkerson and Jimmy Nesbitt with Their Educated Mules, Eko and Will Rogers, and Jimmy Nesbitt and his Chariot.

Donna Melvin, daughter of early part-time rodeo producer and full-time rancher Bill Maher, of South Dakota, told me of his experiences in the 1930s to the early '50s. Bill would travel to the Red Desert in Wyoming, and with the help of Frank Robbins, of Rawlins, Wyoming, and some cowboys he would gather the mustangs from the range. They were shipped by railroad to Ft. Pierre, South Dakota, where they were held in the stockyards. Those that

Jasbo Fulkerson and favorite mule Eko.
(Photo by J. A. Stryker; submitted by Bill Wittliff, courtesy of University of
Texas–Permian Basin Collection)

would not buck were broke for saddle horses and sold to nearby
ranchers.

Donna described her father's rodeos: "Dad would construct a
rodeo arena and holding pens, using railroad ties, cable, smooth
wire, snow fence, barb wire, hog panels, poles, posts and some
rough lumber. Three to five plank chutes, a good sized arena and
some catch pens would complete it. The side hills usually offered
good seating areas for families.

"Dad always had good crowds at his rodeos, as he promoted
ahead of time. He had a fellow who was an artist offer to paint
western scenes on the windows of local businesses," she continued. "Lyle Marshall, of Bonilla, South Dakota, wore a clown suit
and rode in a scoop shovel which was wired to the tail of a wild
horse and it was let out of the chutes to run around the arena.
Sometimes he was announced as a well-known local businessman,
coming out as the next rider. When he came out, his overalls were
fixed to come off. When they did he'd run toward the chutes, as
his pants went trailing the bucking horse running across the arena."

Maher usually had around ten rodeos a season. He would trail drive his stock from one rodeo to the next.

During the developmental years, the earliest rodeo clowns continually improvised, tried new routines, and found what entertained *and* what did not. They were berated and admired during that time. Some cowboys resented the fact that a rodeo clown was paid for each performance. A cowboy had to pay to compete, and when he bucked off and came up with a handful of dirt, instead of pay dirt, he left with empty pockets. On the other hand, cowboys could not help but be appreciative of a friendly assist from the rodeo clown when he happened to get in a wreck.

In written material from the early days, some years not a word was mentioned about the rodeo funnymen. Then in other years early periodicals, such as *Hoofs & Horns,* might have an article in every issue about the current-day clowns. It has always been up to the rodeo clown himself to be his own public relations man and make sure he had representation—to stock contractors, producers, rodeo managers, cowboys, and the media. These earliest cowboy clowns set the stage, and what happened to them would directly affect those who followed after them.

The rodeo audience, however, never required justification of the rodeo clown. The fans accepted him with open hearts and much laughter. They always left a performance well entertained.

A 1937 *Hoofs & Horns* magazine cover showed a cartoon of a rodeo clown on his knees in front of a steer. An article in the same issue described well the role of the rodeo clown:

> At most every rodeo held in the country there is at least one clown and often more. Most of them are, or have been, cowboys and some of the togs they rig themselves out in are plenty funny.
>
> These men work hard for your entertainment and with them on the job there's something doing every minute of the show. They must stay awake nights thinking up some of the stunts they pull. They take plenty of risks also in the rodeo arena. If you don't think so, step into a corral with a wild Brahma sometime.
>
> The bronc riders, ropers, steer riders, bull doggers, etc., cannot be given too much credit for making the Great American Rodeo what they are. You hear plenty of cheers and applause when a bronc rider makes a good ride, or the roper or bulldogger does a neat job. This is as it should be.
>
> But the rodeo clowns fill in the idle minutes between

broncs, steers and bulldoggers, so folks, save a few yells and cheers for the clowns. They will appreciate it a lot, and you know you would sure miss 'em if they weren't there. [10]

Early rodeo clowns were tenacious, creative survivors. They had to be, as there were no guidelines. We will never know how many cowboys attempted to enter this line of work in the earliest days of organized rodeo. Some of those found success and chose to continue as rodeo clowns; some created acts that continue to delight audiences even today, almost a century later.

CHAPTER 2

The Era of the Funnyman

High-spirited Humor

As the rodeo clown developed his profession, his first responsibility was to entertain, to amuse. In contrast to the emotion felt by the rodeo audience when they watched a cowboy ride a wild bronc in anticipation of the life-taking injury he could experience, the rodeo clown could quickly turn their mood to merriment and ease the tension.

In the earliest days, many impromptu actions were taken and the funnymen reacted to what was happening in the arena. As they gained importance in a performance and were called on more often, they began working out routines and acts.

Monk Carden reminisced about acts performed by him and partner George Moens at the Pendleton Round-Up, starting in 1928. "We would rubber band crackers to a mouse trap, with the cheese bait trigger removed. I would hold the trap with the spring flipper held down with my fingers," described Monk. "Moens would shoot blank pistols behind his back, between his legs, and so on. I'd let the trap snap and the cracker would explode. Suddenly his guns would jam. He would turn away, work on them, then fire a couple of test shots in the air. Then he would turn and take aim on the crackers again. About that time two dead ducks would drop from the sky. Actually tossed off of the roof of the grandstand by a friend. Moens would look startled, then look up in the air. He would look at the crowd, pick up the ducks, take a bow and act like he had intended to hit the ducks."

Carden continued, "We would also ride doggin' steers or hang

George Moens and Monk Carden harass a downed steer, 1929,
Pendleton Round-Up.

(Photographer unknown; submitted by Monk Carden)

on to their tails. We would turn flips or do a handspring upon getting bucked off or when we turned loose of their tails."

Many of the early acts were the first of their kind and required a certain amount of fine tuning. Some of the strange contraptions devised by the cowboy clowns created great fun but required working out the kinks to make sure they weren't too dangerous to the clown.

Wayne Ingram and Jane Pattie described Jasbo's chariot:

In Clayton, New Mexico, Jasbo spent the day at the blacksmith's shop supervising the welding of a steel chariot. The two wheeled contraption had a long arched tongue with a hook; the arch allowed the tongue to reach over the chute gate and to be hooked via a swivel snap to the surcingle that was cinched on a bull. The bull was turned out to discover that he could escape neither the heavy, rumbling monster that shadowed him unceasingly nor the vociferous little man clinging to it. The swivel allowed the bull to turn and charge the chariot, but the length of the tongue was gauged just so as to elude the maddened rushes. Jasbo needed all his strength to brace for the jolts as his little cart careened and slid dangerously around the arena.

One jerk on the rope running down the tongue to the chariot released the bull, and the chariot would come to a neck-cracking halt as the tongue dug into the arena sand. Now the bull could reach his tormentor; the sudden release allowing the bull to hit the hated thing with his ton of brute force only built up his fury. It was up to Jasbo's agility to keep the frothing beast on the other side of the chariot until the pickup men could drive or drag the animal from the arena. [14]

No one was safe from the rodeo clowns when it came to kidding. Anyone could be included in the clowns' antics. Jasbo and George Mills were two of the best at teasing cowboys or the audience:

In Great Falls, Montana, the stands were always filled on Saturday afternoon. Wag Blessing had just made a good ride on a stiff-legged bay; as he walked away from the center of the makeshift arena, oblivious from fatigue and relief, he didn't see the black-bearded buffoon who tiptoes behind him, built a loop in his rope and neatly dropped it over the cowboy's head to pin his arms to his sides. The deed done, Jasbo dug his heels into the dirt, braced his stout legs and with amazing strength for a man of his height, he held his thrashing catch until his partner in crime had the victim on the ground.

While partner George Mills sat upon his chest and held his hands, Jasbo reached into his voluminous patched trousers and pulled out a pair of very pink, very large, very feminine panties. He sat upon the cowboy's kicking legs and tussled the garment over his boots and levis to their proper position. To crown the jest, he exchanged his disreputable derby for Wag's new Stetson.

The clowns stood up to survey their handiwork and found it good; they staggered about in fits of laughter. Wag scrambled out of the rope and with the overly large legs of the pink underpants flapping as he ran, he chased the galloping little clowns out of the arena and around the grand stand. [14]

Tin Horn Hank Keenen's son Carl, who traveled with his father and mother when only six weeks old, told: "When I started working with my father, as Little Tin Horn Hank, a single day's clowning for the elder Keenen included riding a couple of steers backwards while holding a suitcase and firing a pistol; riding a couple of broncs holding a suitcase, a blazing .45, stepping off and turning cartwheels; clowning on Steembote; clowning up some

Tin Horn Hank Keenen on Pitchfork, a bucking bronc carrying the suitcase, Oklahoma City.
(Photo by R. R. Doubleday, National Cowboy Hall of Fame Collection)

kind of quick ambulance ride; driving a steer or bull attached to a Roman chariot; trick riding on a mule; shooting act with a pig; a bullwhip act; funnying up the wild cow milking and wild horse race; and fighting bulls when crossbred Brahmas began to replace domestic steers." [22]

Personal news occasionally brought on an additional burst of energy and creativity which resulted in extra laughs:

> Just before the whistle blew for the opening performance at the Providence, Rhode Island Rodeo, Brahma Rogers, a six-foot clown from Tyler, Texas, received a message stating that he was the father of a newly born eleven pound son.
>
> "Young button is fine and healthy," wired Mrs. Mary Rogers, Brahma's wife. "Looks a lot like you. He's smart, too. Told me he did not care for milk but wanted bacon and beans. Has already asked for a big hat, Levis and a horse and spurs."
>
> Brahma let out a howl of joy that could be heard for blocks. Announced that the boy's name would be James—named him after Colonel Jim Eskew of the JE Ranch outfit and then went in to clown. And how he DID clown. Hung to the tails of buck-

ing horses, spit in the faces of the wild Brahmas; horned into the musical act of the Irvins, warbled, "I Am A Proud Papa Now," and roughed up every cowhand that came within reach. Then after the show he dug deep into his old leather pouch and bought several quarts of "wild cow's milk" which was passed around to the boys. [10]

The announcer's ability to banter with the rodeo clown helped to set up the clown's jokes and acts. A few of the announcer/rodeo clown teams were great and audiences raved over them. An example: "In 1937 Homer Holcomb, World Champion Clown, and announcer Abe Lefton teamed up and worked like smooth oil. Both were tops in their respective lines, with Homer doing some trick roping and losing his Levis to show immaculate unmentionables." [10]

Abe Lefton assisted other rodeo clowns as well.

Throughout all performances George Mills and Jasbo Fulkerson, and Abe Lefton, kept the crowds in snickers with their screwball antics, their corny dialogue and their sharp ad libbing. Their frequent "gumming of the works" by refusing to play ball with each other on some of the routines furnished some hilarious entertainment to those who were familiar with their friendly "off stage" feuding.

George and Jasbo found occasion to climb up to Abe's announcers booth armed with a couple of fat clubs. Abe's counter attack consisted of bottled Coke which he generously showered down on George, forcing a retreat. [10]

Gene Lamb described in his 1956 book, *Rodeo, Back of the Chutes:*

Another thing the announcers have to watch for is what the clowns shoot at them as gags. Clowns are notorious practical jokers; it's part of their business. And as explained, without a mike in the arena, they have to let the announcer carry both sides of the gag. It goes like this:

Clown: I just gave my girl fifty dollars.
Announcer: You just gave her fifty dollars? Where is she now, out spending your money on somebody?
Clown: No. She's over in the stands. See that girl with the red dress?
Announcer: Oh. That pretty girl in the stands in the red dress? I see her. She has on a pretty hat.
Clown: Yeh. I gave her that. See that purse she has?
Announcer: You gave her that hat? Yes, I see her purse.

Clown: I gave her that purse.
Announcer: You gave her that purse, too?
Clown: See that little boy beside her?
Announcer: Yes. Yes. I see that little boy beside her. Don't
              tell me—Oh. I see. That's her little brother.

The announcer may get into this repeating routine, and
the gag has to be carried over fast, as he doesn't have too much
time to think what he's saying, and a tricky clown can get him
to repeat some of the damndest things ever heard over a mike.
I've never heard Cy [Taillon] or any of the other long time pros
caught. They know most of the routines too well, and can think
fast enough, but I've really heard some lulu's when a clown can
get an inexperienced, or local announcer involved. [16]

Interviewing Dan Coates, Sr., former rodeo announcer, Lamb
said, "I have seen an announcer kill the clowns dead when they
refused to clean up the jokes and the patter. It's easy to do. The
clown is in the middle of the arena, and no matter how strong his
voice is it won't reach but a few people, so he's wasting time and
lung power if he doesn't have the announcer carrying him over
the mike."

Skipper Voss told of an incident involving an announcer in his
early clowning days:

I was working for Mike Cervi and it was at Las Vegas. Pete
Logan was the announcer. I'd heard Pete could really butcher
an act for a clown. Cervi asked me to do an act and I had a
shooting act worked out with Wiley McCray. I was at one end
of the arena and McCray at the other end. Pete was talking with
McCray but he was totally ignoring me. I kept trying to get his
attention and the more he ignored me the hotter I got. By the
time I got his attention I was really mad. Cervi yelled and told
me to hurry it up. I cut to the end of the act, McCray bends over
and I shoot him in the rear. I am so hot I wait until after the
performance to find Logan. I'm still mad and plan to give him a
piece of my mind. I'm really ready to let him have it. When I
walked up to Pete he said, "Skipper Voss, the best bullfighter
I've seen in years." The wind went out of my sails immediately.
He went on and on about what a good bullfighter I was and
when he was through I had nothing to say.

Charley Lyons told of how he learned to work with the announcer in his early clowning days. Charley was working a rodeo
and Mel Lambert was the announcer. Charley had a few rank jokes

Wiley McCray at Calgary Stampede in 1966.
(Photographer unknown; submitted by Charley and Imogene Beals)

to tell. He'd feed them to Mel, and Mel would just change the subject and talk to the audience about something else. After the rodeo Charley found Mel and was really miffed. Mel told Charley he was too dirty. "Tell some clean jokes and you will do a lot better," said Mel. Charley asked Mel to help him. Together they worked out several jokes that were fitting for family entertainment. From then on Charley and Mel worked well together, and Charley considers Mel a good friend.

Being experienced with animals, especially horses and steers, helped a cowboy clown a great deal when dealing with rodeo stock. It was also the basis for numerous routines:

> Jasbo grabbed the tails of bull-dogged steers which dragged him all over the arena. He hitched rage-crazed Brahmas to his two-wheeled chariot and was given hair-raising rides. He taunted the vicious bulls almost from underfoot, diving into his barrel just as the huge bony skull crashed into it. On other steers he lay with his legs over their eyes and played cards on the big hairy backs with George Mills, who lay nonchalantly on the steer's rump. The audience may not have realized the animals

wouldn't move so long as Jasbo kept their eyes covered, but after awhile he raised the "blinds," and clowns and cards were thrown in all directions. [14]

Buddy Heaton was known to be able to improvise wherever he was, whatever the situation. He was never at a loss for something funny to do. In Oklahoma City, in the indoor rodeo arena, Buddy would often be found wandering around on the catwalks and rafters high above the grandstand. It was not at all unusual to look up and see Buddy's big, baggy pants strolling back and forth. At one performance he got the bull-riding dummy up on the catwalk with him. During a quiet spot in the show, Buddy let out a squeal and pushed the dummy off the catwalk into the air. It plummeted downward toward the arena floor, startling the crowd and everyone within earshot.

The creative mind of the rodeo clown would often work over-time to find unique ways to entertain: "At Cheyenne Frontier Days the champion bronc rider was Gerald Roberts, but rodeo clown Benny Bender brought down the house with the world's shortest parachute jump from a helicopter flown by personnel from Fort Warren, which had become an air training command base." [5]

Benny wasn't alone with that creative genius. George Mills was an on-the-spot creator of much impromptu humor:

> George's favorite partner is John Lindsey. The pair can dope out some doozers. They may deck George out in a properly padded ballerina costume or, as happened once to the large delight of Denver fans, they may lug a box of snow into the coliseum and gleefully snowball the cowboys. When some singers appeared at the same rodeo, George and John solemnly trudged into the spotlight beside them. First, the clowns gestured for the singers to sing louder. Then they joined in the music themselves. Finally, they heartily paddled the vocalizers with brooms. The singers never came back. [10]

Any eager young rodeo clown should take advice from a professional such as Gene Clark. Gene offered, "Rodeo clowns should use common humor that the audience can relate to, especially children. Mothers continually fuss at their children about hygiene and manners. One of the simplest jokes that kids always love is: 'I stuck my finger up the bull's nose and a booger bit me.' Gene also added, "A clown needs to get to the rodeo early and make sure all his equipment is in good shape and that he is ready for all his acts.

Make sure everything works. Mothers and children get to a rodeo first so they can get the best seats, so the children can see. A clown should get with the kids early, have fun with them before the show starts. That sets the mood."

Not all acts turn out the way they are intended:

> One of George Mills' durable laugh-getters involves the age-old clown's tomfoolishness of simply losing his pants. He ties one end of a rope to his baggy jeans, the other he whirls around a running steer. The steer pulls off his pants, leaving George in his lightweight boxing shoes and his long-handles. Hundreds of times he has gone through these unhitches without a hitch. But once at Denver something went wrong, something awful. The rope not only stripped off Mills' pants but his underwear as well, and the sell-out crowd blinked. There George stood as NEKKID as a plucked duck. Somebody ran out with a blanket to wrap around him. But until then, George remembers with a wince, "I just hunkered down low as I could get—way, way down." [10]

Slim Pickens also joined the fraternity of arena funnymen who could be hilarious instantaneously. *Hoofs & Horns* reported:

> Slim has the God-given power to make people laugh and it

comes as natural to him as a duck taking to water. In or out of
the arena, he's the same. Unlike most rodeo clowns, Slim has
no set routine but takes full advantage of any situation as it
arises. During a show he's liable to pop up most any place—in
the stands, on the race track, leading a band and even, on occasion, joining the Indians in their ceremonial dances. He's as
unpredictable as the weather and works directly with and
among his audience. As Dr. I Cutemup, active partner of Digger
O'Dell, the friendly undertaker, Slim is on hand to give first and
last aid to the bronc and bareback riders. When the occasion
warrants and things are running smoothly in the arena he often
dons a painter's cap and overalls and armed with his trusty paint
brush, proceeds to paint the stands, including the seats, posts,
steps and even the spectators themselves. It usually takes some
time for the folks to catch on that it's all a gag and there isn't any
paint in the can or on the brush—and they love it and him for
making them in a small way a part of his act. It's simple things
like this that have made Slim a favorite of rodeo audiences from
coast to coast. [10]

Under the worst of situations the best rodeo clowns could
make the audience laugh:

A downpour drenched the San Angelo rodeo last Spring
and turned its usual arena dust into a soggy bog. During the bull
riding, a Brahma up-ended a rider named Shorty Horn. Before
Shorty could pick himself up, the clown, George Mills, slushed
up and hastily scooped mud on him until the hapless hand was
a small mountain of muck. The customers chortled themselves
hoarse.

Mills, a reddish-maned stringbean, is a wise old-timer at
making mountains out of mud-hills—at dressing awkward, ev-
eryday situations into little comedies which regale rodeo goers.
Once when he and John Lindsey were clowning Denver's National Western a sulky bent a wheel during the horse show.
Before attendants could whisk it out, George hitched John up
to the little cart and they raced whooping around the oval. The
pursuing handy-men were noticeably untickled. But the audience roared. [10]

Occasionally a spur-of-the-moment bit of comedy became a
routine that was used from then on: "Clown Buddy Heaton com-
mandeered the city water truck and proceeded to wet down everyone in range. Heaton and other clowns have continued to use
this act through the years." [15]

From the complete other end of the spectrum was the very

precise and deliberate routine that was practiced to perfection before an audience ever saw it. For example, Dan Coates, Sr., told of an act that Wilbur Plaugher had that involved setting up an outhouse in the arena. The clown is seen going into the outhouse. A funny old car comes into the arena and weaves around. About a dozen fellows dressed in police uniforms come swarming into the arena. The announcer tells the audience not to be alarmed about the police, they are looking for a drunk driver. The funny car continues to weave around the arena. It finally drives up to the outhouse and hits it squarely. The outhouse collapses. All the walls of the outhouse are lying on the ground and there is no sign of the clown who had entered the house before the car hit it.

A comic ambulance comes into the arena, sirens going, and numerous white-suited fellows jump out looking for the clown. They hover over the collapsed outhouse, lifting the boards to no avail. Finally, they all climb back into the ambulance and leave the arena. Shortly, the clown comes climbing over the fence at the far end of the arena. Everyone is confused and baffled as to how he got there.

Actually, there is an unseen hole in the arena under the area where the outhouse was set up. After the clown went into the outhouse he put on a white suit, which was hanging in the out-

house, and climbed down into the hole. When the car hit the out-house and destroyed it, he was still in the hole. When the ambu-lance arrived and the workers got out to search for him, he got out of the hole, with the white suit on, in the midst of the other white-suited fellows, climbed into the ambulance with them, unnoticed by the audience, and leaves the arena. Once out of the arena, he hurried to the far end and, having taken off the white suit, climbed back into the arena, much to the surprise of the audience. Timing and illusion were very important. And everyone in the audience enjoyed trying to solve the mystery of how it was done.

Bobby and Gene Clark were well known for their popular and mystical routines. Audiences and reporters continually made com-ments reviewing their acts, trying to determine possible ways in which they were executed: "Gene and Bobby Clark are well known for their ability to fight bulls and protect bull riders, but they are famous for their comic acts, like their cannon act, 'Kannon Kapers,' which still has not been duplicated. They used the mys-tery of magic with Gene the sharpshooter and Bobby the target holder and using only smoke, Bobby disappeared right before the audience's eyes to immediately reappear at the far end of the arena." [13]

At the National Finals Rodeo Historical Society, get-together

Bobby explained the act:

> Gene would come into the arena loaded with small guns and announce to the announcer he was going to shoot me. He shot, but I just stood there. He used all the guns he had but I just continued to stand there . . . nothing worked. Then the announcer asked Gene, "Don't you have anything new?" Gene tells the announcer he has a new gun that he knows would work. He runs out of the arena and returns with a cannon. Gene fires it up and a big explosion takes place with a huge puff of smoke that completely surrounds me.

> While I'm engulfed in the smoke, I drop down into a trap door that had been placed over a hole dug in the arena prior to the rodeo and covered with dirt. When the smoke clears I am missing. Allowing the audience just enough time to search the arena quickly with their eyes to determine I am nowhere around, a yell comes from the far end of the arena and I climb over the fence and run back to the center of the arena. The announcer spots me coming over the fence, says, "There he is," and all eyes go to me.

> Meanwhile the cannon is pulled over the trap door, and I climb from the hole into the cannon unnoticed by the audience, and the cannon is pulled out of the arena. The audience's

Brothers Bobby and Gene Clark with chimpanzee Moe.
(Photo by Ben Allen; submitted by Bobby Clark)

eyes are glued to my "stand-in" dressed identically to the way I am dressed.

The mechanics of the explosion the cannon makes are different than they appear. There is a Roman candle attached to the cannon. After Gene lights it, he holds his ears. When Bobby pushes a button, four bags of powder explode just as the stick of dynamite explodes.

This act drew everyone's curiosity. Bobby reminisced: "In Calgary a reporter saw me slip into the hole because the smoke cleared a little too soon. Headlines in the local newspaper the next day were 'AT LAST THE CLARK SECRET IS OUT.' " But as the Clarks traveled the country with this act, other observers weren't so lucky to figure it out.

"In Mercedes, California, a fellow came up to me," said Bobby, "and said, 'You boys have a hell of an act, how do you do it?' Of course, we wouldn't tell him. But apparently he watched every performance and one day my stand-in came over the fence at the far end dressed like me but had an ace bandage on one arm. The fellow noticed the difference. I wasn't wearing an ace bandage, my stand-in was, and he came back after the performance and said,

Bobby Clark, C. T. Jones, and Gene Clark in St. Louis, 1971.
(Photo by Bern Gregory)

'I saw it today, I know what you do.' He was sure pleased with himself."

In Cheyenne a woman came behind the chutes, found Gene Clark, and told him that she, her husband and four friends, all from Pennsylvania, had been there for five days watching the rodeo and were totally baffled by the act. The three couples were sitting up nights quarreling over how the act was pulled off. She told Gene they weren't getting any sleep and would he please tell her how the stunt was done so they could finally get some rest. Gene politely told her that he just couldn't tell her, that it was their trade secret and they still had another performance to give. After she begged and begged, looking so tired and dejected, Gene told her that if she came back after the last performance there in Cheyenne, she'd get her answer.

Gene forgot all about the conversation, but no sooner than the last bull was out of the chute and put away she was back at the Clarks' trailer waiting for Gene to fulfill his promise and explain the routine to her. Gene, true to his word, explained it to her in full detail. When he finished she was quiet for a few minutes. Then she looked at Gene, said, "Bull Sh—," and walked off.

The Clarks had another shooting act. Gene, dressed as Speedy Gonzales, Mexican sharpshooter, came into the arena riding full speed on a mule. The mule would stop and Gene would just step off over her head. He wore holsters of ammunition criss-crossed on his chest and a huge Mexican sombrero. Gene announced he would shoot a quick split shot, and Bobby, at the other end of the arena, held up a balloon for Gene to shoot. After much hilarity, Gene shot the balloon. It would break *and* Bobby's pants would fall down.

Not every trick worked as it was planned. Once in a while a routine went awry. It was reported that "Hoytt Hefner down in Georgia was working with a gun trying to get it to shoot behind him. Did. Shot him behind. Cartridge had to be removed by surgery requiring thirty stitches, and Hoytt rode home on his stomach where he will be laid up for a while." [10]

Another report of a shooting routine that did not go as planned went like this: "Bobby Clark, Bakersfield, California, was hospitalized when one of the guns used in the clowning went off in his face and the blank shell wadding was imbedded. He was released and returned home." [11]

On more than one occasion, an act dealing with guns and gunpowder did not work as planned. One such incident put Buck

LeGrand out of commission for some time: "Cowboy Clown and bullfighter Buck LeGrand is scheduled to get back into the arena action April 27 at Mesquite, Texas. Buck was badly injured by an explosion during his clown act at Camdenton, Mo., last summer and has been out of action since. His left leg was mangled in the accident and for a time the doctors thought they'd have to amputate. Buck refused to consider that." [11 (1962)] The *Tulsa Daily World* carried a full report on Buck's accident and said, "Buck now gets around as well as ever, claims he never did walk real straight anyway. After a year on the crippled list a man [who] still has his sense of humor will make it all right." [27]

An accident is never expected, but when explosives are used in each performance, the odds of something happening go up a bit: "Rodeo clown Jerry McMann of Phoenix, Arizona, suffered severe damage to both eyes when his 'hat cleaning' trick exploded in his face during the Coer d'Alene, Idaho, rodeo last month. McMann, who isn't blind but has a few sight problems, underwent two operations, and still had one more facing him. He had no idea what caused the explosion. Frank Ellis, retired rodeo clown, from Saugus, California, filled in for Jerry and evidently didn't have any trouble fighting bulls after a ten year absence." [11 (1974)]

A follow-up article two months later said, "A plastic surgeon performed the final operation on September 17, Jerry McMann reports, and 'I'll always carry some of the powder in my face, but for the most part, after I heal I'll be handsome as ever.' " [11]

Some rodeo clowns don't just become heroes in front of the bucking bulls. *Rodeo Sports News* made this report: "Rodeo clown Wiley McCray is in the hospital in Logan, Utah, caused by a giant firecracker exploding in his face. It was at first feared he might lose his eyesight, but the word is now that his vision will be all right. He will be out of action for some time. Wiley got in front of a kid trying to save him, when he saw the firecracker was about to go off, and did keep the child from harm, and got the full blast right in the face." [11 (1963)]

The comedy car act has always been an audience-pleaser. Clark Shultz, second-generation rodeo clown, told: "The 101 Ranch built a bucking Ford. Roscoe Armstrong, from Florida, told the 101 Ranch they would have to pay copyright royalties as he all ready had a bucking Ford. The 101 Ranch just cut their bucking Ford up and threw it away."

Clark, Charley Shultz' son, continued to tell, "At Marlin, Texas, some Indians in a 1923 Model-T touring car ran into my mother

Early bucking car manned by unidentified rodeo clowns.
(Photo by Dean Photo Service; submitted by Ben Johnson)

and just about killed her. The car was about wrecked but Dad took it anyway. The same fellow that built the bucking Ford for the 101 Ranch said to my dad, 'Charley, let's build you one.' They tried to offset the wheels, but it racked it to pieces." Charley always got six or seven kids from the audience to ride in the back of the car for balance. Charley had his funny Ford until 1958.

Charley Shultz bought a Model-T for Clark. Clark said he would go work a rodeo, then go home and work on his car, trying to get it ready to use. That was in spring of 1948. By 1949 Clark was busy working lots of rodeos with his crazy car.

Clark's car was also a bucking Ford, but was designed differently from Charley's car. Clark's car had dual controls: one set in the front, where one would expect the driver to sit, and the second set in the back seat. Arline, Clark's wife, who was part of the act, sat in the back of the car and could control it with her feet, unseen and never realized by the audience.

Clark would drive the car into the arena. It would buck a time or two and then stall. Arline, dressed in a long dress, big floppy hat, and carrying an umbrella, would be sitting in the back seat.

Clark and Arline Shultz in "Buckin' Ford."
(Photographer unknown; submitted by Clark Shultz)

The announcer would say, "Get that thing out of here." Clark would get out of the car, go around in front of the car, and attempt to start it with the crank. When he did it would go "Clap, Clap," but nothing would start. The announcer would suggest, "Check your water, you may be out of water." Clark would unscrew the radiator cap, and when he took the top off water would shoot twenty feet into the air. When he would put the cap back on the radiator, the stream of water would shoot out the top of Arline's umbrella.

Clark would run to the back of the car to catch the spray of water in his hat. When he would get there it would quit spraying out of the umbrella and start squirting out of the radiator again. He would run back and forth, trying to catch the water. Each time he reached the stream of water, it would stop. He would finally give up and go back to crank the car again—still nothing happened.

The announcer would say, "Well, you've got plenty of water. How about the carburetor? Check it." Clark would look under the hood, then reach in and bring out a little dog. The announcer would say, "No wonder it wouldn't go. Look what was in there."

Clark would try to crank it again. Still nothing would happen. The announcer would then ask Clark, "How far did you come in that car?" Clark would yell back, "We left at daybreak, we've come a long way." The announcer would answer, "You are probably out of gas." Clark would move around to the gas tank and show that he was going to strike a match and look in the gas tank. With that, Arline, still sitting in the back seat, would jump up when she saw what he was going to do. She would jump out and start hollering, with suitcase in hand, and run off about fifty feet and stop. A loud explosion would go off, as if the gas tank had blown up, and lots of blue smoke appeared.

The suitcase Arline was holding would fly open, with clothes and a live skunk tumbling out. Arline, after chasing the skunk and catching him, would head back to where she dropped the suitcase—holding him at arm's length and holding her nose with her other hand. The announcer would then comment, "I see you carry your own perfume, Corral #5."

Arline would gather up all the clothes that had fallen out of the suitcase, stuff them and the skunk back in, close the suitcase, and get back in the car. The announcer would say, "Well, it's gotta go now. You got plenty of gas." Clark would crank it again. The announcer interrupts, "Wait a minute. I know what's the matter. You gotta pull the spark down." (All Model-Ts required manual spark adjustment.)

At this point, Arline would stand up in the back seat and lean over. When he'd crank, she'd reach over to the steering wheel and pull down the spark. It would then start and she would grab the steering wheel, lose her balance, and fall back into the back seat with the loose steering wheel still in her hands. Unseen by anyone else she would proceed to guide the car and control the gas by the levers on the floorboard of the back seat. At this point the car would be going about twenty-five miles an hour in a circle. Clark would take a run, jump over the hood, and walk across the car. Just as he would go off the back, he would grab the back end of the car and it would drag him. His suspenders would get attached, and as they were pulled his pants would fall down. He'd grab his britches, pull them up, run, jump on the running board and back fender, and flip into the back seat. Arline would then move over and he would settle into the seat and take over the controls.

Clark would make the Ford back up and buck. Meanwhile Arline, sitting next to him, would hold up the loose steering wheel. Clark would run the Ford in a tight circle, while Arline braced her feet on the back of the front seat and grabbed hold of Clark's britches to keep from being thrown out. Just as Clark was ready to leave the arena in the car, he would pull a lever that would squirt a spoonful of oil into the manifold. It would throw out a big puff of smoke, as the finale. This was quite an act and always delighted the audience.

"Once at a rodeo in Dallas I had just filled the oil tank with oil and had about ten pounds of pressure. Since just a teaspoonful of oil makes the right size puff of smoke to end the act properly," Clark explained, "I was frantic when I pulled the rope to release the oil and the return spring broke, allowing oil to continue squirting on the manifold. It wouldn't stop. We had so much smoke it completely filled the entire arena. They had to stop the rodeo and wait until the smoke cleared, which took a while. First it rose a little from the ground and just hung there. You could see the horses' legs moving around the arena, but the smoke was still completely blotting out the riders and upper bodies of the horses. Slowly the cloud of smoke rose and dissipated and finally they could resume the rodeo."

Cowboy clowns rode bucking stock every which way they could think of to get laughs. They rode double, backwards, and carried chickens and suitcases loaded with all sorts of paraphernalia. Charley Lyons had a variation of the ride that not many tried. He bolted a washtub to a saddle, and it was put on an exhibition bucking horse. "The audience would be expecting one more contestant to come out of the chute," described Charley, "and there I'd be sitting in a washtub."

Plain old cooking flour was placed in the bottom of the tub so that with each jump of the bronc the flour would fly and look like dust flying. "One time in Fort Worth I put a little too much flour in the tub," said Charley. "The horse came out of the chute and bucked right next to the fence in front of the box seats, where some Fort Worth councilmen and city dignitaries were seated. The flour covered them, too. It was kinda comical to see these prominent men trying to wipe the flour off their dark suits," chuckled Charley.

Other rodeo clowns were interested in copying Charley's washtub routine. After he showed them his bruises, caused by the rough ride, most changed their minds. Earlier arena funnymen had variations of the routine. Tin Horn Hank Keenen had an old tub he cinched on a bronc, and he would sit in it as if he were taking a bath. [38] Steve Shannon used an old wicker rocking chair on the

Charley Lyons rides in metal washtub filled with flour, 1959. This act was too hard on the body and few copied it.
(Photographer unknown; submitted by Charley Lyons)

back of a bull once. He made the ride, but getting off proved to be a problem. He almost broke his back. [39]

Mules and Other Friends

Some of the tricks rodeo clowns taught their animals would surprise anyone, including another rodeo clown. Pinky Gist had an appaloosa mule. During one performance, Pinky asked Charley Shultz to go sit down in the arena. Charley did so, and Pinky had his mule go and sit on top of Charley. The audience laughed, but the joke was really on Charley. The mule would not get up nor let Charley up. No matter what Charley tried to do, the mule continued to sit on top of Charley. This went on for some time, and Charley no longer found it amusing. Finally, Pinky gave the mule the signal and it stood up. Charley never fell for that trick again.

The *Ketch Pen* carried this article:

Every good clown must have a mule, so Hoytt Hefner bought Martha Raye from another good clown, George Tyler,

JERRY
MERILUCH
& FRIEND

and anyone who ever saw them work, knew it was pure delight to watch them.

Hefner worked with most all of the good rodeo clowns of his day, but when he and John Lindsey teamed up there were no holds barred.

Hefner and Lindsey were the originators of riding a bucking horse double. They first tried it on one of stock contractor Homer Todd's horses at Gladewater, Texas. The rider had bucked off, so John and Hoytt climbed aboard. Lynn Beutler, another stock contractor, liked the idea but thought it best to give them a little more protection, so he furnished a special horse for them at his rodeos. The way these two would work this it always seemed to be spontaneous, and not planned. [13]

Mrs. Gertrude Hefner, Hoytt's wife, wrote in a letter: "The first time Hoytt and John rode the bucking horse double the two mounted the horse in the middle of the arena. John in the saddle, with Hoytt behind the saddle with nothing to hang on to. He grabbed John's suspenders. After about three jumps the suspenders broke and Hoytt flew into the air, landing on his back. After the pickup men rescued John, he ran back to revive Hoytt, and a new act was born. Some other clowns tried their luck at the double riding, but gave up. The ground wasn't always soft."

In 1938 whenever the word "Brahma" was mentioned, every-

Hoytt Hefner and John Lindsey riding a bronc. Taken from a 1947 Round-Up. (Submitted by Mrs. Hoytt Hefner)

one thought of a vicious, bucking Brahma—a killer. When the following article appeared in *Hoofs & Horns* in January 1938, it was evident that this act was quite a novelty:

> Something new and different in the way of a rodeo clown was seen at the Chandler, Arizona, rodeo. Brahma Bill Harbison clowning with a Brahma steer. Bill and "Buster" are already familiar to rodeo fans all through the Northwest with their presentation of a Trained Brahma Steer Act, but their clowning is the real climax of the accomplishments.
>
> Buster, transformed from one of the meanest Brahmas in any man's string of rodeo stock, has responded to Bill's skill and patience in a way that has to be seen to be believed. Buster not only does as he is told, but Buster really loves the show, and is as much the clown as Bill is, and Bill is a "natural." Not only the children hail Bill and Buster, but when Bill's novel and amusing make-up, teamed with Buster's flapping ears and high Brahma hump, first enter the arena, the grown-ups too realize that here is something that will bear watching.
>
> Bill exhibits magic powers by pumping water into a bucket right out of Buster's ear. Buster and Bill also do a clown pedes-

tal act which is skill combined with humor, and which gets many a laugh from the stands. Buster alas, drinks his beer out of a bottle, and disgraces Bill by getting a little drunk right out in front of everybody.

But the high spot in Bill's and Buster's clowning is their take-off of "The Law of the Range," the educated horse act so familiar to all rodeo audiences. Buster's performance is faultless, Bill makes of his part something different and real fun. From the moment of their entrance until the final taps they put across an act that is as novel as it is truly humorous. [10]

A trained buffalo was reported in a 1939 issue of *Hoofs & Horns:*

> In 1936 Diamond D. Dewey purchased a buffalo from the Senator Carey Ranch, near Douglas, Wyoming. The buffalo was a year and four months old and weighed three hundred and ninety pounds. He now stands even with Dewey's shoulders and weighs over a thousand pounds. A buffalo deceives his looks. Instead of being clumsy as you would suppose, he is unusually quick and fast in his movements.
>
> This buffalo will eat any kind of feed, even fond of carrots and sugar. He does his tricks at Dewey's command. No whip is needed to make him work. He has been worked on the stage, in theaters and at rodeos and fairs. Dewey also uses a black mule that weighs 420 pounds. He does all kinds of clown tricks, plus a full line of high school tricks, such as walking on his hind feet, turning a somersault, jumps a standard car, spins a flat loop in his mouth. This mule was used in Andy Clyde Comedies in Hollywood last winter. [10]

It has always been known that mules are smarter than horses, but the O'Neill Brothers knew their mule was a cheat: "Mules are smarter than horses. But that does not mean that mules are easier to train or to work with than horses. On the contrary, a horse will not cheat very much as you put him through his tricks, because he is not smart enough. But a mule, though he learns his tricks much more readily, is so smart that he learns to cheat and you have to watch him all the time, told the O'Neills." [10]

In a *Hoofs & Horns* article a few months later, the O'Neills said: "Skimmilk, who is a little lady mule, knows a lot of tricks—more than 30 in all, that includes telling her age, standing with all four feet on a stool less than a foot in diameter, climbs on a small turning stool with all four feet, kicks a football, walks on her hind legs, does an Egyptian prayer, dances and does many other things.

She seems to understand everything we say to her." [10]

John Lindsey's first mule was named Hoover and was given to him by his best friend, Bud Kemp. Herbert Hoover was president at the time, and when an announcer would ask Lindsey why he called the mule Hoover, John would reply, "Because he won't do a d—— thing." [13]

Mules and other animals used in clown routines became part of the rodeo family. One report serves as an example: "Jimmy Nesbitt's little mule, Billy, developed lameness in a front leg soon after coming to Tucson. All through the act at the show every day Jimmy eased Billy along. After the rodeo closed Billy became really sick and Jimmy and wife, Pauline, Montie Montana and two vets nursed him through one night when it looked as if their efforts would be in vain. But Billy is a game little fighter and began to improve. He's doing very well at this writing." [10 (1940)]

Most of the mules that rodeo clowns used were the small kind that made the clown look out of proportion when riding him. But Dick Griffith encouraged Elmer Quait, while both were with the 101 Wild West Show, to work out something new in trick riding. He used a full-sized farm-work mule named Eli: "The first show Eli worked with Elmer was Fort Worth in 1939. Elmer went in with

Jimmy Nesbitt and mule Billy Sunday.
(Photo by R. R. Doubleday, National Cowboy Hall of Fame Collection)

the understanding with the management that if, after the first performance, he was no good that both he and the management
would forget it. But he literally stole the show and worked every
performance. He can do any trick on Eli that any rider can do on a
horse, and is the only person to go under a mule's belly while
running at full speed." [10]

An act that always brought the audience to their feet with
thrills and chills was Homer Holcomb's Brahma bull hitched to a
chariot. *Hoofs & Horns* described this incident involving the act:

> Closest of the recent escapes came at the Amador County
> rodeo at Jackson in the final act as Homer rode chariot behind a
> particularly mean Brahma bull owned by Harry Rowell,
> Hayward, California, rodeo king. In the act the bull is hitched to
> the chariot and held by means of a slip catch that can be re-
> leased should the going get too tough. At Jackson, however,
> this catch failed to work. While the crowd gasped in terror the
> angry bull hauled Homer about the arena at breakneck speed.
> Suddenly the bull halted, turned and started butting the car-
> riage into the fence while Homer tried frantically to work the
> release. Then there was a groan of agony from the rodeo fans as
> the bull caught one wheel of the carriage in a fence post and
> turned the vehicle completely upside down. It seemed that
> Homer must certainly be crushed beneath the heavy chariot,
> but after what seemed an eternity and with amazing "luck" as
> he described it, he came bobbing out of the whirl of dust with
> the bull hot on his heels. Just in the nick of time he leaped to
> the fence to escape the charging bull. [10 (1941)]

There are times when one person's misfortune can be another
person's good luck. For example:

> A turning point in Jasbo [Fulkerson's] life was the acquisi-
> tion of Eko from Sam Stuart at the Buffalo, New York rodeo. It
> was early morning and Sam was taking nips from a flask. Jasbo
> said, "Early breakfast, Sam?"
> "Damn it, man," said Sam coughing and spluttering, "I got
> a notion to bend this gun barrel around your head."
> Now Jasbo noticed for the first time the butt of a pistol
> protruding from Sam's belt. "Sam, don't you know this eastern
> law don't allow no pistol-packin'?"
> "Worse'n that, I been given to understand I can't even
> shoot my own mule with my own gun in this prissy town. About
> one more sip from this jug an' I'm gonna say to hell with 'em
> and put ol' Eko outa his misery."

Jasbo walked over to a stall at one end of the pen, where a little black mule was lying down, head lowered and ears spread. "Aw, what's the matter with Eko?"

"Horse kicked him on the way up here in the train. He's cut awful bad."

"Call a vet, Sam. He may have a chance. You can't just let him suffer like this," said Jasbo.

"Call a vet, hell. He's too far gone for a vet to do him any good. Anyway I ain't gonna let him suffer no more." Sam stowed the bottle carefully and pulled his gun.

"Wait, Sam." Jasbo blocked his path. "I'll call the vet. Give him a chance—O.K.?"

Sam looked steadily at Jasbo for a long moment and said, "If you call the vet, Jas, he's your mule." Abruptly he turned, walked to his car, and drove away.

For several days Jasbo and the veterinarian worked over the dull-eyed Eko. Weak, and shaky from his fight against infection, the small mule finally regained his feet and began to take food. An elated Jasbo took Eko with him to Toronto, where the barns were big and clean, and hot water available. He fussed over the mule like a mother hen until the devil came back into Eko's eyes and his sleek coat glistened over his round belly.

Jasbo schooled Eko for an hour or so every day and built up a considerable repertoire. At the Toronto show Jasbo showed Eko's act to the promoter of the rodeo, Peter Welch. Welch was delighted and offered Jasbo $250 a week for the act. Now here was MONEY. Guaranteed income. No more dependence on luck in the contests for eating money, though any prize money won in the bull or bronc riding would boost his income to more than Jasbo had dreamed. On a cushion of air three feet thick he walked home to tell Madolyn. [14]

For the 1947 Denver show, Jasbo had a major problem:

His mule Mingo had died, so he borrowed a mule named Dynamite, from friend and rodeo clown, Andy Womack. Jasbo had Dynamite in the back of the pickup early one cold morning. He stopped in Wichita Falls and picked up Hoytt Hefner, good friend and fellow clown, and by mid-morning they were in Electra, Texas. Jasbo glanced in the rear-view mirror and saw smoke pouring from the bed of his truck.

He pulled to the side of the road, and the two men were out of the truck almost before it stopped. The bedding straw was ablaze from a passerby's carelessly flipped cigarette. The fire had done little damage to the pickup, but the small mule's legs and belly were badly burned.

The fire extinguished, Jasbo and Hoytt gently lifted Dynamite back into the truck, and a veterinarian in Electra tended the severe burns. By the time they reached Denver, Dynamite had contracted pneumonia.

Jasbo's face was long as he telephoned Andy Womack to tell him of the mishap.

Jasbo looked in Denver and in Fort Worth for a mule to replace Dynamite, but when he failed it was crabby old Eko that he rode in Fort Worth's Southwestern Exposition and Fat Stock Show in January.

The little mule still was possessed of as much fire as he had shown the first time that Jasbo had ridden him, twenty-two years before. Once more in the spotlight, Eko kicked up his heels and performed each trick as one long accustomed to applause. [14]

Charley Shultz had a mule, Judy. She kicked big beach balls up into the rodeo stands. She could kick a long way. Clark, Charley's son, also used Judy in his rodeo clown acts. Clark explained her ball kicking: "If I put feed in front of her she'd kick while she was eating. If I crawled up behind her she'd never move. But if I stood up, she'd really kick at me. I'd get behind her and kneel and say a prayer, then I'd crawl up and get the rein on her to lead her out. She lived to be 30 years old. Then it was because she fell through the ice and drowned that we lost her."

Hoytt Hefner's bronc mule was named Martha Raye: "She had been spoiled and presented no easy task in breaking, but with patience and mule talk, Hoytt made her one of the greatest. Another part of the Hefner troop was Pedro, a young skunk. On a morning when Hoytt ordered his breakfast in the hotel cafe, he orders ham and eggs and two raw meatballs. The waitress with a dumbfound look asks him to repeat his order, the people next to him stop eating and look, and when the waitress goes to the kitchen, the cook comes up and looks. Cowboys are suppose to be sorta 'tough Jakes,' but do they eat their meat raw? The two meatballs are Pedro's daily diet." [10 (1958)]

Dan Coates, Sr., reminisced about a routine John Lindsey had with his famous miniature Hereford bull, Iron Ore:

John comes in the arena dressed like an old sheriff looking for outlaws. The announcer sets up the act by telling, "He rides out of the mountains into the valley, he looks to the east." (John astride Iron Ore looks to the east.)

"He looks to the west." (John looks to the west.)

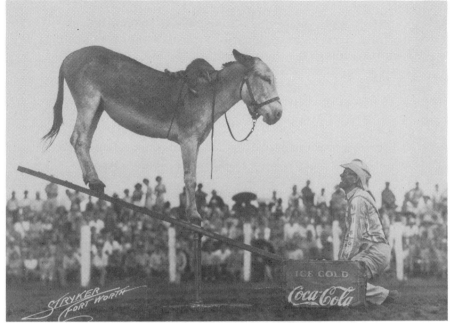

Early-day Charley Shultz performs with mule and raccoon.
(Photo by J. A. Stryker; submitted by Clark Shultz)

Hoytt Hefner astride mule Martha Raye in 1948.
(Photographer unknown; submitted by Mrs. Hoytt Hefner)

"He looks to the north." (John looks to the north.)

"And . . . he looks to the south." (John looks to the south.) Then John shrugs his shoulders signifying he is unable to find the outlaws any direction. Suddenly there is a loud BANG. John falls off his steed, legs trembling.

The announcer says, "Get yourself together," at which time John feels around and discovers he is really all right. He has not been shot.

He proceeds to check Iron Ore and discovers he has been shot in the leg and the leg is broken. The sheriff cries out, "It's broken."

The announcer says, "Sheriff, it's the law of the range, the code of the west. You have got to put that animal out of his misery—you've got to shoot the injured animal."

The sheriff pulls out a long barreled gun from a scabbard on the saddle. He aims at the bull, then he puts the gun down, signifying he just can't do it.

The sheriff takes off his hat and puts it over the bull's eyes; he aims again. But he still can't do it.

The sheriff tells the announcer they have been through too much, they've had a lot of rough times. The sheriff takes out his handkerchief from his back pocket. The dust flies. He bandages Iron Ore's leg with it.

John Lindsey rests on his trained miniature Hereford bull, Iron Ore.
(Photo by J. A. Stryker; submitted by Bill Wittliff, courtesy of
University of Texas–Permian Basin Collection)

He mounts the bull—another shot rings out—and the sheriff falls from the saddle.

The announcer asks, "Will the loyal steed help the sheriff like the sheriff helped his mount?"

With that Iron Ore nuzzles the fallen sheriff, lies down next to him, the sheriff throws his leg over the bull's back. Iron Ore gets up with the limp sheriff lying across his back and rides out of the arena. At that time the announcer says, "Life's blood is drained out and they go over the Great Divide—Together."

This, of course, was a very clever take-off on the famous "End of the Trail" performed so well by Cecil Cornish and his horse, Smokey.

Some old-timers just can't quit, as witnessed at *Hoofs & Horns* headquarters: "Who should come visiting us a few days ago but our old friend and yours, Pinky Gist, as spry as a cricket he is these days, having recovered from the partial stroke he suffered last year. He and his two fat little mules, Mickey (age 30) and Freckles (age 28) have clowned several shows this season and have several more to do." [10 (1950)]

Other accounts of visitors to the office that year were:

Who should come calling a couple of weeks ago but Zeke and Cele Bowery with their "baby," the two year old chimpanzee, Marie. They have had her about six months and she was wild as anything then—bit and scratched on the slightest provocation—but now she is a very well behaved little lady. And it is remarkable how many things they have taught her. Zeke has her take part in his clowning act, but it is Cele who has done most of the training and Marie clings to her much as a real child clings to its mother. She rides the little spotted pony, Champ, in parades and grand entries, sitting up in her own little hand-tooled, silver mounted saddle that Red Allen, saddle-maker in Colorado Springs, made especially for her. [10 (1950)]

But all chimpanzees aren't the same. Gene Lamb described another:

Andy Womack of Phoenix has an older chimp with the interesting name of Cousin Hugo. He is used only in the bull riding, and then fastened with a chain where he can't get near anyone. The chain is snapped onto the cable from which the stuffed dummy used during the event is hung, and Cousin Hugo perched on top of the dummy. When the bulls come out he will jump up and down, hang wrong side up and make passes at the bull. If the bull takes after the dummy up the cable will go

Andy Womack and trained chimp Jocko.
(Photo by J. A. Stryker; submitted by Bill Wittliff, courtesy of University of
Texas–Permian Basin Collection)

Cousin Hugo screaming insults in chimp language. When not in
the arena he is kept in a barred compartment in a trailer, and
even then the clowns have to keep an eye on him to keep some
kid from slipping up and poking at him through the bars. Cousin
Hugo will poke back and he isn't playing. [16]

Slim Pickens' eight-year-old mule, Judy, a half Shetland-pinto
and half Spanish burro, gave him a time:

Judy is definitely a character and as unpredictable as her
master. She often upsets the apple cart and Slim along with it by
doing things her own way at the most unexpected moment.
During the two months they are home from December to
February, Judy leads the Pickens' a merry chase. She turns on
water taps and forgets to turn them off. Opens gates and lets all
the other stock out and almost laughs her fool head off watching Slim and Maggi trying to get them in again. She can untie
just about any kind of knot, and after two months of putting up
with Judy's antics the Pickens family just naturally have to start
rodeoing again to get a little peace and quiet. [10 (1951)]

Wilbur Plaugher had a wonderful act which involved a dog herding ducks.

> Wilbur comes waddling out into the middle of the arena with a sack over his shoulder; the sack has four or five large white ducks which apparently escape. After a little patter with the announcer, giving the ducks time to scatter a ways, he unzips his oversized jeans, and out comes a little black and white dog. The dog takes off after the ducks, and the ducks head for Wilbur who is holding open the sack, and in they go. Once in a while a duck will miss the sack and have to take another circle around to get in the sack. Usually the dog will run into him full tilt, and the duck goes rolling, scrambles to his feet and heads again for the sack.
>
> "Many tricks have been played on me," told Wilbur, "but having my regular ducks switched almost gave my trained duck dog a nervous breakdown. The new ducks had never seen a dog before and scattered like quail. I had another act in which I fired a shot toward the roof of the arena and a dummy duck was suppose to be dropped by a prop man up on the catwalk. The next time I shot, a mallard duck would be let loose. Well, I let the gun roar once and nothing happened. Then twice, and finally at the third shot, both the dummy duck and the mallard were slung down. The prop man had gone to sleep. [10 (1951)]

Some of the glitches that happened in an act not only caused a clown to wince at the mistake, but at times grimace in pain. *Hoofs & Horns* reported: "Once when the Old Grey Mare was picking up Ken Boen by the seat of his Wrangler jeans, the horse bit down so hard that he hurt his lip. This infuriated him so much he gave Ken a hard shake, hurting it even more, which made him throw up his head and raised his upper lip, and so appeared to laugh. Many audiences have enjoyed his famous 'horse laugh' since for he repeated the same thing in each succeeding performance thereafter." [10 (1951)]

And sometimes it was the clown who felt it: "Wiley McCray helping Jay Sisler and his Australian Shepherds, in the shooting part of the act, really suffered the damages. Every time Stub and Shorty (Jay's dogs) went after those big clown pants they got more than just pants, result being several bandages and much iodine and finally a leather in-seat sewn in the overgrown levis." [10 (1952)]

And sometimes they just got into trouble. Gene Lamb wrote:

> Buddy Heaton usually improvises as he goes along, but he does have one act that he uses in conjunction with his clown-

ing and bullfighting. This is a horse named El Rocco, a beautiful animal of mahogany color. Buddy sometimes improvises with El Rocco. During the Denver rodeo one year when working with George Mills they waited for a lull in one of the horse show events to put their plan in action. The Denver rodeo is held interspersed with various horse show classes sandwiched in between rodeo events. The one Buddy and George were waiting for was a jumper class. Quite a few of the jumpers had been faulting, and the judges declared a time out while the grooms went around straightening up standards and poles. As soon as they were through, and before another jumping entry could be signaled in, the gate on the far end of the arena swung open, and here came Buddy, in full clown regalia, mounted bareback on El Rocco. El Rocco was trained to do standing jumps straight up in the air, throwing Buddy up so that he would come down astride several times, then off onto the ground the last time.

A three- or four-foot running jump was nothing, around and over the jumps he went, Buddy waving his arms and legs and slithering back and forth. Buddy and his horse may not have placed as to form, but there was no doubt about their jumping ability. The caper almost created a storm, but was settled by the clowns apologizing to the judges and the jumpers. I don't know what form the apology took; knowing the clowns they probably ended up saying, "We're sure sorry our horse jumps better than yours." [16]

But not all tricks were played by the rodeo clowns; some were played on them. In an article by Willard Porter in the *Daily Oklahoman,* he relayed:

Before his death in 1974 John Lindsey told your reporter about one occurrence at Clovis, New Mexico. Following the bronc riding, it was the custom at Beutler Brothers rodeos to put a horse called Star, Jr. into the chute for the clown to ride. The gentle horse would deposit the clown onto the ground while the crowd laughed. But there was another horse in the string called Old Star, a wild, fierce bucker that wasn't any fun at all to climb aboard. The mounts bore a startling resemblance to one another.

"You get the picture, don't you?" Lindsey asked me. I had to nod yes.

They switched Old Star for Star, Jr. and Lindsey never knew it until the gate opened and the bad horse lunged into the arena.

"I threw away my suitcase real quick," he said, "and it opened up in the air and a lot of strange clothing floated out.

The crowd laughed, they always did. And I guess they thought it was extra funny that I was on that real tough bucking horse instead of the cream puff I usually rode. Anyway, I hollered for Slim Whaley, the pick-up man, 'Get me off. Get me off,' I yelled. He was laughing harder than anybody but he came and got me. Cowboys love to see a clown get in a jackpot, but they'll go to bat for you when they have to. They don't like to see anybody get hurt. Then it's no longer fun." [24]

During the early '60s the Society for the Prevention of Cruelty to Animals started cracking down on the rodeo world and criticizing various treatment of the stock. After a calf roper roped and tied his calf and judges okayed it as a good catch, Wes Curtis and Sammy Reynosa had a routine of tying a Roman candle to the tail of the calf so it stuck in the air about four inches above the calf's tail. When the calf was untied and ran to the ketch pen, one–two– three flares would shoot up into the air. Mel Lambert, a conscientious and serious rodeo announcer, was always prepared to handle any incident. He would take great pains, prior to the release of the calf, to prepare the audience, "These Roman candles are specially made and they will not harm the calf in any way."

Wes Curtis and mule Porky. A commercial artist today, he designed the drawing for the dust cover of this book.
(Photographer unknown; submitted by Wes Curtis)

Wes decided to play a little trick on Mel, so he visited the local slaughterhouse where he bought a calf hide. The calves being used for roping were all Herefords, so it was not difficult to buy one that looked like the calves being used. Wes asked the man in charge of the fireworks display that ended each performance if he would prepare an explosion in the ketch pen just as the calf entered the pen from the arena.

At the next performance Mel gave the audience his usual lengthy assurance the animals would not be hurt. "The Roman candles were specially prepared not to harm the calves," and so on. Wes and Sammy attached the Roman candle to the calf's tail as usual and the flares shot skyward, as planned. Just as the calf ran into the ketch pen from the arena a huge explosion sounded — *BARRROOOOOOM*...

Everyone's ears were ringing just as Wes ran back into the arena from the ketch pen, dragging the calf hide behind him. Smoke was coming from the hide from a carefully placed smoke bomb hidden under the skin.

Mel Lambert was speechless.

Bobby and Gene Clark had miniature mules. Bobby used them in a Roman riding act. He would stand on their backs as they jumped hurdles. They used scaled-down hurdles identical to the full-sized ones used for regular-sized horses. After each jump the hurdle was raised gradually, making the jump more difficult.

The hurdles were finally placed above the mules' heads. Bobby would then bet the audience he could jump the hurdles even at that height. No one in their right mind would believe him. He surely couldn't jump those little mules over hurdles that were higher than they stood. Bobby still insisted he could do it.

A bet was made. Bobby would get those miniature mules running as fast as their little short legs could go and as they approached the hurdles the mules would go *under* the hurdles, but Bobby would jump *over* them. It was a clever act, and Bobby would collect every time.

Training animals to do what is expected and to *not* do the unexpected sometimes requires drastic measures. For example:

Buck Robinson of Oklahoma City works a bear. Usually he fastens the bear to a post in the arena during the bull riding event, and it's quite a sight to see a bull come bucking out with a cowboy doing his best to stay on and at the same time keep an eye on the bear, who makes a swipe at the bull whenever he comes close enough. One hot day the bear was unusually irri-

table, and while Buck was moving him around, the bear reached out and bit Buck on the end of the nose. Buck didn't give way to fury; he thought it over calmly for at least three seconds, decided it would do little good to cuff a bear, and be damned if he didn't bite the bear soundly on the leg. The bear had pretty good control, too. Instead of him going into a fury, he thought about it over a second or two then crawled up his pole crying piteously. As far as I know that ended the biting match. [16]

Wes Curtis used various acts during his career. One act included chickens. When Wes came home for a few days and put the chickens in the yard to act as "normal" chickens, all was well unless Wes went somewhere in the familiar pick-up. As the vehicle left the yard, the chickens could be found running down the road after the pick-up—wings outstretched and running as fast as they could. Afraid they were being left.

Frank Rhoades told the following account in the *Ketch Pen:*

In 1970 I came up with the idea of the Roman Chariot Race. Jiggs Beutler hired Tommy Sheffield and me with this act. Tommy couldn't even drive a pair of mules. My chariot was to blow up, and the mules were to drag me for a ways. When I started to drag Tommy run over me in the other chariot. Hadley

Barrett was laughing so hard that he almost fell out of the announcer's stand. Jiggs was laughing and said we should do that again the next night. I said, "You'll have to hire another clown, because I am going to kill Sheffield." Next season I teamed up with Rick Young. We had lots of fun and many wrecks with the chariot. Once the chariots were running and I fell out of my chariot backwards. Rick thought I had a heart attack and died. Then there was the time we were at the rodeo in Florida. The chariots were running as fast as the mules could pull them, and the neck yoke on Rick's chariot broke. The tongue of the chariot fell and stuck in the ground. The chariot stopped but the mules kept running. Rick fell out of the chariot and under the mules. One of the mules kicked him. When he got up he commented that this was harder than fighting bulls. [13]

Tommy Lucia, who clowned for twenty-three years, has a comedy act that also tells a lesson:

In His Glory is a six year old horse with an unusual deformity—a grossly exaggerated swayback. Bob Tallman, announcer of the Southwest Exposition and Livestock Show in Fort Worth said, "This horse and man are living proof—no handicap should make you want to quit." Although the routine is comedy Lucia hopes to bring a feeling of hope, not pity, to people who see In His Glory perform. "We all need a booster shot from time to time," he said. "People can plainly see all the good things he can do. He has magnetic charisma, he's feisty and he's obviously happy to be alive. I think this act helps PRCA rodeo spectators appreciate rodeo people more. It's another way of showing them that we truly care about our animals, and draws us closer together with our fans." [12 (1988)]

Announcing the retirement of Roger Mawson's Old Gray Mare at age thirty-two brought some memories of earlier days: "In 1956 Roger and his Old Gray mare joined Bill Estes on a trip to France for a rodeo tour. They sailed on a ship and Peggy (The Old Gray Mare's real name) had to be in a crate she could barely turn around in. The trip took 21 days, weather was terrible on the high seas. She was tired, seasick and hadn't had any exercise. She recovered quickly, however, and they performed and traveled Europe for three months.

"After arriving back in the U.S. they started traveling the rodeo circuit. 'No matter how sore she got from traveling she had always given me her best,' Roger said." [11 (1975)]

Dale Woodard has worked with several trained pigs. One of them, called Gorgeous George, delighted in jelly beans and hot cakes. The pig went blind and worked by voice command the last year he worked. "Dale is a natural at communicating well with animals. He wants them to like what they do. For example, he doesn't ask his chickens, Blinkey and Machine Gun Joe, game chickens, to perform at night because they go to sleep when the sun sets." [12 (1990)]

For every story about an animal told here there are hundreds more that haven't been told. Animals are very special to rodeo clowns. Their time spent with these highly trained friends doesn't stop when they leave the arena. They are with them daylight to way past dark, seven days a week, continually training and practicing. Even the glitches don't just happen.

Getting attached to their animal friends also causes a great sadness when something happens to one of them. *Hoofs & Horns* reported this loss:

> Ken Boen for many years has had his specialty act with the Old Grey Mare and was planning to retire his companion in the act—whose real name was Tony. Then a few weeks ago a gate was accidentally left open and Tony, together with Ken's other horses, got out on the highway and Tony was hit by a car and left with a badly mutilated leg. After several days treatment by a vet who amputated the leg, Tony developed hyperstatic pneumonia and died with Ken's arms around him.
>
> We can imagine Ken's grief at losing his faithful friend in such a tragic way.
>
> Tony was buried directly behind Ken's house in Ft. Smith, Arkansas, in the sitting position he was so famous for, with his pipe and covered with a Blue Bell Wrangler blanket. He advertised Blue Bell Wrangler jeans in the act.
>
> Tony was the only trick horse that ever repeated five consecutive years in Madison Square Garden and Ken had turned down hundreds of offers to buy him. In 1944 Ken refused a Radio City Movie contract because of a foot injury that Tony had and Ken thought the work in the movies would be too hard on him.
>
> Ken has a young Old Grey Mare which he has been using of late because of Tony's advancing age, and he is fortunate that this young horse escaped injury.
>
> And so the Old Grey Mare has passed on to greener pastures where there are no injuries and no limitations of age, but where he is probably still listening for his master's voice. [10 (1951)]

WAITIN' IN THE BULL PEN

MACK BERRY

Another sad demise hit the 1951 rodeo circuit: "Zeke Bowery's chimp, Marie, died when a stray dog rushed her and she ran up a telephone pole to a live wire and was electrocuted." [10 (1951)] In 1953 this death was reported: "Jo Jo, Bennie Bender's famous mule, has passed on to his reward. Jo Jo recently retired after 19 years in show business and one of the most traveled mules in the country. He had been taught to evade bulls and broncs in the arena, but no caution as to cars. He wandered onto a highway and got struck by a motorist. Next day Jo Jo was buried on a hill near his winter home, Selby, South Dakota, and the family mourned his death. 'It was like losing a member of my family,' Bennie said." [10 (1953)]

Another sad day was in 1968: "Whirligig, Mac Barry's clown mule, died apparently of a twisted intestine, last month at an estimated 38 years old." [11 (1968)]

In 1970: "Bobbie Hill is lamenting the loss of his famous little jenny, Rose Bud, which passed away this year at the age of 31. This little trick star was given a fitting burial. She had toured the rodeo circuit and been in nightclub acts and stage shows with Bobbie for years. She was originally owned by Al McMillan, formerly a clown and bullfighter throughout Idaho and Utah." [11 (1970)] And 1972: "Larry Clayman lost his trick horse at Waynesboro, Va., during the rodeo there last month. He got loose from his stall and wandered out on the highway and got hit by a car." [11 (1972)]

As many a rodeo announcer has said: "And as they go to the Great Divide—let us hope that it is filled with tall grasses and cool water for our dear departed friends."

Antics Outside the Arena

All the hilarious things rodeo clowns did and were accused of doing weren't done just in the arena. In fact, there are probably tales that no one will ever hear because they are so wild.

In his book, Foghorn Clancy tells this story:

> I was rooming with Red Kelly during a rodeo and they started a dice game. Some cowboys accused a gambler of cheating. As the gambler left he heaved a heavy water pitcher at Kelly and knocked him cold. The cowboys gave the gambler a real working over. People ran out of their rooms to see what was happening but they subdued them. The next day Kelly had gone to the fair ground when Red Sublett dropped in to the room to talk about the fight before we went out for the performance. Other cowboys dropped in until there were six of us. Then in came two plain clothes detectives to start their own investigation.
>
> We claimed we knew nothing but they got sore and took us to the district attorney's office. They wanted someone to plead guilty, but we said "nothing doing." They let everyone go but Red Sublett and myself. It was getting close to show time. The boys who had been released reached the grounds and told Kelly that his clown and announcer were down at the jail. Kelly got the secretary of the fair to phone the police and ask them to let us go and they would pay the fine.
>
> When Foghorn got to Dallas for the State Fair he thought the incident over but two fellows showed up and he ended up paying $60 odd dollars for he and Red to close the matter. [4]

Another early incident happened in Kansas City, 1922, and isn't it funny how the rodeo clown always seems to be along? Bill King explained:

> Two or three days before the rodeo was to start Fred Beebee came out to the barn in a great big white car. It was a retired fire chief's car and was a seven passenger job with gold colored trimming and it had a huge pair of steer horns mounted on the front of the radiator. I believe it was a "Willis Knight"

car. It was a big touring car with the top down.

He asked some of us if we wanted to take a spin. So Sammy Garrett, Red Sublett, Guy Weadick, Cliff and I got in and Fred BeeBee took off. We went down in the main part of the city to Twelfth Street where BeeBee had set up the headquarters for the rodeo in the Washington Hotel. After leaving there, we went over on Fourteenth Street. BeeBee had been in Kansas City quite a while and kind of knew his way around so we stopped at a Speak Easy (prohibition days term for a saloon) for a few drinks. When we left there we were "feeling no pain" and had bought a quart of their white lightning to take along. We were rolling along pretty good on Thirteenth Street when a car started to pull out from the curb and BeeBee swerved to miss it. Something happened and we turned the car over onto its right side. Well, we all rolled out, the bottle of whiskey which had been laying in the bottom of the car went sliding down over that rough brick pavement about twenty feet. What kept it from breaking, I'll never know, and remember, this is during PROHI-BITION! Well, we sure did some scrambling. I recovered the bottle, we tipped the car back on its wheels and got on our way without too much commotion. [7]

Another account in King's book told:

Tommy Douglas, one of the early rodeo clowns, had gotten a ride for himself, his little mule and a trunk with a carload of performance horses being shipped from California, and had a clowning job someplace close to Omaha, and was needing transportation pretty bad. He had slipped his mule, his trunk and himself into one of the empty doorways along with two or three other fellows, thinking the train would have to stop in a place like Omaha. But the train never stopped, just slowed down to ten or fifteen miles an hour going through there. Several of us fellows knew he was on the train, so we were watching out the windows. When the train started picking up speed we saw this big trunk go out the door, then this mule's head appeared, but there were two blocks passed before the mule got shoved off, and we were moving pretty good. Tommy bit the dust, as the saying goes, when he bailed out. By the time we got out of sight, the little fellow had gathered his mule, and rode him back to gather up the trunk. That was the last time I ever saw Tommy Douglas. [7]

The Madison Square Garden Rodeo was always quite an event for the cowboys. They all looked forward to it. Today they have many fond memories of the time spent there during the rodeos.

For years there were more than thirty performances in the Madison Square Garden Rodeo. This description is of one of those performances:

> The rodeo season opened with a parade in New York. People lined the sidewalks to see these unusual types in the city. The clowns rode their miniature mules. Jasbo's new mule, Gravel Gertie, was one of the smallest. Her dainty legs looked as if they would splinter beneath Jasbo's 175 pounds.
> "Hey George," Jasbo would cry to George Mills, the other clown of those days. "Betcha can't catch me," and off he would charge across the sidewalk and into a department store at Gertie's top speed. Behind him George rode Eddie in close pursuit. Heaven help the working girl and her dignified customers as the wildly yelling, grease-painted clowns urged their wicked little mules at a run through the aisles. [14]

Rodeo clowns take on many roles, and although they have one thing in common—humor—they are described by fans and friends in varying ways. Wayne Ingram and Jane Pattie had this to say about the beloved Jasbo:

> Jasbo's friends said they never saw him angry. He was an incessant prankster, or was being made the butt of the joke himself, and he seemed to enjoy one as much as the other.

Jasbo Fulkerson watches bronc rider as he contemplates a later catch.
(Photo by J. A. Stryker; submitted by Bill Wittliff, courtesy of
University of Texas–Permian Basin Collection)

After each night's show he had a few drinks of Lord
Calvert's and ate a steak the size of his hat. Ordinarily he was
drafted immediately into a party to which he supplied most of
the action. Frequently after these evenings of revelry it occurred
to him to call a friend on the telephone, usually Tad Lucas, and
plead with her to listen to him sing, "I Mighta Gone Fishin," at
three in the morning.

However, he was equally philosophical one morning when
the bellboy at the Broadmoor Hotel in Colorado Springs took
one look at Jasbo's form stretched out in the lobby and ran
screaming for the switchboard operator to call the police and
an ambulance because "a little man had been butchered." The
evening before, Jasbo had lingered too long and actively at the
bar of the Levi Strauss Room. Wandering into the lobby and
coming upon a plushy sofa, he melted into it for a moment to
rest his eyes. He was still out cold when the party broke up and
Tad Lucas spotted him.

With her were Carl and Bernice Dossey, Doff Afer and
Frank Moore from New York, no group to forego the opportunity to dish up a bit of Jasbo Medicine. While Tad and Bernice

smeared him lavishly with lipstick, the men chanced upon a bottle of hotel ink and, using tissues, splotched a number of very nasty looking bruises on Jasbo's peacefully relaxed face.

The bellboy discovering him the next morning could not believe a man could absorb such a vicious beating and still be alive. Jasbo, stumbling blearily to his feet and gazing into a wall mirror, was inclined to agree with him. [14]

Jack Long, rodeo historian, trick rider, and former rodeo clown told me that George Mills drank a lot of whiskey but never seemed to be drunk. Once at a rodeo in New York he was standing over his clown trunk, looking into it. He turned and called to Dick Griffith, "Hey Dick, you want a drink?" Dick, not one to refuse, ambled over and looked in the trunk, expecting to see all the usual clown paraphernalia, make-up, and props. Nope. The trunk was full of liquor bottles—nothing but liquor.

Jimmy Schumacher and Wes Curtis were clowning the Salt Lake City rodeo when Roy Rogers and Dale Evans were featured as guest entertainers. The rodeo committee went to great lengths to make sure Roy and Dale were comfortable. They provided a luxurious trailer house near the arena. Workmen spread small pebbles and made a walkway from the trailer door to an opening into the arena. On each side of the pebbled walkway was a border of larger stones, and potted plants were placed about every four feet on either side. It looked grand.

Wes and Jimmy observed the development of this elaborate decor for the stars and decided they should have the same facilities. Jimmy moved his small, beat-up, well-traveled trailer next to the Rogers' trailer. Wes made a trip to the city dump. They lined a make-shift walkway with old tires. Instead of potted plants Jimmy used old tin cans filled with weeds.

One of Roy and Dale's adopted daughters took a liking to Schumacher's son and spent many hours playing in the front yard of the Schumacher weed-decorated trailer. Roy and Dale enjoyed the joke immensely. The Salt Lake City Rodeo Committee did not share their feelings.

When former rodeo clowns reminisce about some of the tricks they pulled on friends and entertainers, they tell it as if they were innocent bystanders who merely observed the event. For example, Bobby Clark remembered: "Roy Rogers had a shooting act that he performed at rodeos. Somebody bought some dead pigeons and when Roy would shoot, somebody would throw down a dead pigeon from the rafters above the arena."

Bobby also remembered another mischievous event: "The Sons of the Pioneers would perform their theme song, 'Cool Water,' whenever they performed at a rodeo. It was always fun to dump a five gallon bucket of water on the singers in the midst of their song."

During the National Western Stock Show and Rodeo in Denver, Larry McKinney, John Routh, and Chuck Henson, along with other friends from the rodeo, decided after quite a few drinks to visit a strip joint called the Stage Door. By the time they arrived they were plenty drunk. After watching the paid entertainers a while, Larry, Chuck, and John decided they could strip too. They got on stage, but the management was not too keen on the idea. In spite of the management's requests for them to leave the stage Larry, Chuck, and John started to remove their clothing, piece by piece. The management, getting no results, tried other means, and the three were finally subdued—by mace in the face.

Many rodeo clowns have entertained at hospitals throughout the country. Pete Peterson learned through his many visits that it is not always easy to determine from a hospital audience how much they are enjoying an act. Some patients' medical problems are not always distinguishable by sight. Pete learned to watch the eyes of his hospital audience. No matter what the illness of the patient, he could find the real appreciation in their eyes.

Buck LeGrand's a real "show must go on" kind of guy. At one rodeo he arrived with a cast on his leg, which had been broken some time before. When it was time to go to work as a rodeo clown, Buck merely took the cast off and went to clowning.

Another time, when not enough contestants had arrived to make a good showing, the producer asked Buck if he would participate in the bucking horse contest. Although Buck had four broken ribs, he agreed to do it. When he came out of the chute on the first horse, he landed real hard. He got up, left the arena, and it was obvious he was in pain. Without saying a word he just lay down under a wagon behind the chutes. Bobby Clark asked him if he could help. Buck just said, "Leave me alone." Once Buck got his breath back, he was up and back at work. It's hard to keep a good rodeo clown down.

Cowboy clowns have always tried new animals in their acts. They have bought and borrowed various animals, always attempting to find something new for the rodeo audience:

Fess Reynolds thought up a Liberty Zebra Act, and bought

four of the sport model jackasses, had them unloaded in New
York. One of them died in quarantine, but Reynolds and his
helper started west with the other three.

Along in the middle of the great American desert (in the
middle of the night) they stopped to rest. The helper looked in
the back and one striper was down. When they dropped the
tail gate to get him on his feet—striped blurs—they all took off.

They caught one when it was blinded in the glare of the
headlights of an approaching truck, and shoved it back into the
trailer.

They spotted another "spotter" down the road, so Fess got
on the fender with a piece of rope, looped at one end, and off
down the road and across the country they bounced, coming
up to the animal Fess roped him; the helper slammed on the
brakes, and Fess continued to bounce—along behind the zebra.
Fess said he knew if he let go that's the last they'd ever see of
him.

These were small animals, and none too sturdy after the
long trip and long haul, so when the roped animal tired a little,
Reynolds crawled up to him and bulldogged him down. They
got him back into the truck and gave up for the night. After a
few hours sleep they lost interest in the last zebra, and took off
down the road with the other two.

Next day on down the line a piece in the paper explained

the mystery. "Dead Zebra Found by Highway." Fess figured he
just laid down and passed away from exhaustion and excite-
ment. And so through *Rodeo Sports News* we solve the other
mystery of "where did all them damn Zebras come from." [11
(1959)]

Buddy Heaton buys and sells horses. At home in Hugoton,
Kansas, he has a yak. "I was told you couldn't train a yak to ride,"
said Heaton. So he immediately decided to saddle break him. While
trying to saddle the yak it turned and bit Buddy on the hind side. It
made Buddy so mad he tied a bear he owns in the saddle on the
yak's back and let them go. Buddy said they were all over the place.

A rodeo arena wasn't the only place where a rodeo clown
performed. There was no telling where you would find them. For
example: "Buddy Heaton was a crazy clown. Huge man of 240
pounds who wore hair down his back and a long Buffalo Bill
handlebar mustache. 'You know Buddy was in President Ken-
nedy's inaugural parade,' said Skipper Voss. 'Nobody knew how
he got there, because he apparently didn't have a parade permit.
But there he was, riding that buffalo, in the parade for the President of the United States.' " [16]

Another Buddy Heaton incident, as told by Gene Lamb, occurred in Calgary: "Heaton had a substantial bet on a particular
horse in a race at the Calgary Stampede one year. He watched from
the infield as his choice faded badly around the final turn. This so
infuriated Buddy that he jumped on his pet buffalo, an animal he
used in his act, and rode straight on to the race track and toward
the oncoming horses. It caused somewhat of a commotion. Jockeys and horses scattered in every direction to avoid the wild man
on the speeding buffalo. No, they never asked Buddy Heaton back
to Calgary again." [16]

Dan Willis, auctioneer today but former rodeo clown, relayed
the following story:

> We were in Louisville, Kentucky, and heading back to
> Texas to the Texarkansas Rodeo. Kajun Kid drove a big Chrysler
> and he always let me ride with him.
>
> It was going to be a tough ride to get there in time for the
> rodeo because of the distance. Toward the end of the last Lou-
> isville performance a bull had me up against the chute. Kajun
> yelled to John Routh, the third clown in the arena, "Help, John,
> he's killin' my driver." Kajun always told me, [said Willis], "I
> don't want a bunch of those bull riders in my car drinking beer."
>
> Well, the rodeo was over and we headed toward Texas. It

started to rain. About ten miles down the road we saw a soldier hitchhiking. Kajun told me to pull over and pick him up.

During the course of the trip, we found out the soldier was coming from his mother's funeral and trying to get back to camp. We drove a few miles more and Kajun told me to pull in at the next cafe. "I heard this is a good place to get a steak," said Kajun.

Before we got to Texarkansas we took the soldier right to his base, which was 100 miles out of our way. We got to the rodeo 30 minutes before the performance was to begin.

There is a constant supply of Kajun stories. One involves a bet Kajun had made on an important sporting event to be shown on television. He was really looking forward to the game on TV. It was July 20, 1969, and NASA had sent a man to walk on the moon for the first time. All TV stations were tuned in to this awesome world-wide event. Everyone in America, that is except Kajun, seemed to hang on every word about this history-making feat.

Dan Willis knew Kajun's desire to see this special game. Although it was untrue, Dan told Kajun that the TV network had canceled the showing of the game because of the space shot to the moon. Kajun ranted and raved. He was so mad he fussed, "I'm so tired of that moonwalk. They aren't on the moon anyway. They are in someone's pasture. Everyone knows the moon is yellow."

Marie Whiteman, former rodeo timer, used to write a column for the *Rodeo Sports News* entitled "Things & Stuff." In it she reported, "Ike Thomason was up in the bareback bronc riding in Little Rock Tuesday night and was sitting by the chute with his head in his hands and sniffing and sneezing and Jimmy Schumacher walked by and said, 'What is it, Ike?'

"Ike answered, 'I'm up in the bareback tonight and I've got Asiatic Flu.'

"Jimmy says, 'What's his number?' " [10 (1957)]

It is not enough to dodge Brahmas during a show; some cowboy clowns seem to like to walk right on the edge. *Rodeo Sports News* reported: "Clown Jim Hill of Enid, Oklahoma, reports he sure will be glad to fill his book and start doing safe things like bullfighting or riding. Jim recently, in fact on Friday the 13th, joined an elite group known as 'Loyal Order of White Fangs.' It is for people who have survived the bite of a deadly poisonous snake. He and companion, Steve Cox, had captured a rattlesnake and were transferring the reptile from a sack to a jar when it got loose. They were both bitten on the hand and treated and held for obser-

vation at St. Mary's Hospital in Enid." [11 (1973)]

Sometimes fearless funnymen forget what is happening in the real world: "Chuck Henson tried to leave Tucson to go to the next rodeo with 20 pounds of black powder, but they wouldn't let him take it on the airplane." [13 (1986)] Damned inconsiderate of them, Chuck thought.

At the 1988 National Finals Rodeo Historical Society's Awards Program, D. J. Gaudin (Kajun Kid) was honored and was introduced by Mel Lambert, announcer and longtime friend. Mel had this memory:

> We announcers serve as projectors for the rodeo clowns. I couldn't understand Kajun because of his dialect for quite awhile after I met him. But I want to thank these rodeo clowns. Without them we would have been rather dry. Sometime back Kajun had collected and made some black strap molasses. He had some at a rodeo, I tasted it, commented on how much I liked it and Kajun sent me a bucket of it.
>
> Well, apparently the rough treatment by the U.S. Postal Service jarred the lid loose. It sat in my mailbox just long enough to attract a swarm of bees. The sorghum was running down the post of the mailbox and it turned the box completely black with bees. We couldn't get the mail out for days. I finally poured

diesel oil all over it, set fire to it, burned it to the ground and put up a new mailbox. Thanks anyway, Kajun.

Gathering information to compile this book uncovered many stories. It is a shame not to be able to include each and every one. Interviews and visits with rodeo clowns made me realize there is not just one type of person that becomes a rodeo clown. Personalities included extreme extroverts to very shy men—and everything in between.

One very late night during National Finals Week in Las Vegas, a group of retired rodeo clowns, cowboys, and friends continued the revelry they are so good at. We had been partying since early evening. One of the retired rodeo clowns asked me, in a seemingly serious manner, if I had ever made love to a rodeo clown. I replied that I hadn't.

With a little twinkle in his eye he said, "Well, we may not satisfy you, but we'll put a little smile on your face."

How They Became Laugh-getters

Seldom does anyone really know how they plan to spend their life and make a living. After the earliest plans to be a fireman, a policeman or a cowboy are past, a person grows a little older, matures some, and starts thinking more seriously. Or do they?

The following accounts will prove there is really no rhyme or reason as to who decides to become a rodeo clown.

Jasbo Fulkerson:

As a youth Jasbo rode steers at North Fort Worth Stock-yards (1924) and he tried riding bulls. He saw Red Sublett clown. Jasbo rode bulls, trick rode and bull-dogged. Later as he sat with Madolyn in the stands between the steer wrestling and bull riding events, he suddenly said to her, "Just look at every-body, Baby. All scrunched down in their seats, pullin' their hats down over their ears. Never any laughs from start to finish. What they need is a clown act, and I just figger Eko and me can give 'em one."

He discussed the idea with Welch (rodeo promoter) who encouraged him wholeheartedly, because so many of the cow-boys were refusing to ride bulls, unless there was a clown there ready to attract the bull's attention from a fallen rider. Madolyn made Jasbo some loud, baggy shirts and a ridiculous big vest emblazoned with mules, while Jasbo worked Eko's tricks into a comic routine that started as a filler to amuse the spectators while the chute-handlers were preparing for another event. Quickly this act became so notable as a crowd pleaser that Welch began to feature it. [14]

Homer Holcomb:

Another man who had made a business of following the rodeo in the precarious occupation of a rodeo clown, a man who because of his ability in the work need not take a back seat for anyone, is Homer Holcomb. He was formerly a world's relay riding champion and all- around contestant, in his seventeen years of being "funnyman" for rodeo, he has earned a reputation of fearlessness that few possess. [15]

Benny Bender:

When Benny Bender was fourteen he began breaking horses and at eighteen first rode at a rodeo. At the suggestion of the McMackin boys he started clowning, but also kept on contesting, riding broncs and bulls.

While clowning some shows for Guy Weadick in Canada, the latter took an interest in Bender and gave him some valuable pointers in the business of clowning.

His mule, Joe Louis, has become one of the best trained mules in the business, and with him Bender has clowned shows, big and little, in the United States and Canada. Each year they have new tricks and add more contracts to their score. [10 (1939)]

*   *   *

One day after a bad spill, a cowboy picked Benny Bender up and set him right side up on shaky legs. With an arm around the game buckaroo the rodeo man said, "You've got what it takes, Benny. Why don't you learn to clown? I'll show you."

Benny got a lump in his throat at the magnanimity of the offer. The friend was Jimmy Nesbitt, a great clown in the rodeo world, and one of Benny's heroes of the arena. [10]

Hoytt Hefner:

As a youngster Hoytt Hefner knew he wanted to be a clown, to make people laugh and to protect cowboys. He and his three brothers put on their own rodeo in the barn lot, inviting all the neighbor kids. He was raised on a ranch near Wichita Falls, Texas. At age 17, Hoytt went to the Fort Worth Stock Show and Rodeo and entered the bareback and bull riding. [13 (1987)]

*   *   *

Jimmy Schumacher and his famous barrel after (1951) he removed the bottom. (Photographer unknown; submitted by Jimmy Schumacher)

Hoytt Hefner decided he was getting a little too many rings on his horns to be a rodeo contestant any more, so he began clowning and bull fighting. [10 (1950)]

Jimmy Schumacher:

Jimmy Schumacher worked for Clyde Miller's Wild West Show in 1936. He was 16. In 1945 he won the bull riding in Calgary, and in 1946 and 1947 won the bareback riding. He became friends with George Mills and in Phoenix in 1949 word was received the other clown, Jasbo Fulkerson, had been killed in an auto accident. George gave Jimmy some of his clown clothes and some tennis shoes, that were too small for him, and put him in the barrel, and this is where he stayed until he retired in 1970. [13 (1986)] ·

Wilbur Plaugher:

"During the war, rodeos were sometimes unable to get bull-fighters to protect the riders," told Wilbur Plaugher, in an article in *Hoofs & Horns* entitled "My Life as a Rodeo Clown":

Since I rode bulls I would often protect my riding buddies and soon I was in demand as a bullfighter. It was during the repair of a broken chute that Wilbur, the clown, was born. The producer wanted me to do something funny to keep the crowd from getting bored. I was very shy, quiet and unfunny. It was unbelievably difficult for me. I was like the dummy in Charlie McCarthy's act. Then the announcer began to tell jokes that he credited to me and the audience roared. Doing it that way made it easy.

When I was offered pay for clowning I was convinced that I could be funny, and with the help of a wig and makeup to hide behind, my career was born. My first act included a pig and a bottle and was not too funny, but I discovered a brand new thing: there is a kind of magic that takes place between an audience and a performer. A relationship begins and you have but one desire—to please them and hear their response. Nothing else seems to be as important as the result of this communication. It's thrilling, rewarding, and very addictive. I've come to realize there is no point of saturation and a performer can never really get enough. [10 (1951)]

Ken Boen:

At the age of fifteen Ken Boen bought a two-year old grey

Ken Boen and the "Old Grey Mare." When the mule died, Ken buried her in this position with her Wrangler blanket and pipe.
(Photo by J. A. Stryker; submitted by Bill Wittliff, courtesy of University of Texas–Permian Basin Collection)

horse and began teaching him tricks to relieve the monotony of farm life in his Danville, Illinois, home. Soon he was exhibiting the horse at nearby fairs, calling him the "Old Grey Mare." Thus began his career as clown with his act of that name. [10 (1951)]

George and Hank Mills:

Ranch-raised near Grand Junction, Colorado, George Mills and younger brother, Hank, were jockeys before they decided in the early '30s, that they preferred chute gates to starting gates. It was as barebackers that they first went their winning ways. For three years running, 1939, '40 and '41, Hank topped that event at Madison Square Garden, and George stood second. That last year, '41, George won the IRA bareback championship and in a neat turnabout, Hank galloped right in behind him. By then, George already was sitting high as a funny-businessman. He began clowning a few small shows. He studied the tricks of older clowns and for a year traveled with one of the best, Jimmy Nesbitt. When Jimmy was hurt in New York in 1938, George subbed a few performances. And two seasons later, in his grey wig and old man's get-up, he became a regular at both the Garden and Denver—two big timers he's performed for 14 straight years now. For ten of them, his partner, the man in the red barrel, was Jasbo Fulkerson. "Nobody," he says, "could beat Jasbo working that barrel. He brought the idea into the rodeo business." [10 (1954)]

Frank Curry and Jim Wise:

Both Frank Curry and Jim Wise, who will clown at the California Rodeo at Salinas, have unusual backgrounds. Curry is probably the only rodeo clown ever to come out of New York and has been dubbed "the Manhattan Matador." He got his early training as a clown with Ringling Brothers Circus and was introduced to rodeo clowning by Casey Tibbs. Wise is, as far as we know, the only saddle bronc rider to enjoy tangling with the bulls, and almost certainly, the only member of the board of directors to clown intentionally, that is. [11 (1966)]

Quail Dobbs:

Rodeo fans all over the Upper Midwest and even the nation are familiar with the fine bullfighting and humorous antics of diminutive Quail Dobbs of Coahoma, Texas. Quail spent most of the summer working rodeos for Bob Barnes and it wasn't long before a very interesting rumor about Mr. Dobbs began circulating behind the chutes. It seems that Quail "had it made" long before getting into the rodeo game. According to rumor, Quail gave up the security of the top position among

Famous trick rider and early-day lady bronc rider Tad Lucas was recruited to clown on occasion. First time was when Jasbo was killed.
(Photographer unknown; submitted by Mitzi Riley)

the toy makers at the North Pole to lure bulls from fallen cowboys in warmer climes. [11 (1971)]

An occasional woman tried her hand at rodeo clowning from time to time. It was never considered a "woman's career," and no woman stayed with it very long.

One of the few who was accepted as a rodeo clown, just as she was at every other endeavor she tried, was Tad Lucas:

> She competed in rodeo longer than any cowgirl, even taking a brief turn in the arena as a clown. "In 1949 I was offered the job by Vern Elliott. Jasbo Fulkerson had died and a replacement was needed during the Denver Stock Show. Clowning is not only for laughs but a necessity, especially in bull-riding, where the clowns dash in at their own peril to distract the bulls, allowing the riders to escape the horns of the wild animals. Two regular clowns John Lindsey and George Mills and I worked up an act in which I sat in the audience and heckled the clowns, and finally in a fit of anger they hauled me from the stands to see if I could do a better job. The act was so real that the crowd stopped us and wasn't going to let them take me.

When we reached the arena, the two clowns would push me in the barrel, just as the bull would send it careening across the arena. When the Brahma knocked me halfway out of the barrel, George and John would stuff me back down. I was badly bruised but it was a lot of fun." Lucas continued clowning for 13 performances at the Kansas City Rodeo. [17]

Juanita Gray:

Juanita Gray, trick rider, explains how she became a clown. "It was in Beeline, Texas. One of the clowns got hurt the night before. I always wanted to try and finally producer Earl Sellers let me. I was on the fence most of the time. Once I stumbled over the other clown, and the bull went over the top of me. The next day in Corpus Christi they told me they would give me $150 more to do the act, but my husband Weaver told me if I got hurt we would miss the ten day rodeo at Elk City, Oklahoma. That was the end of Juanita Gray, bullfighter." [17]

Dixie Reger Mosley:

Dixie Reger Mosley worked alongside her father and a trained steer. At 5½ she trick rode on a shetland pony and toured with the H. E. Ranch Show. Later she performed as a clown and bullfighter at many of the Girl's Rodeo Association rodeos. [17]

In 1951 Willard Porter wrote an article in the *Hoofs & Horns* magazine about Dixie Lee Reger:

Today Dixie is considered to be the queen of the girl clowns. Actually she is the only official GRA clown. Tad Lucas used to help Dixie out at the approved GRA shows, but since Tad has quit clowning Dixie is now on her own. She knows her business, too, having also started this line of rodeo work when only a child. At 11 years of age she clowned a show at Wichita Falls, Texas, that was promoted by Fay Kirkwood.

Dixie thinks clowning is about the toughest job there is in rodeo. "Believe me," she says, "a two-hour show is hard work. It really takes it out of you—especially if you've got to clown the show alone." [10 (1951)]

Bonnie Eloise Williams:

Bonnie Eloise Williams started in rodeo by being a trick rider. She wanted to add a matched pair of horses for a Roman riding act but could not afford them. She did buy a pair of mini-mules. After an assist from Glenn Randall, Bonnie named them Ziggy and Punkin. In 1979, in Denver, a stock contractor was trying to decide between Bonnie's act and a barrelman. Bonnie told him if he hired her she'd be his barrelman too. And so Bonnie Eloise Williams began her rodeo clowning career.

CHAPTER 3

The Bullfighter

Introducing . . . The Brahma Bull

Most sports records are made to be broken. The speed it takes a runner to run a mile has decreased as the athlete has developed. The title for most home runs by a big league baseball player has passed from one player to another throughout the years. As the sport of rodeo develops and cowboys begin to master their techniques in each event, the stock contractors and producers work just as hard to make the challenge even greater. One of those challenges has been the introduction of the Brahma bull to bull riding.

Willard Porter recorded this about the event: "Verne Elliott introduced Brahma bulls to bull riding in the late 1920s in Fort Worth. He said they would offer some fight, as the grown steers cowboys had been riding would just run off the minute the cowboys dismounted. He also said the loose hide on a Brahma bull would be more difficult to ride. Homer Holcomb was a clown working for Elliott at that time and he became the first Brahma bull fighter." [18]

Gene Lamb wrote in his book *Rodeo, Back of the Chutes*: "The Brahma Bull can claim credit for a lot of employment in Rodeo, because without him there would be little need for the clowns. Up until the 1920s Bull Riding was not a predominant event in Rodeo. The 'bulls' might be real bulls, they might be range cows, they might be good sized steers: in fact, they might be anything that could be remotely considered a 'bull.' With the development of the use of the Brahmas in the Bull Riding, the event began to assume more importance in the arena. There will always be much argument as to where the Brahmas were first used, and by whom. They are usually accredited to Verne Elliott, who has been in the Rodeo stock contracting business for about forty years. Verne used a couple of the Brahmas at Fort Worth, Texas, in the '20s, then took some elsewhere when they proved to be crowd pleasers." [16]

A 1954 *Hoofs & Horns* article about Red Sublett told: "The advent of the Brahma came after most of the pioneer rodeo comics were through. Sublett, however, had much experience with them. He was riding and clowning with Brahmas in Texas, and then elsewhere for McCarty and Elliott, at a time when the hump-backed bovines were an unknown nemesis in other parts of the country. Sublett's spectacular set-tos were an inspiration to many youngsters who later cut themselves a slice of fame and fortune in rodeo. Red Sublett was a broth of a boy and born too soon. It should have been so that he could be clowning today—in rodeo's heyday." [10]

As mentioned earlier, it was always a concern of the rodeo producer to keep the cowboy or cowgirl challenged. This account regarding Cheyenne, and changes made at Frontier Days, reflected what was happening in other parts of the country as well:

> From 1918 to 1936 both the bull riding and bareback riding were exhibition events. The riders were paid from $3.00 to $5.00 per ride but soon cowboys began to take less pride in actually riding the animal, thinking only of the fee to be received. As a result, in 1932 the Committee decided to pay only if a qualified ride was made. This helped somewhat but in 1936 the Committee sensed the opportunity to make these two events into spectacular and competitive contests. Brahma bulls were used. These animals are very difficult to ride, oftentimes charging the rider when he is thrown or jumps off at the conclusion of his eight second qualifying ride. Here the rodeo clowns, bullfighters actually, become a necessity. They distract the animal's attention through the use of capes and other accessories until the rider can scramble to safety. [5]

In 1941 a *Hoofs & Horns* article began:

> A body full of knitted broken bones—a heart full of kindliness and understanding and a homely face full of smiles and good cheer—that's Homer Holcomb, rated in most circles today as the world's greatest cowboy clown.
>
> His legs, arms, chest, head and hands are knotted and gnarled with injuries suffered in his daily grind of facing danger

Homer Holcomb bullfights with cape.
(Photo by J. A. Stryker; submitted by Bill Wittliff, courtesy of
University of Texas–Permian Basin Collection)

to save cowboys from that, self-same danger. Yet, in true parlance of his trade, it's still "Laugh, Clown, Laugh."

Despite this fact Homer still has several score enemies.

Enemies that carry a hatred in their black hearts for the clown. Hatred that would bring him death at least 3,000 times a year were it not for his cunning and alertness.

These enemies robbed of hundreds of victims by the wiry clown are Brahma bulls, vicious, ornery critters that feature rodeo entertainment throughout the nation.

At least 3,000 times a year Homer rushes in to protect bull riders after they have jumped or been thrown off Brahma bulls. At least 3,000 times a year Homer waves his red cape in the face of a maddened, pawing, snorting Brahma; taunts him to give chase; escapes by clever footwork then scurries to the nearest barrier bare seconds before slashing horns lash out, capable of tearing him to shreds. Then while mounted riders finish the job of sending the infuriated beast out the exit gate, Homer tips his hat to the crowds, fans posterior in derision and carries on with the show.

Everyone agrees that the Brahma bull is the meanest ani-

mal on earth. It is a Texas bred cross between the compara-
tively gentle Brahma of India and evil dispositioned Mexican
longhorns. Result is nearly a ton of concentrated dynamite. An
animal with the strength of a Sampson, cunning of a fox, sight
of an eagle, speed of an antelope, and the vile heart of a Black
Widow spider. [10]

A Madison Square Garden Rodeo program of 1947 titled the
event "Wild Bull Riding." The purse was $24,910, and the entry
fee was $30. The program prepared the audience by its descrip-
tion:

The Brahma bulls and steers used in this event are wild
and vicious, they are more like jungle beasts than domestic animals, their principal range being the salt grass marshes of the
gulf coast country they are known to be the quickest of action
of any animal their size in the world, are big powerful brutes
with bucking prowess unsurpassed even by the greatest out-
law bucking horses. In this event contestants really do risk life
and limb, and the rodeo clowns also come in for their share of
risk in trying to attract the attention of the bulls from the rider
when the rider is trying to dismount or is thrown, as the Brahmas are quick to turn upon a human being in an effort to gore
out his life.

Buck LeGrand leaps the bull.
(Photographer unknown; submitted by Charley and Imogene Beals)

No wonder the crowds looked forward to this event.

Sport between animal and man has been a challenge for thousands of years. In 1500 B.C., in the Aegean Age,

> one theme that appears often, both in Crete and in Mycenae and Tiryns in Greece, tells us that the favorite sport of the old sea peoples was the cruel one of BULL-GRAPPLING. Young men and girls seem to have been trained to perform in the bull ring; for the artists have painted them often in the act of catching the bulls horns, or flying over the bulls back to be caught by another acrobat waiting with out-stretched hands.
>
> Menos was king of Crete, a sea king of great power. At Knossos was his palace where Daedalus built the famous Labyrinth. It is believed that youth and maidens were sent to be devoured by the Minotaur—half bull, half human—but by the inscriptions it is said they were sent to be trained for the dangerous sport of bull-grappling in the Labyrinth. [28]

The sport of man versus bull has taken different forms throughout centuries past. However, there seems to be no record of a human challenging a bull with a bent for humor—until the rodeo clown.

Duties of the Daring

Once bull riding became a regular event at rodeos across the country, the demand for more bullfighting rodeo clowns increased quickly. Many arena funnymen had been entertaining audiences from the arena with a well-trained mule, a beat-up jalopy, or just their continual patter with the announcer. To be expected to assist a rider off the bull safely, especially after the Brahma was introduced, was not a part of the profession that every rodeo clown could adjust to with ease. Some took to it better than others; some chose to find another way to make a living.

An untrained eye may not notice that the rodeo clown takes on an air of seriousness when the bull riding is announced. He may continue to ride the cowboys unmercifully about their spills, even take his hat off to fan their behind-side after a rough landing. But under his breath he will be asking if the rider is OK. He appears to the audience as a nuisance to the riders of the event; however, without his presence many of those riders might hesitate to compete in this event.

It is not something that is obvious, this air of protective responsibility, because the clown/bullfighter does it with such ease.

Since he is dressed in such outlandish garb, the audience continues to snicker and hee-haw at his every antic. However, the illusion is strictly to keep the audience up. The clown actually faces a
killer each time the chute opens. The bullfighter tries to keep the
attention of the bull directed toward him. Once the bull rider hears
the whistle, he attempts to get his hand loose from its tightly
wedged position between the bull and the rope he has been holding on to, so he can jump, slide, bail out, or take whatever exit
looks the safest.

Many times the rider's choice of departure and what actually
happens don't mesh. But the bullfighting/rodeo clown is there.
He knows most of the bulls that are being ridden. Although there
are many stock contractors across the country, a rodeo clown will
work for one or just a few during a season and very quickly become familiar with that contractor's bulls and their maneuvers and
tactics.

The arena "bull-baiter" may dodge and dive and seem to be
out of control. He may dart from one side of the bull to the other.
But rest assured each move has a reason, and the timing that the
clever, precise clown uses is closely calculated to allow him just
enough of a chance to move out of the way of the charging bull. By
this time the rider, who has gotten off the bull, recovers his foot-

ing and hopefully makes it to the safety of the fence—thus allowing the bullfighter the option of heading the maddened bull toward the exit or toward his partner in the barrel or his dummy full of straw.

The veterans are many: "Jasbo Fulkerson, George Mills, Hoytt Hefner, John Lindsey, Homer Holcomb, Elmer Holcomb and Jimmy Nesbitt are only a few who have carved a place in this work. Years of experience as active contestants in the many contests of rodeo have given them a sincere appreciation of what is expected of them. The knowledge of what the cowboy contestant experiences in active participation makes these men acutely aware of every serious and dangerous moment. During the bull riding contest the clown must be constantly wide awake and aware of what is happening, for his work demands a clear head, a strong heart, shrewd observation and an unfailing sense of timing." [15]

Jack Herman was quoted in a 1945 issue of *Hoofs & Horns* as saying, "Now the bulls have taken over. A clown needs to be a clever bullfighter. If a clown gets hooked in the pants the people think it's funny. It's like the olden times when the gladiators fought hungry lions in the Roman arenas. The more risk to life and limb the more laughs from the populace." [10]

Jimmy Nesbitt taught George Mills how to fight bulls. Jimmy

Wright Howington staying one move ahead, British Columbia, 1977.
(Photographer unknown; submitted by Wright Howington)

was considered the best in his day, until George came along: "It is commonly conceded that George Mills is beyond a doubt the best bull fighter in the game. He seems to be almost fearless and often allows the bull—one without horns—actually to toss him into the air and butt him along the ground just for the fun of it. He takes more chances than any other clown. George Mills is not only a clown and bull fighter of excellence; in 1941 he won the RAA Champion Bareback Riding event. He is a bull rider of ability. Riding bulls and experiencing their various actions, he knows how to help the other riders out of the tough predicaments they get into." [15]

The bullfighting segment of rodeo clowning was bluntly defined by the following quote: "Often the clown's skill makes the difference in whether the cowboy goes to the next rodeo, hospital or a morgue." [19] Enough said!

In rodeos, the stock used in bucking events gets a reputation just as the cowboys do. Although the money a bull earns is not counted in points as a cowboy's earnings are, it does earn for the bull's owner the reputation of having good bulls that buck hard

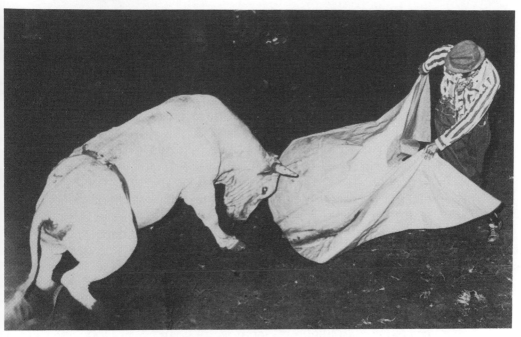

Wes Curtis toys with irate bovine.
(Photo by Foxie; submitted by Wes Curtis)

and give a good show. A cowboy can get a higher score on a hard-bucking bull. The cowboy will then want to go to more rodeos where the stock is furnished by a stock contractor with that reputation, and hopefully will end up the year with more winnings, more money, and more points. The stock contractor will be offered more rodeos, and so it is a win-win situation.

Bulls normally buck with some consistency. Cowboys who have had experience riding certain bulls will pass information to those fellow bull riders who draw that same bull at later performances. Bullfighters learn very quickly the habits and patterns of various bulls. Cowboys also question the bullfighters in preparation for their next ride.

If the bullfighter is not familiar with a bull, he may study him in the pens, before the performance: "Some of the animals will have long and pointed horns. In that case the clown can feel fairly certain that he is not particularly dangerous. If he was, the horns would very likely be cut off or at least shortened. If he sees a young bull with signs of recent dehorning, he can be fairly sure that here is a bull to watch." [16]

A book written by an anthropologist, not a seasoned rodeo fan, described the bull as such: "The rodeo bull is viewed as not just unfriendly, but as an actively aggressive enemy who takes pleasure in injuring a man. Expressing this hostility, the announcer may tell the clown as he enters the arena, 'That bull could make a shish-ke-bob out of you and he would like to do it.'

"Another announcer made this more graphic, describing, 'Chunks of clown meat on a bull's horn.'

"At Calgary the crowd was told: 'This bull got a clown down a few weeks ago in another rodeo, and the clown is still in the hospital in Lethbridge. He's in rooms 20, 21 and 22!' " [20]

Bullfighters come and go. Cowboys, too. The world of rodeo is exciting. Those who are good at it make it look so easy. Beginners observing the experts may decide it can't be that hard—and it seems *so-o-o* exciting. And a new bullfighter is born.

First of all, he puts his costume together. A beat-up hat, some baggy britches, a wild-colored shirt, and a pair of "running" shoes. Then comes the make-up. Most rodeo clowns have distinctive faces, using the same face each performance. Some "expert" advice from existing bullfighters, and now all he needs is a job.

A few stock contractors are approached, but no one needs a new bullfighter. Dejection begins to set in. But wait—a bullfighter got hurt? The stock contractor has a rodeo and no bullfighter? It doesn't pay much? The beginner will take it. A job. He's in business.

At the first performance, what had looked so easy and simple now seems to have slipped the new bullfighter's mind. He can't remember a thing. It's all a blur. He feels sick at his stomach. Will he live through it? Everybody is yelling at him. Where's the chute? God, that bull is huge. Do I stand this close? Why am I doing this? And the chute gate opens and the first bull and rider come out.

Somehow he gets through his first bullfighting job. It wasn't as easy as it looked. There is so much to think about. There is so much responsibility resting on his shoulders. "Is it really worth it? Do I really want to do this?" he asks himself. Maybe he will make a successful bullfighter. If he is quick enough, alert enough, can learn the bulls well enough. Maybe. Time will tell. If he can out-think them, out-smart them, *and* out-run them. Well, maybe. There are many variables in the final results. Just look at the ever changing list of rodeo clowns, bullfighters, and barrelmen advertising from one year to the next.

It has never been a secret that rodeo clowns do get knocked

*Artist Orren Mixer painting of Charley Beals riding a Brahma. Clowns
are Hoytt Hefner, Jasbo in the barrel, and John Lindsey.*
(Painting is owned by Charley Beals, submitted by
Charley and Imogene Beals)

around quite a bit. A perfect example is "good old Jimmy Nesbitt,
who fought the bulls to a standstill, and then fought them lying
down on the ground after he had been tossed ten feet in the air."
[10 (1945)]

The bull riders are the greatest admirers of these fearless
funnymen. Hoytt Hefner is one of the professionals who has been
appreciated by the cowboys he saved. One cowboy expressed his
feelings toward Hoytt by saying: "Why man, I'd come out on a
rattlesnake upside down, even if I knew I'd get bucked off, 'cause
I'd know Hefner'd be there to take it off me." [10 (1950)]

Slim Pickens was also applauded by the bull riders he was
there to protect. Slim was considered to be a natural at both comedy and bullfighting chores.

The riders seemed to have the confidence that Slim would be
there for them, if they got in any kind of a wreck. Although he was
the only rodeo clown to don a toreador suit to bullfight, he was
very serious about his business. He said he gained his skills from
the good old school of experience and hard knocks:

It was while riding the starvation circuit that young Slim first tried his hand at the art of bullfighting. At a certain show, the boy contracted for the job failed to show up, so when the rodeo management offered a reward of good hard spending money to the cowboy fool-hardy enough to take his place, Slim being a little braver than usual that day, volunteered. The memory of that first show is still a little on the hazy side but apparently he came out of it alive and kicking. Some time after this he was shown some home movies of himself in his debut as a rodeo bullfighter and it almost scared him to death. As time went on, he worked several more of the smaller shows to help compensate for the money he didn't win other ways for even a cowboy has to eat once in a while. He admits to being plenty scared until he finally found the cure at a small show in California. They turned out the biggest blackest, meanest-looking bull Slim had ever seen and with every move he grew bigger and blacker and meaner-looking. Slim says he just stood there trembling in his boots because the minute that bull left the chute, he knew that was the one with his number on it, and right then and there he received his baptism of fire. When the dust in the arena had finally settled and things more or less had got back to normal, Slim found to his amazement that he was still in one piece and not too badly hurt. After that he lost his fear but never his respect for the rodeo Brahma. [10 (1951)]

Some rodeo clowns were short on responsibility and on occasion would not show up for the next job. That caused room for others to try their hand at the jobs. "Mr. Bullfighter failed to show up and Earl Sellers asked Ike Tacker if he would fight the bulls. So, Ike, always trying then as now, to please and cooperate accepted the job. Ike said he had no intention of making it a continual thing but it turned out that way. In 1945 the Sellers' hired Ike to work all their shows as the clown and bullfighter." [10 (1953)]

In 1954 George Mills was interviewed for an article in *Hoofs & Horns*. He had earned $25,000 the year before in twenty-one dates, which was good money in those days. As one of rodeo's great funnymen he was asked what makes a good clown: "Guts mainly. You get scared of them bulls, and they're going to hurt you. But you've got to have respect for them." [10 (1954)]

Junior Meek was praised by former rodeo clowns George Taylor and Dan Willis, for his abilities as a bullfighter: "He was one of the first great stand-up bullfighters. He would jump the bull. He'd take a running start right for the bull's head. The bull would lower its head as Junior approached. Junior would step on the bull's head,

Junior Meek outruns Brahma at Pendleton, Oregon, 1965.
(Photograph by Bern Gregory)

lift himself up, run down the bull's backbone and off the back end. Then he would go down on his knees and tip his hat to the audience."

Taylor and Willis added, "Homer Todd had the toughest bulls. They were all white and their horns went straight up. Junior done things no one can do. He'd grab 'em by the horns and throw 'em down." Junior's talents as a steer wrestler came in handy even in bullfighting. He went to the National Finals in 1966 in Steer Wrestling.

A 1959 program for the Fort Worth Southwest Exposition and Fat Stock Show called the rodeo clowns "Life Guards." That year Junior Meek was the daredevil outside man and Jimmy Schumacher worked the barrel.

Larry McKinney also had the ability to jump the bulls. In fact, during a gathering of retired rodeo clowns in Roseburg, Oregon, in 1986, Larry, then in his late forties, showed the audience he still had the knack. He jumped a bull and never touched him.

Wick Peth became one of the best bullfighters of any era. The son of stock contractors from Washington actually grew up helping his family determine which Brahma bulls were good rodeo stock and which were not.

An early *Hoofs & Horns* article, prior to Wick's taking up the profession of bullfighting, reported: "The Peths are planning a trip to California this fall to purchase more Brahmas. The ones they have now aren't tough enough to suit Wick, the youngest of the Peth boys. Wick thinks if a bull doesn't throw him and walk all over him, he's no good so they get rid of him and get some more. The other Sunday Wick attempted to ride 8 bulls, one right after another. He's quite a boy, this Wick Peth, and although he doesn't do it professionally, he's a dern good little bull fighter." [10 (1949)]

Wick's popularity among the bull riders is obvious. He went to the National Finals eight times as bullfighter and was an alternate three times. He used to keep notes on the palm of his left hand of the homicidal habits of the bulls out that performance.

A *Life Magazine* article about Wick entitled "Behind the Funny Act, A Life and Death Job—Rodeo Clown" made this assessment:

> He has the speed and reflexes of a quarterback and the dedication of a surgeon. He has broken his fist on a bull's nose. And he has traveled miles to visit a hospitalized bull-rider who was hurt at a rodeo Wick didn't even attend.
>
> Wick saved Billy Mills at the Snake River Stampede. Wick came in like a bullet and jumped, head on, astraddle of the bull's neck. He yanked the rope free of Bill's pinioned hand, slipped off and slapped the bull's nose until he'd drawn him far enough away so that the other cowboys could lug Billy to the chutes.
>
> "Brahmas don't drop their heads and charge," said Wick. "They keep their eyes riveted on a man until the last second and then hook one horn with the speed and accuracy of a fencer." [29]

Wick today professes that he is *not* funny. "One time I forgot to wear make-up and Cy Taillon said, 'Why bother? You're not funny anyway.' " From that day on Wick did not wear make-up. Wick says, "Doug Allen once said I was about as funny as a funeral in the rain." But as he says it the corners of his mouth curve upward into a slight smile. "I never had any talent; the other guys were bad and just made me look good." Who says Wick isn't funny?

In 1954 Wick could not find his clown pants, and the performance was a short time off, so he borrowed a pair from Sammy Reynosa. Sammy being shorter than Wick, the pants were tight in the crotch. So Wick simply cut out the crotch. This was the begin-

Wick Peth and Wilbur Plaugher distracting the bull while rider Carl Nafziger exits. Later Nafziger trained 1989 Kentucky Derby winner.
(Photo by Ferrell; submitted by Charley and Imogene Beals)

Wick Peth at 1989 Cowboy Clown Reunion in Roseburg, Oregon. Who says he's not funny?
(Photo by Gail Woerner)

ning of the short bullfighting skirt that so many rodeo clowns wear in bullfighting today.

Wick said one of the biggest changes for the bullfighter came about in 1960. Prior to that time it was not mandatory that the clown be up in front of the chute when the bull rider nodded to be let out of the chute. But from 1960 to now (1993) it is a requirement that the bullfighter be in front of the chute when the gate is opened.

The legendary Wick Peth, described in earlier days, was built for his sport: "In his mid-forties, Wick has the body and stamina of a man twenty years younger. Wick works out between performances, jogs, and tapes his ankles and thighs before each rodeo. He has quickness, speed, and is constantly on the move, somewhat remindful of a roadrunner or will-o-the-wisp. Wick will race in through a bull's path, beating the animal to no-man's-land, or run behind a bull, grabbing its tail." [21]

Skipper Voss started bullfighting in 1972. In less than a year he was being called one of the best bullfighters around.

Skipper started his career in South Texas. When he joined the PRCA he worked for Tommy Steiner, a stock contractor. *Rodeo Sports News* reported: "Skipper seems to have built-in radar with the bulls on the other end. He can sure get their attention and after he does he makes some passes at them that could even wake up the dead." [11 (1973)]

He went to the National Finals Rodeo as bullfighter in 1974, and his expertise there was described: "Voss stepped in front of a rider about to be freight-trained (run over with a full head of steam), taking the brunt of the bull's charge himself; the times he's jumped completely over a bull or let one charge him while he was on his knees; the way he'll leap right into the well (inside a spinning bull) to get a rider clear. Cowboys love Skipper, but some rodeo officials do not. Skipper resents what he feels is the second class citizen treatment rodeo clowns get and often speaks his mind." [21]

Over the years Skipper has not been hesitant to speak his mind over the treatment of rodeo clowns—by the association, not the cowboys.

Some of the newer indoor arenas used for various sports, not just rodeos, are so large that even when converted for the rodeo they may cause some problems for the rodeo clowns. The size of the Astrodome in Houston, Texas, as an example, presented a safety factor during the bull riding. Quail Dobbs, Kajun Kid, and Wilbur Plaugher were the protectors: "The only protection in the middle of the arena is Wilbur's hanging dummy and during the first performance Quail made a fine leap to safety atop the dummy with a pair of horns directly below." [11 (1975)]

Throughout the years many changes have been made and new ideas are constantly being used. One of the greatest was the origination of the barrel. Depending on the size of the rodeo, as few as one rodeo clown may be used, or as many as three. The barrel is usually the only source of protection sitting in the arena during the bullfighting for the bullfighter and barrelman. Some rodeo clowns do work both as bullfighter and barrelman. Some work only one classification. A bullfighter can work alone, but a barrelman will not work without partnering with a bullfighter.

There are times that a bullfighter will switch from the responsibilities of the bullfighter to being a barrelman. It is sometimes more practical as the bullfighter grows older and realizes his limitations in out-maneuvering that deadly critter. Sometimes limitations aren't just a limitation of age.

Jasbo Fulkerson was the first rodeo clown to use a barrel.

Because of his daring and thorough knowledge of the animals, Jasbo's fame as a bull-baiter spread rapidly. Here his short stature was responsible for his famous trademark—the big red barrel. While he could sidestep the rushes of the bulls for a long time, his stubby legs handicapped him in a long run to the arena wall—a race he was bound to lose.

He needed a sanctuary in the center of the arena, and he hit upon the idea of a barrel. An ordinary wooden cask wouldn't do; the staves would splinter and fly apart with the first crash of the bull's skull. For reinforcement he fitted some old automobile tires around the barrel, which served admirably as shock absorbers as well as girders. A coat of bright red paint and he had a home away from home.

A workman rolled Jasbo's familiar red barrel to the center of the arena and set it upright. Out ran the little hobo and jumped into the barrel, head and feet disappearing last, up popped his head still wearing the derby, to receive his applause with a solemn bow.

Jimmy Nesbitt followed Jasbo, and the two clowns joked raucously with the announcer until the first contestant in the bull riding called for the chute to be opened and the bull's fury to be released. If the cowboy went the full eight seconds, Jimmy and Jasbo were on hand to keep the bull's attention while the contestant jumped clear. If the rider were thrown, the clown's job was to divert the bull from the fallen man, giving him a chance to reach the arena fence—a job as ticklish as tripping through a den of riled up rattlesnakes.

According to their usual tactics, Jimmy dropped back to a slightly safer spot behind the barrel and Jasbo slid into the barrel from his seat on the rim, emerging immediately to hurl strident taunts. The bull charged. Jasbo sailed his hat at the brute and dropped out of sight just as the quivering express train smashed into the barrel and sent it bouncing. The Brahma veered toward Jimmy, who sprinted for the fence. To cover him, Jasbo stuck his head out of the barrel, shouting and shaking his fist at the infuriated animal. The bull's hot eyes stared at the hated little man in the tire-covered barrel; he backed a step or two and pawed the ground. With his next charge the crowd's laughter changed to screams of horror. The force and fury of his rush had wedged the bull's head in the open end of the barrel. Jasbo was trapped.

The bull's massive head blotted out all light. Jasbo felt the barrel lift into the air. The animal's hot, wet breath blew into his face as it bellowed with rage.

The excited spectators were on their feet, screaming. For the moment Nesbitt and the cowboys were frozen in their steps. The bull charged blind around the arena, wildly slinging his head.

Jimmy came to his senses and ran shouting to the pickup men. "Somebody—quick—get a rope on that bull!" Before either man could build a loop, the bull slung his head and the barrel flipped end over end through the air. There was no sign of Jasbo as the barrel dropped to the arena floor and bounced a few times before rolling to a stop.

Two loops dropped around the bull's head. The crowd was silent as the cowboys ran toward the barrel. As they raced up, a startling array of patches backed out and straightened up to reveal Jasbo's rumpled head with wig askew. His nose bled, but he was grinning. [4]

Barrelmen tried many different types of barrels and various inventions within the barrel: "The simple barrel is a standard steel oil drum of considerable size with some padding inside, and a couple of hand grips welded to the interior; the outside is rubber-coated, usually with car or truck tires that fit tightly over the barrel, with the barrelman inside, the rubber absorbs some of the shock, and the shock is tremendous." [16]

Gene Lamb wrote:

Jimmy Schumacher of Phoenix, Arizona, claims credit for originating The Walking Barrel and has applied for a patent on

Jimmy Schumacher sits atop his patented barrel.
(Photo by DeVere Helfrich; submitted by Jimmy Schumacher)

it. This isn't too elaborate an affair. It is the standard barrel with both ends open. The barrelman can stand up and shuffle around with the barrel covering about half of him, holding it off the ground with the hand holds inside. In case the bull charges he just lets it drop, and goes down inside. He thought up the idea at the rodeo where a small-headed and hornless bull got his head inside the barrel with Jimmy. His head didn't come out as easy as it went in, and there they were, Jimmy and a bull breathing in each other's face—and both of them wanting out, and willing to make any arrangement to get out. There wasn't much the bull could do to make sure the incident didn't happen again, but Jimmy made sure. He got him a big hammer and chisel and knocked out the bottom of the barrel. Now if the bull comes in at one end, and indicates he wants the barrel for himself, Jimmy goes out the other end and lets him have it. [16]

Jimmy Schumacher's "walking barrel" was introduced to the public in Fort Worth in 1953. He filed this barrel to be patented February 8, 1954. It was given patent number 2,809,035.

And then there was another version of the barrel:

Billy Keen knew bulls, especially the ornery, hard-headed

Brahmas that give the fans goose bumps and make them happy that they're in the stands and not in the clown's place in the arena.

Billy also knew that this very orneriness and stubbornness, that was such a selling point to the fans, was sometimes a dead spot in the clown-bull routine. Many times the routine was slowed down by the bull's uncooperativeness with the barrel. Either the bull would ignore the barrel, passing it up on his way to the livestock exit, or the beast would just stand snorting and pawing at it.

Up to that time the idea was for the bull to come to the barrel. Sometimes this worked and sometimes it didn't. Well, Billy figured it would be far better and quicker if the barrel went to the bull. It was just that simple. And from this reasoning, in April, just before the spring and summer rodeo circuit got under way, he perfected his original mechanical barrel—a clever contraption, padded and braced like ordinary bull barrels, with wheel and such maneuverability that Bill Keen has earned the title of "the guy who really chases the bulls." [10 (1951)]

Another description by Gene Lamb in his book went like this:

Billy Keen who runs back and forth between Sand Point, Idaho, and a couple of towns in Florida has a gadget he calls "Billy Keen's Bull Machine." This is a specially made barrel. The opening in the top is standard size (about 16 inches across), and swells out from the top down to about four feet across. A heavy leather cover is laced over padding on the outside, and three or four slits are cut clear through cover and steel about a foot down from the top.

Through these slits Billy can peek out and see what the bull is doing. On the bottom are three wheels, rubber tired and sturdy, one of them runs free on a swivel joint, and the other two are chain geared to the inside where separate cranks can turn each wheel independently.

Billy can squat down inside, turn both cranks, one with each hand, and move forward or back, while peering through the slits to see where he is going. By turning one or the other of the cranks separately he can turn right or left. It's an upsetting sight to see this funnel-shaped object rolling around the arena, and no one in sight. Probably pretty hard on a bull's nerves for the first time.

If the bull knocks the barrel over and the other clown is not near, Billy can shift his weight and it will right itself onto the wheels. Once the barrel was setting just right and the bull hit it and instead of going over it went straight ahead on the wheels. The wheels turned and fairly fast, and the cranks went around

Bill Keen's Bull Machine totally confuses the bull.
(Photographer unknown; submitted by Charley and Imogene Beals)

like a windmill. The inside of the barrel was only as large as absolutely necessary, and there wasn't any space to spare for the two whirling cranks and Billy's head. One of them whacked him, and he went out like a light. [16]

In a 1958 issue of *Rodeo Sports News,* the following prayer was written:

"Oh Lord, please answer this short prayer
Please bless our clown, with speed to spare." [11]

Even the notorious bulls became famous—or infamous: "This old Brahma, Jasbo, is one of the stars of Leo Cremer's string of rodeo stock, and he has earned the respect, if not the love, of most of the top notch bull riders of today.

"Jasbo acquired his name the first time he bucked out of the chute. He hit Jasbo Fulkerson's barrel, knocked it over and then tried to get into the barrel with Jasbo. He seemed to have a special mad at George Mills, for he never fails to fight him every time George is in the arena when Jasbo comes out." [10 (1948)]

Some of the bullfighters of rodeo fame learned their profession by also studying Mexican bullfighting styles. Elizabeth Atwood Lawrence examined the differences in the events: "Rodeo bull fighting clowns are actually brave and skillful men, but their grotesque costumes and antics belie this. Rodeo's bull event is frequently compared to the bull fight, and I suggest that the ridiculous character of the rodeo clown represents the antithesis of the matador. For the Spanish bull fighter is elaborately dressed, an explicitly sexual figure, prepared for a serious ritual. The clown on the other hand, as a buffoon, acts to defy and divert the deadly serious nature of the bull riding." [20]

Slim Pickens donned a fancy toreador outfit but fought the bulls with humor. Gene Clark studied in Mexico to learn the art of bullfighting south of the border. A 1949 Toppenish Rodeo account told: "Bob Clark, up and coming young rodeo clown, helped Slim Pickens clown, while Bob's older brother, Gene, who has earned quite a reputation in these parts with his exhibitions of fighting rodeo Brahmas in the traditional toreador style, came in right handy during the bull riding. With thirty riders to go each night they were turning the bulls out fast and furious, and all three bull fighters had their hands full, but did a swell job." [10 (1949)]

Two years later another article said: "Gene and Bobby Clark of

Gene and Bobby Clark on their teeter-totter, outsmarting the bull.
(Photographer unknown, submitted by Gene Clark)

Bakersfield, California, rise to success—international favorite in Canada. Gene got his first break in 1947 at Omak, Washington, to sub for Wilbur Plaugher and had fans on the edge of their seats with his colorful dramatic Spanish style." [10 (1951)]

An article in 1952 reported: "Bobby Hill plans on teaming with Joaquin Sanchez. Joaquin attended a Matador School in Mexico for seven weeks and is one of the few rodeo clowns practicing Spanish bullfighting techniques." [10 (1952)]

In an interview Gene Clark explained some of those techniques: "In Mexican bullfighting you study the bulls. You need to learn how they move, what they think. Are they right-horned or left-horned?" He also said, "A bull will favor the longest horn, the one that sticks out toward the front the farthest."

Gene went on to say that there are two kinds of bulls—the offensive and the defensive. You either play *to* the bull or it will watch you and see what you do, then play to the bullfighter.

A 1957 article in *The Evening News* from Harrisburg, Pennsylvania, quoted Gene as saying, "You can never underrate a Brahma. That's asking for trouble. They may be wild as hell but they're smart. A Brahma is a defensive fighter. He wants for you to make the first move. The bulls in the rings of Mexico always take the offensive. A Brahma will try to sucker you into a wrong move. I've fought 'em both." [30]

Jasbo told in his book: "You remember I went to Mexico a while back to study that trade. It didn't help me much, because the bulls the matadors use are especially bred for that purpose. They shut their eyes when they charge, but a Brahma charges with his eyes wide open. Another thing, when a Mexican bull enters a ring, it's his first fight and his last. These old Brahmas fight almost every day, and they've learned lots of mean tricks. You'll never see a matador fighting a Brahma." [14]

Occupational Injuries and Then Some

Rodeo life is not for the timid, nor the weak, nor for anyone who gets concerned about a few injuries. Rodeo clowning is even worse. It takes tape, thread, bolts, and screws to keep some of these fellows going. It also sometimes takes pills, potions, and maybe booze to ignore some of the more severe damages. But these cowboy clowns never admit to being hurt. If they are unconscious, then maybe the medics can get them to the hospital or get them repaired before they wake up and insist on getting up and getting back out there to do their job.

Through hundreds of interviews done to compile this book, I never heard a rodeo clown admit he had been badly hurt. The injuries they had sustained were discovered through other sources, such as the book *Jasbo* by Wayne Ingram and Jane Pattie:

> The cowboy's ride fell a few seconds short of the required eight. George Mills and Homer Holcomb's fast waltz around the bull distracted him until the cowboy reached safety.
>
> It was Jasbo's squat figure, as he dropped into the barrel that attracted the immense gray Brahma. His small hot eyes watched the clown's jack-in-the-box procedure only a moment before he lowered his head and thundered across the arena to hit the barrel with the impact of a locomotive, or so it seemed to the occupant of the barrel. The barrel spun crazily back and teetered over as the bull followed with another quick charge. His massive head disappeared into the barrel with Jasbo.
>
> George and Homer worked dangerously close to the bull, feverishly trying to free its head. The pickup men had their loops built to rope him when the barrel was tossed free. The two horsemen quickly ushered the Brahma out of the arena.
>
> George took one look into the barrel and groaned. Gently he helped the dazed and badly injured clown out into the circle of horrified cowboys. The horn had entered Jasbo's temple, curving behind the left eye.
>
> With a swing of a powerful arm, Jasbo freed himself of helping hands and stood erect, swaying generously. He announced, his speech thick and slurred, that he was completely all right and required no assistance, and that the thought of going to the hospital was laughable.
>
> The doctor worked over Jasbo and finally told Mrs. Fulkerson, "He's had a very serious injury, and it almost cost him his life, and it may yet cost him his left eye, we're going to need your help."
>
> For thirteen days and nights, Madolyn applied cold packs to Jasbo's eye. After two months the doctors told him the injury was permanent. The eye would have to be removed.
>
> When ready to go to work after the operation Jasbo said, "If you see one of them Brahmas sneakin' up on my blind side, how about hollerin." [14]

Accidents were not uncommon, but they did little to slow down the rodeo clown: "Another case of 'on with the show' was the work of Skeeter Crist, the clown, who broke a bone in his arm at the outset of the show, but went on working and the audience never knew of the accident." [10 (1940)]

Ma Hopkins, editor of *Hoofs & Horns* for many years, wrote: "Got some fine rodeo action photographs from Devere Helfrich taken at the Fortuna rodeo. One of them showing Felix Cooper a split second before bull, Mush Hop, lit with both feet on Felix's chest, breaking his breast bone.

Felix had a badly crushed chest and collar bone and was expected to be on his back for at least three weeks." [10 (1941)]

And some have injuries on top of injuries: "Bobby Clark of Bakersfield, California, who had been working with several broken ribs, while clowning at the Sidney, Iowa, Rodeo suffered a severe concussion and internal injuries when one of the bulls charged him, pinned him against a gate and gored him before rodeo workers could get him away. Late reports say he is recuperating and getting along fine." [10 (1953)]

Jasbo had his fair share of accidents and injuries: "At the El Paso rodeo Jasbo gave his best, the El Pasoans continued to cheer. For two days all went smoothly. On the third day at the early show, one particularly enterprising Brahma knocked the barrel on its side and rammed a horn inside it. The bull trotted away, but Jasbo did not come out. George rushed over, took one look inside, and motioned for the ambulance. The bull was herded out of the arena and several cowboys rushed out to lift the limp figure onto the stretcher.

"Jasbo regained consciousness in the hospital; he had eleven stitches in his head. When asked what happened Jasbo said, 'That fool bull decided to crawl in the barrel with me, and it just got too damn crowded.' " [14]

Another early arena laugh-getter also had his share of injuries:

> When Homer Holcomb was sent to a hospital after having his leg broken in the last performance at the Denver Stock Show and Rodeo, he woke up, of all places, in the maternity ward.
>
> "Although a bit surprised, it didn't seem to cramp his style, and he clowned right through his hospital days.
>
> After a couple of weeks in the hospital, he went to Hayward, California, where he has been making a good recovery, and will be out in circulation very soon. Homer received the injury when he ran in to protect Dick Griffith who had been thrown from a fighting Brahma bull. The bull caught Homer and tossed him around pretty rough. But he'll be right back helping the boys out as soon as he gets steady on his pins again. [10 (1941)]

An article quoted Homer as saying: " 'I'd watched that bull all

MATURNITY WARD

week, and had decided he wouldn't fight. Dick Griffith rode him
and when Dick hit the tanbark I drew the bull away from him and
past me, with the cape. Then I stepped away without looking back
at him. Next thing I knew, he had me.' " [10 (1941)]

Not all injuries happen without a little help—maybe from Doctor Calverts. Wayne Ingram and Jane Pattie wrote:

> It had been raining for days on the open arena in Dublin,
> Texas. Mud was knee-deep, rodeo attendance was negligible;
> nobody was cheerful, except Jasbo. The pelting rain was cold
> and his feet were white and wrinkled from prolonged soaking,
> but he ducked into the clown room at intervals for a swig of
> "anti-freeze."
>
> "Jus' nothing like Dr. Calverts to stave off pneumonia," he
> announced contentedly.
>
> After several such excursions his leaps into the barrel be-
> came slower and slower, until the performers felt that the next
> murderous rush of the Brahma would mean his last mortal mo-
> ment on this earth. Finally, with a wild bull hot behind him,
> Jasbo slogged through the mud seeking the sanctuary of his
> barrel. The bull was fast closing the gap when Jasbo reached
> the barrel and leaped mightily. Lord Calverts does little for one's
> gymnastic ability, however, and Jasbo's feet did not clear the
> ground.

The charging bull lowered his horns for the impact. With a tremendous effort the clown hauled his sodden frame over the lip of the barrel and toppled in, head first; just as the bull's skull exploded on the staves. When the barrel stopped rolling, the spectators waited for the ridiculous wig-capped head to bob out as usual. None appeared.

Running to investigate, the cowboys found Jasbo curled happily in the bottom, passed out cold. They let him nap there until the show was over, when several of them carried him out to the stock pens and tossed him ceremoniously into the horse trough. [14]

The following reports are just a sampling of the injuries rodeo clowns encounter in their chosen professions.

Sometimes the impact is too much to overcome: "In 1945 Homer Holcomb was so badly injured that he had to retire from the business. A big gray Brahma bull, owned by Harry Rowell, hit him so hard that his back was broken and one leg shattered in 12 places." [18]

"Hoytt Hefner was injured the first afternoon of the Denver show and spent several days in the hospital with broken ribs. 'But it's all in the game,' he said." [10 (1946)]

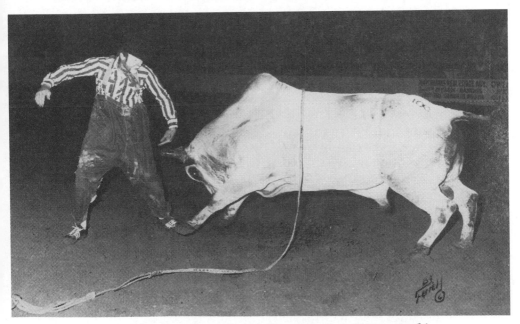

Junior Meek makes it look easy. Cleburne, Texas, 1964.
(Photo by Bern Gregory; submitted by Charley and Imogene Beals)

In an article on Bennie Bender in *Hoofs & Horns,* written by Joe Koller, Bennie defined a rodeo clown/bullfighter's life: "A contestant makes one or two falls an afternoon. The clown makes a dozen. Clowns are not immune to bruises, aches and busted bones. Sometimes a wise crack covers pain just as our rag suits cover the bandage and tape that help hold us together. And another thing—A clown that takes one bad jolt gets back into the arena for another jolt to make good on his contract. He can't afford to feel sorry for himself or get cautious. A cowboy can set one out if he's bunged up. But not the clown. There is no substitute for the clown. And there's no one to do the bull fighting for you." [10 (1955)]

Reports of injuries to Bennie Bender came in from time to time: "While clowning the show at Lusk, Wyoming, a bull hit him and broke his pelvis. Bennie did not seem to think the injury was too serious and was making a good recovery for which we are thankful." [10 (1948)] Also: "Bennie Bender, well known clown, was seriously injured in the Days of 76 show at Deadwood. A vicious Brahma bull rammed Bender against a fence post as he was trying to make a getaway. Hospital reports state no bones appear broken but there was heard of other internal injuries." And another account reported: "Bennie Bender lived up to the cowboys best tradition when he left the hospital bed at Deadwood to resume commitments in the clowning and bullfighting field the rest of the season." [10 (1951)]

Never say never to a rodeo clown: "Slim had a close call Sunday when a rough Cuff Burrell bull knocked him over the railing driving Slim's head into the inner wall and bruising him up quite a bit. Slim was soon back in the arena, however, and demonstrating his uncanny skill with the bullfighting cape." [10 (1949)]

This story is reminiscent of by-gone days: "One year in Hope, Arkansas, a bull hooked Hoytt Hefner and by some freak accident Hoytt's suspenders got wrapped around the bull's horns, and each toss of the bull's head, Hoytt would fly out to the end of the suspenders, then come down with a bone crushing blow and light on the bull's head. The crowd thought it was part of the act, but the cowboys knew better and someone ran out, cut the suspenders. Hoytt's back was broken, but not his spirit." [13] A later article followed up: "Hoytt Hefner did a masterful job taking the bulls off the cowboys even though he was working with his recently broken back in a cast." [10 (1951)]

These bull-baiting laugh-getters seem to have an unusually optimistic way of looking at their injuries: "George Mills had been

Hoytt Hefner "flies" off bronc.
(Photo by J. Homer Venters; submitted by Charley and Imogene Beals)

mauled 'less than a guy would think.' The bulls have broken his left leg twice, an arm, both ankles several times, and 'no telling how many ribs.' Only once have 'they had to pack me out.' That was at Buffalo, New York. He was grabbing at the fence to hoist himself up when a bull nailed him, crushing his leg. His latest injury had nothing to do with hoofs and horns.

"Usually Mills' wounds are produced not by the business end of a Brahma's horns but by the barrel. A bull will thump the barrel and slam it against the clown standing behind it. Most of his trouble, however, is caused by unfamiliar bulls. 'You can tell what the others'll do. But the new bulls do first one thing and then another.' " [10 (1954)]

A Stockton, California, report in 1957 said: "One of Christianson Brothers' bulls kicked Slim Pickens in the face and sent him to the hospital at Stockton where it was said they took 10 stitches in his face. Slim was hurt Saturday night and had to cancel out the rest of the rodeo, but was back next week working in the picture, 'Big Country,' starring Gregory Peck which they are making over near Farmington, California." [11 (1957)]

"Waco Hard on Horses, Cowboys and Clowns" was the title of this article: "Warren Antley hit in the face by the horns of a charging bull flashed a toothless grin after the first performance, when the bull's horn knocked out the front teeth of his dentures. Injured in the first performance Pistol Holliday continued to work the bulls with a cast on his foot until the cast broke loose, and he had to return to the hospital for observation." [11 (1957)]

"Ronnie Rossen rode on a bull with a blind side. Wick [Peth] did the only thing he could; angling from behind, he put on an incredible burst of speed and jumped directly onto the bull's head. He knew No Doze would toss him into the air with all the incredible pent-up power of his massive neck and head, but maybe when he threw his head he would miss Ronnie.

"The split-second move almost worked perfectly. No Doze sent Wick six feet into the air and his horns did miss Ronnie. Then, before Wick could recover his feet, the bull bucked again and one lashing hoof struck Ronnie as he lay on the ground, rupturing his liver and collapsing a lung.

"In the hospital the next day realizing he could have been dead if it weren't for Wick, Ronnie asked how Wick was. Answer: 'He didn't get racked up but Wick's in one of them real black moods of his 'cause the bull wrecked you.' " [29]

Jack Long once said, "I was always lucky enough to get hurt on the last performance of a rodeo so I could usually have enough time to heal up before the next rodeo."

The injuries kept coming:

"Goldy Carlton was injured at Carlsbad, New Mexico, when a bull stuck his head inside the barrel, carried it around for awhile and then threw it to the ground with quite an impact." [11 (1958)]

"The second night at Lovington Ronnie Webb, who was working the barrel for Ken Boen, as well as contesting, took a bad fall from Bull No. 13. The bull stepped on him, breaking two ribs but when the ambulance arrived he refused to go to the hospital. In fact, five minutes later he was back in the barrel and was able to finish the rodeo." [11 (1958)]

"Bullfighters had a rough time at Phoenix with those fighting bulls, but went over big with the tremendous crowd. Kajun Kid was hit Friday afternoon and hurt his previously injured knee, so Larry McKinney subbed for him the rest of the rodeo. Wick Peth injured his right hand which swelled up and looked like it was broken, but he was able to continue. Jimmy Schumacher just missed being gored when one bull stuck his horn in the barrel." [11 (1962)]

"Chuck Lorimer wants to thank the committee at Redwood City for paying his hospital bill and expenses when he received broken ribs and ruptured kidney from that Brahma bull." [10 (1941)]

Once in a while a little reverse humor sneaks in: "Wilbur Plaugher was down with the flu but went on to clown and was hit by a bull. The bull is O.K." [11 (1963)]

Also: Buck LeGrand was knocked cold inside the bull barrel at Houston. Ten minutes and several stars later he was ready to go again." [11 (1963)]

But this is serious business:

"Joaquin Sanchez who is quite a bullfighter, besides clown, was badly mauled Friday night when he was hit and knocked down while trying to get Hank Sproul loose who was hung up in his bull rope." [11(1963)]

"A bull hit Mac Barry at Eugene knocking him half way across the arena. He came out of it with a broken arm and sufficient shock to keep him hospitalized one night, but was able to face the critters the next evening." [11 (1963)]

"Clown and bullfighter Gene Clark who was injured at St. George, Utah, rodeo in September is back on the active list now, his broken jaw healed and he is ready to rodeo." [11 (1963)]

"Wick Peth got a horn high on his right leg and they had to take about 15 stitches. This is nothing to Wick however. He left the arena only after the wound was bleeding quite badly and then only long enough to get the bandage slapped on. I think he missed one, possibly two bulls out and was sewed up later. That bull by the way appeared at Mt. Vernon with shorter horns. Somebody got busy and sawed them off." [11 (1964)]

"Jimmy Schumacher was by the office last week, right after the Pine Bluff, Wyoming, rodeo. Jim had just gotten a cast off his arm. He broke it in Price, Utah, in July, but didn't have to lay off because of it. History is that a bull stepped in the barrel, breaking his left arm, and skinning up his head. Most people with a skinned up head and broken arm don't get them that way, but I'll take his word for it." [11 (1964)]

"We also heard from Wick—healing up from an injury he received in Nampa. He'd been fighting a bull and ran to the fence, jumped up on it to let it pass. As he went by, the end of his horn hit Peth just above the heel, nearly severing the achilles tendon. They put him in a cast to keep the leg bent until the tendon healed." [11 (1964)]

Wick did take his share of knocks: "Wick Peth, working closer fighting bulls in the mud at the Mt. Vernon, Washington, rodeo got caught and tossed in the air, butting heads with the bull on the way down. Wick was cooled out but except for a few stitches in his head, is OK now." [11 (1966)]

One incident occurred when Larry McKinney and Jimmy Schumacher were clowning at the Mandan, South Dakota, rodeo. The final bull of the performance "ripped Larry a good one"—but Larry didn't even realize he'd been hurt at the time. It wasn't until after the performance and they were back in the clown room. Jimmy asked McKinney if he were all right. Jimmy had seen the bull and Larry tangle and was sure the bull had done some damage. Larry said he didn't think so, and continued taking off his make-up. When Larry stood up there was a big pool of blood where he had been sitting. The bull had indeed done some serious damage.

Jimmy rushed McKinney to the hospital, where it took over 100 stitches to repair the injury. Although the bull's horn had ripped Larry from stem to stern, it hadn't even ripped his clown pants.

True to rodeo clown tradition, the following midnight, Larry snuck out of the hospital and was on his way to Belle Fourche with

Larry McKinney jumps bull at Salinas, California, 1960.
(Photo by Milne; submitted by Larry McKinney)

Schumacher. Two weeks later he was back in the arena clowning.

The reports continued:

Bill Lane who was badly gored at the Porterville rodeo, suffering a broken jaw and punctured artery while getting a bull rider loose who was hung up in his bull rope, is recovering at home in Oakdale and expects to be ready to work the Livermore rodeo." [11(1966)]

"Tom LeGrand, up and coming young clown and bullfighter, from Morrison, Oklahoma, was hospitalized in Kansas City with possible internal injuries, July 18, when he got caught by a bull and was badly gored." [11 (1966)]

"Frank McIlvain, rodeo clown and bullfighter from Mesquite, Texas, broke his left arm just below the elbow when hit by a bull Friday. He'll be out all season." [11 (1967)]

"Clowns, George Doak and Larry McKinney, who worked Caldwell, Idaho, the latter working on a broken leg as he had also done at Salt Lake City. Not as agile as usual he was bumped a couple of times." [11 (1970)]

"Karl Doering was stepped on by a bull and required several

Bobby Romer and Vold's B6. This was a Top 10 Photo of 1975.
(Photo by Bern Gregory)

stitches in his leg, but it didn't keep him down." [11 (1974)]

"Nampa rodeo clown Wiley McCray who has been jumping headlong into his barrel for more years than he'd like people to know—misjudged slightly and had to have eight stitches taken." [11 (1975)]

"Romer Gored Again" was the title of an article reporting: "Bobby Romer was gored during the last performance at Kissimmee, Florida. Romer finished the event and was then treated. Same leg in which he was severely gored during the rodeo in El Paso." [11 (1978)]

"Chuck Henson suffers injury at Little Rock—suffered a broken foot during the rodeo, a bull hit the barrel, which in turn struck Henson on the heel with such force it jammed his toes into the ground and broke them." [11 (1978)]

"Butch Lehmkuhler of North Platte, Nebraska, suffered severe facial injuries during the Pleasant Grove, Utah, prorodeo. Swanny Kerby's blue Mexican fighting bull #23 got his head in the barrel and crashed Lehmkuhler's right cheek. Required 235 stitches and a nine day stay in the Provo hospital." [11 (1982)]

Some of these injuries are too close: "LeGrand, fighting bulls at Fort Worth, was pinned, and butted, against the chutes during the last night of competition, and suffered a badly broken right collarbone. It was a closer call than Buck realized. Doctors at Ponca City operating on his shoulder Tuesday to insert a metal pin, said the jagged end of the bone could have severed an artery in the hard twisted, little Oklahoman's neck had he raised his right arm to any extent." [11 (1968)]

"George Doak, who clowned the Syracuse rodeo, had a narrow escape when a bull got back into the arena from the unsaddling chutes and blind-sided George. Luckily he escaped with cuts and bruises." [11 (1968)]

"Gene Clark, who worked the Livermore rodeo with his brother, Bobby, recently had a close call while trying out some bulls down at Apatzingan, Mexico, about 1200 miles below the border. He was hooked in the right side of the face and nearly lost an eye." [11 (1968)]

"Larry McKinney had one of those days. A bull ran over him during the afternoon performance, dislocating a shoulder. He was taken to a local hospital where he was put into a brace, and returned to the fairgrounds for the evening contests. Another big bovine tramped him, dislocating the shoulder again." [11 (1969)]

"San Francisco Cow Palace: Wick Peth doing a fine bullfighting job but pulled a torn tendon—Buck LeGrand flew in." [11 (1967)]

"Clown Chuck Henson will probably be out of action for the rest of the '73 season with a badly broken leg and ankle. He had been playing with a bull and when he leaped up on the fence in front of the grandstand, his foot got caught. The bull hit the leg and shattered it.

"Mike Cervi who hasn't clowned in 20 years filled in capably for Henson until Jim Bob Feller could be called in. Mike worked with Wiley McCray in the barrel and fought bulls one performance." [11 (1973)]

At the Fort Worth rodeo: "Clown George Doak was hooked in the back by a bull. Tommy Sheffield took over the clowning chores for the rest of the rodeo." [11 (1975)]

Over the years the list goes on and on. Imagine how many injuries were never spotted by media people and never revealed by those brave men. It is a dangerous profession, no doubt about it. The accident is there, just waiting to happen. These bullfighters and barrelmen are betting that their keen eyes, their sense of timing, and their knowledge of the bulls will keep it from happening. Unfortunately, that is not always what happens:

On May 6, 1989 it all nearly ended for Dean Steed who was critically injured while saving a bull rider at the Hyrum High School Rodeo in Hyrum, Utah.

He successfully got the cowboy's hand free from the bull and out of harm's way. But in doing so, Steed was caught by one of the bull's horns and tossed in the air before the enraged animal placed a heavy hoof squarely on his back.

Steed sustained a broken vertebrae which has left him paralyzed from the neck down.

Steed has movement in his arms. Months—years of therapy are ahead of him. He is bound to a wheelchair from which he is staging the greatest battle of his life.

Steed's career has spanned some 22 years. He joined the PRCA in 1975. Since then, he has painted his face, pulled on a baggy pair of Wrangler jeans and an old pair of football cleats and made a living by thrilling rodeo crowds with crazy—but fun—antics.

"There's an adrenalin rush like no other you can get when facing fear," Steed said. "When you risk and conquer the odds and can laugh in the face of danger.

"The smile of a child who is delighted at your foolishness. The shared laughter with a teenage cowboy who reminds you of yourself so many years ago. These are just a few of the reasons that you keep going back.

"It's a hard life—traveling from one show to the next, spending summer weekends working, sometimes doing two performances a day. But it's a way to act out and make your dreams become reality.

"Cowboy clowns are part crazy and part stubborn mule," Steed said. "They're just big kids who've found a way to stay young in a grown-up world." [11 (1989)]

Not all injuries to these arena funnymen are caused by the bulls. "Homer Holcomb was kicked over and under an eye by Jasbo Fulkerson's mule in Ogden. Nine stitches were taken." [10 (1941)]

And if that weren't enough: "Homer Holcomb sure had tough luck when he slipped on a rug and broke his hip on the same leg that was broken last year. Then to add to it, the pin holding his hip in place slipped out and had to be replaced." [10 (1946)]

Some days it just doesn't pay to get out of bed: "In 1931, at Red Bluff, California, a bad horse fell with Tin Horn Hank Keenen. His foot caught in the stirrup. The horse struggled to its feet and ran off, dragging him down the field, kicking him in the face before he was rescued. He had an ear almost ripped off, broken cheek bones, nose, and both jaw bones. He had two dozen stitches taken in his right shoulder, 50 in his head and face. Not expected to live, he was unconscious for nine days. Yet 17 days after the accident occurred, with his jaw wired together and his head in a cast, he was back clowning. He wore a large, floppy sunbonnet so his face couldn't be seen." [22]

Scotty Bagnell had a series of bad luck breaks: "He is fast to pick up where the other fellow leaves off and is right in there clowning his act when a cowboy has made his try at riding and needs a bit of bull-detouring. But from wins to down falls is an expected cowboy's route, and at Tucson's Hutson Stable rodeo a bronc he was riding fell on him breaking his hip. At Portland on Christianson Bros. famous Brahma Leppy he unfortunately broke his hand while attempting to make a ride. Next May he rode a saddle bronc at Colville, Washington, and broke a leg which indicated doing a few shows clowning only, together with a shift or two at judging just to keep his hand in and the gas gauge up on truck and trailer.

"Not satisfied, old Lady Hard Luck trailed him all the way to Red Deer to see him again break the same leg on a saddle bronc ride." [10 (1951)]

The timing of a mere broken bone sometimes wasn't as convenient as a fellow would like. For example: "Paul's Valley, Oklahoma, Fess Reynolds got a broken ankle while riding a bareback horse. Instead of going to the hospital immediately he continued to clown the show and made quite a run when he roped a calf and tied it in 19 seconds. Then he worked his Liberty Brahma bull act. His ankle had swelled so that he had to leave the arena for it was broke in three places." [10 (1951)]

Another incident hurts just to hear it: "Chuck Lorimer who clowns at Bob Barmby's rodeos was badly injured at the Woodland Rodeo when he was smashed against the fence by a bucking horse and suffered a broken pelvis bone." [11 (1958)]

But if an injury slows a fellow down in one way he can probably work another way: "Joaquin Sanchez was unlucky enough to get kicked in the instep by a horse just before the Bakersfield rodeo and couldn't do his bullfighting chore, so they wired Wick Peth at Albuquerque to come and fight bulls along with Bill Lane, while Joaquin tried his hand at the pickup chore with Lee Olivera of Marysville." [11 (1962)]

Some accidents just have no bright side: "We regret the accident befalling Canadian rodeo clown and bullfighter Wayne Hale of Bassano, Alberta. While performing in a hockey game, Wayne fell on the ice and broke his neck, causing partial paralysis. He works for the Kesler rodeos." [11 (1970)]

And although some accidents are just bad, they could have been worse: "Tim Womack worked only two weekly rodeos at Cowtown, New Jersey, when an auto accident side-lined him for the rest of the year. A tractor trailer rig jack-knifed and hit him head on in the rain." [11 (1970)]

And another one: "Inimitable clown Quail Dobbs jumped off a truck and rebroke his leg prior to the rodeo. He had it in a leather cast but had to replaster it and went on with his work in the barrel. Bunky Boger and Dan Willis joined in clowning." [11 (1977)]

When does a bullfighter or barrelman decide it is time to quit, retire, or do something else? There is no right time. Each case is different. Some rodeo clowns let their past injuries make that decision for them. Sometimes they are forced to quit. Others make their decision based on a variety of reasons.

George Doak said, "I quit when the expenses got heavy and I still had my health. I lost the 100 percent 'want to' that I used to have for rodeo clowning."

Skipper Voss reflected, "I craved bulls. Today the thrill of rodeo is gone. I can't get up for the competition."

Although Dale Woodard now does the barrel honors, he told, "I quit fighting bulls when I was 35 because I lost my overdrive gear. I couldn't get away anymore," he said. "As I got older I found I was already in that gear. There was no reserve. I knew I needed to make a transfer." So he jumped in the barrel. [12 (1990)]

Bulls Zero — Clowns Win!

The purpose of the bullfighter and barrelman is to help the cowboy, who rides the menacing Brahma bull, dismount and get away without injury. The Brahma and other bulls are capable of violence and fury. The responsibility lies with the rodeo clown to make sure the bull's aggression is directed away from the cowboy. It keeps the rodeo crowd holding their breath and causes them to scream in fear during the bull riding. Anyone who has ever been to a rodeo knows during this event anything can happen.

When all goes well, it is the greatest:

Joe Orr came out on a bull named Destiny at Salt Lake City. Joe joined the birds on the third jump. Destiny whirled fast and hooked Joe before he could roll. Then the bull backed up for the BIG THING, but Jimmy Nesbitt came out of the dust and slapped that bull square in the face. Jimmy was clowning the show and while I've watched Jimmy fight bulls all over the country he outdid himself at Salt Lake.

Jimmy never used a cape, but he saved the lives of seven boys with absolute disregard for his own life. Four times death missed Jimmy by an inch, and the crowds went crazy. Hubert Sandall came out on a monster named Black Devil. The bull cleared the chute and went into a whirligig dumping Hubert on the third spin. Jimmy jumped that Devil bull like a cat and drove it back with rights and lefts to the nose.

Then he side-stepped when the Devil rushed him with a left hook, and by that time Hubert was dragged to safety. To Jimmy Nesbitt, this is all in his day's work. [10 (1940)]

A book entitled *Black Cowboys* gave the following account of Willie Smokey Lornes:

A friend was selling popcorn and he and Smokey were standing around shooting the breeze when chute No. 3 opened unexpectedly and out came this bull. The animal made a quick selection of the popcorn man and started butting him up against the bucking chutes, and the bull was too close for Smokey to be able to distract him. Smokey started around the ambulance, which was always on hand for such emergencies, but the bull spotted him, took off after him, cut him off and made him head for the opposite fence way across the arena. About midway, however, the bull stopped and Smokey turned and called to the bull, "Here kitty, kitty" and started to go back around toward the ambulance, but the bull still wouldn't let him get by. He kept cutting Smokey off. The one thing this did was keep the bull distracted long enough for the other men to put the popcorn man in the ambulance and take him away. [1]

Hoofs & Horns was always there to report the current happenings, including the "wrecks":

"Jasbo Fulkerson had a favorite saying, 'Look out, cowboy, that bull, she's a makin' for your bo-hind.' " [10 (1944)]

"During the first show Jasbo was hauled off to a hospital following a blow on his head when a Brahma booted the chariot over on him." [10 (1945)]

"The agile and daredevil George Mills was always on hand and turned in the usual number of lifesavers. To pay tribute to George for saving the lives of many of them at the various shows, the cowboys presented him with a trophy, a small but sincere way of showing their appreciation and gratitude." [10 (1945)]

"George Mills, rodeo clown and bull teaser, had a narrow escape at the Buffalo rodeo. George made a run in front of a vicious fighting bull, succeeded in getting the bull to charge him and then George ran for the catch pen gate to get the bull to make an exit from the arena. George slipped and fell, wrenching his ankle and bruising it so that he was unable to work the remainder of the engagement. The bull? It slipped also which was the only thing that saved George from more serious injury." [10 (1943)]

"Slim Pickens was the bull fighter at the Clovis rodeo. A very bad Brahma bull leaped out of the arena onto the track. As usual, it was crowded with people, men, women and children. Slim leaped the fence right along with the bull, and the result was that in all that crowded mass of people, not a soul was hurt. Slim held the attention of the bull until help could arrive. Those bull fighters are not out there just to be funny." [10 (1947)]

"Chuck Mulhair and Art Savage clowned the shows, and fought the bulls to a fare-thee-well. You ever see this Mulhair person run right up a wire fence with NO HANDS? What some folks won't do for money. John Hawkins made a nice 8-second ride on old HoseNose, and then rode 50 seconds longer because he couldn't get off. Chuck Mulhair finally tolled the bull after him, and Hawkins took off at a dead run. So did Mulhair, and he ran right up that wire fence like a turpentined cat." [10 (1949)]

"I have been hearing reports about Wiley McCray and Zeke Bowery who have been clowning together this summer. They have worked out a routine that is witty and clean and keeps the crowd roaring. Their bullfighting is something to watch, too. One time Zeke had to jump in the barrel head first to escape a bull which was hot on his heels. The bull batted the barrel around the arena for five minutes or more but couldn't jar Zeke loose." [10 (1949)]

Hoofs & Horns printed this story of Pancho Villa, the rodeo clown: "George Ritchie was his name but few people knew it. He was an illegal alien in the U.S. and he knew that sooner or later he would be caught and deported. He joined the J. E. Ranch Rodeo where Colonel Jim Eskew had a brindle bull called Bull Durham which was made to order for Pancho's act. Even in contest this bull was always put in the chute to be the last bull ridden, and was an exhibition. Some of the contract riders would ride the bull which was not a hard bucker, they would jump off and the bull

Wiley McCray keeps the bull on the far side of Billy Keen's Bull Machine.
(Photographer unknown; submitted by Charley and Imogene Beals)

would run to the catch pen end of the arena and there would be Pancho—waiting. Pancho would immediately go into his teasing act, the bull would lunge at him and he would turn his back but the bull had a lot to do with making the act such a sensation. This Bull Durham would not strike Pancho head on, but would rush up, lower his lead and with a quick upper-cutting motion of his head, strike the nervy cowboy just below the hip pocket, thus bodily lifting him up and hurling him straight up into the air a distance sometimes of 15 to 18 feet." [10 (1951)]

And this funny story concerned Ken Boen:

"How high can you jump? Ken Boen, top-notch bull fighter, clown and steer wrestler was asked.

" 'Depends on how close the bull is—just as high as necessary to get out of reach,' answered Ken.

"In Baton Rouge, Louisiana, his height of six feet two and one-half inches once enabled him to grab an iron railing atop a cement wall nearly fourteen feet above the ground. Headed toward the wall, with the bull only a breath behind—too close to dodge, and nowhere to escape—he scrambled up the wall like a soldier run-

ning an obstacle course. Next day, he tried to scale that wall, just
to see if he could, but found it impossible to get anywhere near the
top without the stimulus of a bull snuffing his hip pocket." [10
(1951)]

Some dangerous situations seem funny after the scare has
passed:

> One of those bits of rare humor that might have taken a
> more serious trend was witnessed at the Coliseum of the Louisi-
> ana State University at Baton Rouge. It was a thrilling sight to
> see Jim Patch, a cowboy from Miles City, Montana, a small husky
> lad, coming out on the back of the famous bucking bull, Yellow
> Fever. Jim was riding the beast with a skill rarely seen except
> among older and more experienced men, and was doing a fine
> job. Turk Greenough, one of the judges, moved in for better
> observation of the ride, distracted the animal, and the beast took
> after him. Climbing for a high spot, Turk was knocked off his
> perch, only to fall directly on the back of the animal and to take
> Jim with him to the ground. At this moment Jimmy Nesbitt took
> the cue, he dashed in to bring the bull away from the tangle of
> legs and arms of the men rolling in the dust, to save their lives—
> and to save this humorous incident from turning into a harrow-
> ing experience.
>
> Jimmy Nesbitt is famous for his clowning; to see him work
> with his famous straw-stuffed dummy is a hair-raising experi-
> ence that one seldom finds in any other sport activity. In the
> same show at Baton Rouge, Jimmy tangled with that tough bull
> Spillum of the Leo Cremer fighting stock. While Jimmy was less
> fortunate than the contestants of the previous exhibition, this
> occasion afforded perhaps one of the greatest displays of clown-
> ing and bull fighting that has ever been seen by the followers of
> rodeo. This big bull had thrown his rider and started for Nesbitt
> who whirled away, seeking safer pastures—his foot slipped and
> he went down to be tossed some feet up in the air by the beast.
> Catching the falling man on his horns, Spillum tossed him again.
> The clown rolled like a ball and after a few hazy moments gath-
> ered himself together to go back and gave that bull and the
> audience a taste of real courage and slap-happy fearlessness. He
> used his straw dummy as a shield, and there was hardly a spot
> where he did not whack that animal with the flat of his hand.
> The spectators screamed themselves hoarse in horror and sheer
> delight over his daring. It is said that Jimmy was a sore boy for
> days from the pounding he took from this treacherous animal.
> [15]

Baggy britches can cause mass confusion:

Bill Landis works Ray Hix's bull Snuffy at Grass Valley, California, in 1963.   (Photo by Milne; submitted by Donny Landis)

Up in Willitts, California, this year Bill Landis slid between injured cowboy, Steve Butin, and a Mack Barbour Brahma and took the bull by the horns, literally. In the confusion that followed, Steve escaped, Bill turned loose his unorthodox hold, and the bull hung up in the waistline of his oversized clown pants. Fortunately enough, the baggy jeans were equipped with a two-way stretch, or maybe the bull was plain discouraged. At any rate, he took off in a hurry. So ended a spectacular rescue with history repeating itself. Exactly one year before, also at Willits, Bill had saved Steve in almost the same manner. Only that time there had been no room between the bull and the fallen cowboy. With no other choice, Bill stepped directly on Steve, slapped the bull in the face and turned him. And Steve, with the imprints of Bill's boots in his ribs, was carried off to safety.

A smear of grease paint, the sorriest looking wardrobe this side of skid row and a natural ability to make people laugh go into Bill Landis' role of rodeo clown. "Excuse me while I go dress up like an idiot," is a favorite parting expression of his, but no one knows better than his fellow cowboys just how serious he is about his job. At Santa Rosa, California, this year he took a bull's horns in his stomach to save an injured boy from being gored. The force of the blow made him sick a little while later, but the crowd never had a chance to know. A steady patter of jokes, a lifelike imitation of a bucking, bawling Brahma and a fence climbing technique that would shame a cat kept the spectators happy. And Bill didn't leave the arena until the last bull and rider were out of the chute.

Following the pattern of Bobby and Gene Clark, whom he considers the best bullfighters in the arena today, he started fighting bulls on the head, and found out he liked it. His method of darting in front of a bull brings the spectators out of their seats when he slaps a bull on the nose, the crowds go wild. Wes Curtis, whom he also admires as a great bull fighter, trained him in some of the finer points of the profession, and of course, some of his tricks have been learned the hard way. Bill makes no claim to being a hero. He's just as much afraid of the bulls as the next fellow when he's looking at them. But the fear seems to go away when he gets into the arena. "I like to play with those bulls, most of them, anyway. A few old bulls I hate, and I wish I could tear 'em apart. It's a feeling I can't explain." Once after a particularly dangerous performance with a fighting bull, Bill was asked to describe his reaction. "You know how you feel when you've just finished riding a terrific bucking horse? You're sitting high, and you feel so good, you're almost insulted if somebody comes up and talks to you. Well, that's how it is when you turn in a good performance with the bulls. For a little while, you're just too happy to bother with anything." [11 (1954)]

Sometimes the players are putting the crowd on: "Everett Colburn's bull #44 lowers his outsized horns in rank fashion, paws up a storm in the arena dirt and acts in general as if he will rend George Mills asunder. The truth is, #44 is a phony. Even when he butts the barrel, it is a gentle nudge, and George can lead the fierce-looking Ferdinand around like a puppy. #44 appears to love it. And Mills bears such an affection for #44 that when the bull dies he will have its head stuffed over the fireplace at his 100 acre South Dakota ranch." [10 (1954)]

A true Texan, George Doak relayed the following happening. In 1961, at Pendleton, Oregon, George went to the Kiwanis Club before the afternoon performance. In an interview, a local reporter asked George if he knew about the notorious fighting bull "Little Mexico." George told the reporter he was aware of the bull and that Little Mexico was in the Brahma bull riding that day. "But you have to remember," continued George to the reporter, "I'm from Texas, and all I've got to say to 'Little Mexico' is 'Remember the Alamo.' "

During the afternoon performance of the rodeo, Little Mexico got hold of George and had him on his horns. But instead of throwing George over his head, he pushed George in front of him and pinned him up against the wall of the arena. Out of the corner of his eye, George saw the rodeo producer (who owned the bull) reach over to open the gate that let the stock out. Just as Little Mexico headed for the open gate George jumped away from the wall, looked right at the producer and shouted, "Remember the Alamo!"

George was an athlete in high school, and although a Canadian pro-football team representative tried to sign him, George turned them down. He never wanted to play football. He just wanted to be a rodeo clown. Contemporaries say George was a smooth bullfighter and always made it look easy. In fact, they feel he never got the recognition he should have received because he never looked like he was working.

Bob St. John summed up the profession of rodeo clown/bullfighter in his book *On Down the Road:*

> Some people enjoy making others laugh, which isn't too difficult to understand. But it is difficult to reason why a man would cover his face with paint, dress up like a scarecrow, and attempt to appear as if he's charging a windmill, when, in reality, he's putting his well-being, maybe even his life, on the line. This man is paradoxical, almost a foil in the event as a whole. He might take more chances than anybody in the arena, but few people other than the cowboys realize what he is doing, what he has done. His victories are not recorded in a won-lost column, in money winnings, though his losses are usually stated in broken bones. I don't know. Perhaps I see him as a fine rider in a thoroughbred race. Only thing, he is riding a donkey. [21]

CHAPTER 4

Better Organization and more Recognition

Rodeo Gets Organized and Wins Coverage

Rules of the rodeo varied from one rodeo to another in the early days. However, as cowboys started attending rodeos in communities other than just their own, there was more need for continuity.

In 1929 the Rodeo Association of America was formed. It was the scheduling organization of rodeo committees that created unity among producers. The association established a point award system (one point per each dollar won), standardized events, rules, regulations, judging, refereeing, timing, and arena conditions, but had no legal right to speak for the cowboy.

At the Boston Garden Show in 1936 a strike of the cowboys took place. They were resentful of rules that were detrimental to the contestant and tired of purses that were too small to even allow the winners to pay their expenses. The cowboys signed a petition and refused to compete in the Boston show. The petition read: "For the Boston Show, we the undersigned demand that the purses be doubled and the entrance fees added in each and every event. Any contestant failing to sign this petition will not be permitted to contest, by order of the undersigned." [3]

The result: "Determined to go on Colonel Johnson attempted to find other riders. One hundred thirty cowboys were reportedly enroute to New York from a Chicago show, but when they learned of the situation they backed the strikers and refused to come to Boston. Sixty-one top names in rodeo watched and boo-ed from the stands the first night as stable grooms, chute men, ex-jockeys, and Wild West show performers tried to ride saddle broncs, while the band played, 'Empty Saddles in the Old Corral.' " [3]

The newly formed organization was named the Cowboy's Turtle Association. There were no restrictions as to membership. Their main goal was to secure a fair deal for the cowboy as well as the rodeo organizations. Rodeo clown Hoytt Hefner signed the document forming the Turtle Association. Among the signatures on the original document is a big, black, marked-out name. This was the signature of Jimmy Nesbitt, who said he had second thoughts after he signed it. He was definitely with the cowboys, and they all knew that, but he felt Colonel Johnson would fire him from clowning if he saw his signature. Jimmy admitted later it was the worst job of clowning he ever did, as he would not help those men the Colonel brought in the arena, trying to make a rodeo out of civilians because the cowboys refused to perform. [13]

The association grew: "The Cowboy's Turtle Association raised its dues on January 1, 1940 from $5.00 to $10.00 per year. By August of that year the Association had 1,346 members. Provisions were made to include not only contesting cowboys but also contract performers, such as cowgirl bronc riders, trick riders, trick ropers, clowns and announcers, who by this time had begun to play increasingly important roles in rodeo performances." [3]

In 1941 the Cowboy's Amateur Association of America was founded. The rules were the same as those of the Turtle Association, except that a definition of amateur was made: "An amateur is defined as a person who has never belonged to any rodeo association, and upon seeking membership has never won more than five hundred dollars (in any one year) at rodeos. When, at the end of the year, any one member has won this sum of money, he becomes a professional." [15]

In 1938 the Southwest Rodeo Association was formed to give the contestants from that area of the country special awards at the end of the season. In 1942 the name was changed to National Rodeo Association and membership came from Oklahoma, Texas, New Mexico, primarily, and Kansas, Missouri, Arkansas, Louisiana, and Colorado. Other areas to follow with associations were Midwest, Northwest, Pacific, and Eastern.

The year 1945 was a big year for change in the rodeo world. The Cowboy's Turtle Association changed its name to Rodeo Cowboy Association. The reason for the change was that "the name 'Turtle' has no bearing or no connection with the West, is confus-

Charley Beals and George Mills, former rodeo clown, talk of old times at Cowboys Turtle Reunion, 1977.   (Photo by Bern Gregory)

ing to the public, and is entirely out of place for the purpose of the organization." [13]

In the spring of 1946 the Rodeo Association of America and the National Rodeo Association combined to form the International Rodeo Association. The main thrust of this organization is in contests which are open to all who wish to enter.

In 1949 the National Intercollegiate Rodeo Association was formed. This organization was influential in placing rodeo into the area of sports. Scholarships were given to worthy recipients who attended various colleges in the western United States.

The word "Professional" was officially placed in front of the name Rodeo Cowboy Association in 1975 and from then on the organization has been known as the Professional Rodeo Cowboys Association (PRCA).

Throughout the life of organized rodeo a variety of periodicals have covered the sport. The earliest recognized was *Billboard,* known as the world's foremost newspaper on entertainment. Rodeo information fell under columns that covered Wild West shows.

In April 1915 *The Wild Bunch* began. It was the first publica-

1943 Hoofs & Horns *cover featured Polly Burson Mills and George Mills. Polly was trick riding at that time.*   (Submitted by Jack Long)

tion strictly for Wild West show trade and was printed monthly.

Hoofs & Horns, established on July 14, 1931, was published monthly. For many, many years the magazine was published by Ethel A. "Ma" Hopkins, managing editor, in Tucson, Arizona.

Other periodicals to follow were *The Buckboard* and *Rodeo Sports News,* which later changed its name to *Pro-Rodeo Sports News.* Over the years some periodicals have been directed to the seniors, the retired, or "the over the hill gang." Those have been *The Wild Bunch, The Ketch Pen,* and *The Arena Spotlight.*

Rodeo has evolved, and as the years have passed organization and documentation have taken place. "Gradually other people connected with rodeo on a contract basis felt need for group support and began joining the Association as members in good standing. Naturally the clowns were all contesting cowboys, and added to the trick group there were quite a few members who already were primarily contract members, so there was no objection to those who were solely on a contract basis joining the Association." [16]

Membership in the various organizations did not assure a secure future for rodeo clowns. There were no rule books or lists of do's and don'ts for arena funnymen to follow. The earliest rodeo clowns did set some of the precedents that were followed throughout the years. But, just as in all professions, as the responsibilities grew so did the profession. The income should have grown too. But there were no guarantees, and it was up to the cowboy clowns themselves to make sure they were looked after both monetarily and in recognition.

Some years in the periodicals, especially *Hoofs & Horns* (which was *the* magazine of the rodeo world), there were articles each month about the rodeo clowns of the day, their animal friends, and their specialties. Then years would go by when not a word was written about the men in baggy britches and painted face. Rodeo clowns continually had to fight for recognition. There was no union or pay scale to determine they were being compensated fairly. It was strictly up to the clown himself to make sure he was paid a fair wage.

This was not just a problem for the rodeo clown. It was a situation to be reckoned with for all contract members. As the PRCA organization developed, rodeo clowns held positions on the board representing all contract workers from time to time (Bobby Clark, Chuck Henson, Jerry Olson, and Jerry Wayne Olson to name a few). Organized representation has become an accepted fact in the last thirty years. However, today rodeo clowns, bullfighters, and barrelmen still negotiate their own compensation just as they did in earlier days.

D. J. Gaudin said that when rodeos were first being televised Cheyenne Frontier Days was picked for the TV screen. Kajun was clowning, and when the television representative came to him and offered him $150 a performance Kajun refused. The TV rep said that was all they could pay. "Well, just shoot around me then. Don't put the cameras on me. I want $500 a performance," insisted Kajun.

Little did the TV rep realize that Kajun had done six television spots on the Chevy Show earlier and had been paid $500 for each spot. The representative finally agreed, and Kajun got $500 a performance at Cheyenne—and the cameras didn't have to shoot around him.

In the 1960 account *On Down the Road,* Skipper Voss expressed his resentment of the "second class treatment" rodeo clowns get: "I just feel clowns should be treated more like cowboys. They took the National Finals Rodeo shield off our buckles, which they had no right to do. Then they don't even want us at the

championship banquet. Clowns get no credit, but I'd like to see what would happen without us out there. We pay dues like the cowboys, and we're a part of the show and should be treated equally." [21]

Recognition was hard to come by. And when it did come, who should it come from? These questions went 'round and 'round the rodeo world. In 1960 the bull riders voted on the rodeo clowns to work National Finals as bullfighters and barrelmen. After all, weren't they the ones being protected by these bull-baiters?

In 1970 an article reported: "Clown and bullfighter committee presented a list of 10 names from their ranks on the basis of performances worked and how many years in the association. The commission selected one at random by drawing from a hat, the other nine were voted on—Kajun Kid was selected from the draw, Bobby Clark came out high on the vote. Alternate will be Wick Peth. Five names were presented for barrelmen—Wright Howington came out on the draw—Alternate is Wiley McCray." [12 (1970)]

In 1973 this announcement was made: "Contract acts [are] released from membership, in order [that] they can perform their specialty acts where ever they choose—at the request of contract director, Jerry Olson." [12 (1973)]

Karl Doering, rodeo clown and bullfighter, wrote a column

Kajun Kid at 1970 National Finals in Oklahoma City.
(Photo by Bern Gregory; submitted by D. J. Gaudin)

called "Hornin' In" for the *Pro-Rodeo Sports News,* and in one issue he wrote:

> Christmas came early for the Baggy Britches Bunch at the
> Canadian National Finals held in Edmonton, Alberta Coliseum
> NW September 12. The following is an excerpt from CCA Sec-
> retary Manager Berry Tibbitt column "Chute Talk" in the *Cana-
> dian Rodeo News.*
>
> "The Edmonton Exhibition Association has announced that
> it will present gold and silver buckles by Olson Silver and
> Leather of High River, Alberta, to the clowns and bullfighters
> participating at the CFR, this will not only apply to the 1977 but
> will be retroactive to CFR, in 1974. They recognize the fact that
> while the bull fighters are truly athletes in their own right but
> they have no chance to win a championship as finalists do.
>
> "Bullfighters at Canadian Finals 1974, Karl Doering, 1975
> Kelly LaCoste and Larry Clayman, 1976, Kelly LaCoste, John
> Taylor and Mickey Bagnell, 1977, Jimmy Anderson, John Taylor
> and Chuck Henson." [12 (1977)]

The following year Karl wrote:

Most any bullfighter worth his salt has been run over a time or two. It's an expected by-product of the profession. After you sort out all the parts and find nothing is sticking out through the skin, you can sort of smirk to yourself while soaking in the applause from the five dollar seats.

"By gun, I saved ol' what's his name a bad hooking; bet he won't forget to give me his vote for the finals."

Well chances are ol' what's his name jumped the far fence and never looked back on his way to the airport. To top it all off he probably won't even return his ballot for the finals anyway.

Now speaking of getting smoothed out, there isn't a bull living that could hold a candle to Canadian bull rider Mark Garstad on his arena exit. When you took a contract north of the border, one of the first items of business was to check the bull pen and the entry list; not necessarily in that order. When Mark decided to get off, your best lick was to run in front of the bull and make sure he got to you first. At least the bull didn't wear spurs. [12 (1978)]

Jerry L. Olson had to resign his director's post in 1987. The reasons follow:

The PRCA Board of Directors accepted at its July 7 meet-

Jerry Olson taunts bull at Odessa, 1964.
(Photo by Ben Allen; submitted by Charley and Imogene Beals)

ing the resignation of Jerry L. Olson as the contract personnel director, a post he'd held since January, 1986.

In his letter of resignation sent to the Board, Olson said, "At the present time I have to be more concerned about my personal welfare. I do not think I can be fair to the people who elected me to this position when I have to be more concerned about myself than the problems that arise."

Olson was injured last December when the three-wheeled all-terrain vehicle he was driving crashed near his home in St. Onge, S.D.

He was knocked unconscious and laid in the pasture for eight hours before being discovered. Doctors said he injured his brain stem apparently when his head hit the ground during the crash.

Following the injury, he showed symptoms similar to that of a stroke. His speech was somewhat slurred and he suffered some moderate paralysis. He is still recovering.

Olson has been replaced by Hadley Barrett, who was elected Contract Personnel Director by the Contract Personnel Executive Council. Barrett of North Platte, Nebraska, is a PRCA announcer. [12 (1987)]

The following year Jerry's son, Jerry Wayne Olson, took a seat on the board representing rodeo clowns and bullfighters.

In a *ProRodeo Sports News* article, Jerry Wayne is quoted as saying: "A good act complements the standard events and adds to a rodeo's entertainment value." The article went on to give various cowboys' opinions of specialty acts they truly felt were exceptional: "Quail Dobbs' car act is my favorite," said Bruce Ford, five-time world bareback riding champion. "It's been around as long as I have. I've seen it hundreds of times, and I still laugh. Quail's an entertainer. He knows how to get his crowd going."

Bud Munroe, the 1986 World Saddle Bronc Riding Champion, also enjoys rodeo's added acts. "Good acts add to a rodeo. All of us in rodeo are entertainers. Acts break up the monotony of the rodeo, and at the same time give the contractor extra time to do things like run stock in. It's important to have something flamboyant enough to keep the crowd's attention while all this takes place.

"Butch Lehmkuhler's trampoline act is one of my favorites," said Scott Kesl of Lemhi, Idaho. "He's really good and acrobatic. Tom Feller's buffalo is great, too."

"Jim Bob Feller's old woman cracks me up," said Dennis Humphrey of Cheyenne. "It really looks like he's riding an old woman."

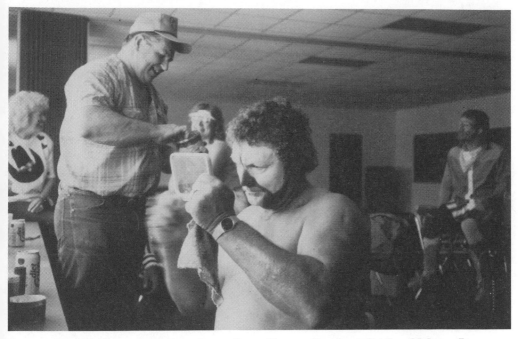

Junior Meek applying clown face. George Doak and Allen Nelson, Jr., getting ready. (Photo by Gail Woerner)

"You'd be surprised how many 50, 60 and 70 year old people come up to us after a rodeo," Olson said. "We really seem to appeal to them."

Rodeo is often called America's original sport. It evolved on ranches of the Old West into its present form. Specialty acts weren't far behind those original rodeos, according to Olson.

"Rodeos have always been celebrations," he said. "Without all aspects of the rodeo business, the celebration's cut short.

"Nobody likes half a party. Bring on the clowns." [12 (1988)]

Karl Doering, rodeo clown and bullfighter of Roseburg, Oregon, was responsible for starting a Rodeo Clown Reunion. The first was held in June 1974, and has been held in Roseburg every three years through 1989. I attended the event in 1989.

Seventeen rodeo clowns arrived in the friendly Oregon town of Roseburg to enjoy a five-day Cowboy Clown Reunion. The clowns ranged in ages from twenty-eight to eighty, and have been entertaining rodeo audiences for the past sixty-one years. A handful are still at it.

The purpose of the Cowboy Clown Reunion is to give retired

Cowboy Clown Reunion attendees prepare for fishing trip in Roseburg, Oregon, 1989. Left to right: Wayne and Cecil Cornish, Larry McKinney, Jerry Mariluch, Mac Berry, Wick Peth, and Charley Lyons.

(Photo by Gail Woerner)

rodeo clowns an opportunity to get together, reminisce, enjoy some fishing and golf, and do some entertaining once more.

Being a first-time attendee I had no idea what to expect. Long-time friend, Gail Gandolfi, of Belmont, California, also attended. Gail, an artist, has been responsible for many of the caricatures and drawings throughout the book. We found out soon after we arrived it was all we could do to keep up with these zany characters, despite several of advancing age.

Since the first reunion in 1974, it had been held in conjunction with the Umpqua Valley Roundup. After Karl Doering's death in 1983, the event was coordinated by Mac and Katie Barry of Coburg, Oregon.

The headquarters motel that opened their doors for the rodeo funnymen had to relax a few rules and be willing to look the other way on occasion. When cowboy clowns, wives, children, grand-children, and friends congregated there was no telling what might occur. Pets—an array of dogs, a cockatiel and even an aged Sicilian donkey—were in attendance. Room doors were left open, and

Madcap merrymen at the reunion, Mac Barry and Wayne Cornish.
(Photo by Gail Woerner)

jokes, laughter, and song wafted out into the parking lot, from daylight 'til dawn the next morning.

Imagine the thrilling surprise to the unsuspecting family from the eastern United States, on vacation in the Northwest, that discovered the rest stop they had chosen that night was filled with rodeo clowns, wherever they looked. The children were ecstatic.

The reunion kicked off with a deep-sea salmon fishing trip. Lunches were packed and heavy jackets were recommended just in case. Jokes were shared about former fishing trips of heavy seas, high waves, and those who had hung their heads overboard "donating" their lunches to the denizens of the deep. Luckily, this year the day was perfect, sunny, with just a hint of a breeze.

All seventeen rodeo humorists returned with salmon to take home. Wayne Cornish, of Waukomis, Oklahoma, was the winning fisherman, having caught the largest salmon—eight and a half pounds.

A Cowboy Golf Tournament was held at the picturesque 64 Veterans Administration Golf Course in Roseburg. Observing, noting, and trying to photograph these crazy clowns as they made ready for the Great Golf Challenge merely reconfirmed to me that clowns have a never-ending comedic view to everything.

"Hey, they want me to play this game with only two balls," yelled one character.

"How do they expect me to wash my balls in this contraption? It's too tall and there's no stool to stand on," complained another.

"These are left-handed golf balls," cried another.

And off they went, some using only one club for the entire game—a wood. Others, more experienced golfers, insisted on at least two or three clubs.

As they made their way up and down the fairways we found some of the competitors "mooning" their opponents in an attempt to distract them from the game.

Jerry Mariluch and Frank McIlvain used their clubs to form a V on either side of the 9th hole assisting Mac Barry's ball to go in the hole as he putted with a wooden rake he picked up in the last sand trap. Several other billiard-type shots were attempted here and there on the green.

To my knowledge a winning team was never determined, but for that matter, there were no losers, either.

After being treated to a complementary steak dinner, the former arena funnymen donned their make-up and baggy britches and headed to the Veterans Hospital to visit with patients. Wes Curtis had his very authentic-looking stethoscope hanging around his neck. He announced to several patients that he was the new doctor and had been assigned to their case. The patients might have grinned a little, but they never turned him away. One real, honest-to-goodness physician put his stethoscope to Wes' head and announced, "There's nothing in there."

Monk Carden directed hospital hallway traffic with his bull-fighting cape, which showed an arrow making a ninety-degree turn upward. With seventeen very eager cowboy clowns darting in and out of rooms, there was total chaos. Patients, doctors, and staff participated, and giggles to guffaws were heard throughout the entire complex.

Monk, age eighty, began his rodeo clown career in 1928 when he and partner George Moens were hired to clown the Pendleton Round-Up. Their burlesque acrobatic act continued to be a part of the Round-Up and other area rodeos for the next ten years. Monk said this was actually before bullfighting was part of a rodeo clown's realm of responsibility. Brahmas were only used in exhibi-

MONK CARDIN
(OREGON)

tion rides in the Northwest during his era (1928 to 1938). Carden was presented a wristwatch by the Roseburg Rodeo Committee for being the oldest clown in attendance.

The first performance of the Umpqua Valley Round-Up rodeo featured all seventeen former rodeo clowns in costume in the arena. Announcer Bob Tallman, on horseback in the arena, introduced each one as they joked and heckled the cowboys, teased the audience, and thwarted the stock. Those who had been primarily bullfighters stayed close to the chutes, ready to assist, if necessary. Habit, no doubt.

Other funnymen roamed the arena and the bleachers delighting the audience with their antics. Sammy Reynosa roped a loose bareback bronc, and when the horse hit the end of the rope Sammy flipped high into the air and landed on his back on the ground, to the hysterical laughter of the crowd.

During the calf roping Jim Hill and Wright Howington approached a tied calf determined a fair catch by the official judge. Before he was released, they baby powdered him profusely and let him go. The humiliated calf ran to the nearest exit.

Wes Curtis and Wayne Cornish roamed the stands, sat on ladies' laps, and revived their favorite tricks up and down the aisles. Many old-timers in the audience must have had a touch of déjà vu

Sammy Reynosa, son and grandson enjoy reunion, 1989.
(Photo by Gail Woerner)

Wright Howington and Frank McIlvain still rodeo clown in Fort Worth and Mesquite, Texas, respectively.
(Photo by Gail Woerner)

or, to put it in terms more western, it must have seemed like the good old days, seeing some of the same routines and costumed clowns that had been entertaining similar audiences for over sixty years.

The following morning was the annual Rodeo Parade, and these madcap men were ready—early. Costumed, they helped wives and other family members, and friends, and one old Sicilian donkey onto the back of a flatbed truck to join in the fun. As the parade made its way up and down the streets of Roseburg full of youngsters and parade watchers of all ages, the rodeo clowns not only waved and threw candy to the onlookers but some hopped on and off the truck "capturing" innocent by-standers. Wick Peth, Charley Lyons, and Greg Doering assisted the "captured" ones onto the truck.

It was hard to determine who had the most fun, those on the truck or those watching the parade. That evening at the rodeo performance, when ribbons were awarded and trophies given, Sammy Reynosa accepted the First Place Float trophy, on behalf of the group.

All rodeo clowns were eligible to win a Remington rifle and scabbard donated by Jack Saulls, long-time committeeman from the Columbia River Pro-Rodeo Circuit. Larry McKinney, rodeo clown-bullfighter from 1955 to 1977, won the rifle.

Although activities were planned and organized daily, the spontaneity of the cowboy clowns continued to flow as bubbles from an uncorked bottle of champagne. Their way of looking at everything, no matter how minor, has such a crazy, zany approach.

Although a depressing subject was seldom mentioned by these ageless humorists, they did discuss with affection and re-spect the cowboy clowns who have died. The fun their deceased brothers enjoyed at earlier reunions was recalled with humor and love. They will long be remembered.

Bill Landis and son Donny signify the passing of the profession from father to son. Bill clowned from 1948 to 1970, and Donny started his career in 1973. Donny and Charlie "Too Tall" West were clowning the Roseburg rodeo. Donny's Wild Cantabeetalope routine is one not to miss.

Enough stitches have gone into these fellows to make a pile of quilts. But it doesn't slow them down. Nor do they let a few aches and pains bother them. Life is too much fun.

These paradoxical characters are a very special breed. They have a toughness that goes beyond description. They have a hu-

Behind the chutes at Roseburg. Left to right: Jim Hill, Donny Landis, Charley Saulls, Bill Landis, Jack Saulls, Larry McKinney, Wayne Cornish, Frank McIlvain, Butch Robinson, Mac Barry. Front row: Charley "Too Tall" West and Cecil Cornish.   (Photo by Gail Woerner)

Donny Landis works his "Cantabeetalope" to the delight of a rodeo audience.   (Photo by M. Bowman; submitted by Donny Landis)

morous angle that comes through in every situation. They have a protective tendency that doesn't disappear after the bull riding is over. It extends beyond the cowboy, their family, one another, and beyond their own selves. The rodeo clown—a true American hero in painted face and baggy pants.

Representing 419 years of combined rodeo clowning, those attending the 1989 reunion were Sammy Reynosa of Redwood City, CA; Donny and Bill Landis, Fresno, CA; Jerry Mariluch, Elko, NV; Charley Lyons, Saint Ignatius, MT; Wick Peth, Bow, WA; Butch Robinson, Yerington, NV; Howard Arnew, Grass Valley, CA; Wes Curtis, Oakland, OR; Wayne Cornish, Waukomis, OK; Jim Hill, Enid, OK; Mac Barry, Coburg, OR; Greg Doering, Roseburg, OR; Larry McKinney, Frazier Park, CA; Monk Carden, Pendleton, OR; Wright Howington, Colleyville, TX; and Frank McIlvain, Balch Springs, TX.

Others attending were Cecil Cornish, Enid, OK; Bill Shaw, long-time director of Pendleton Round-Up, Pendleton, OR; Jack Saulls, Moses Lake, WA; and sons, Jack Jr., and Charley, plus assorted families and friends.

During a brief meeting it was decided to hold the next reunion in 1991 at Moses Lake, Washington, hosted by Jack Saulls.

Jon Temple, Wright Howington, and George Doak sign autographs for Special Olympians at Texas Summer Games in Denton, 1992.

(Photo by Gail Woerner)

Opportunities to reunite and reminisce are most important to these over-the-hill humorists. During the year, many attend the Rodeo Historical Society gathering of old-timers during the National Finals Rodeo in Las Vegas. Although they don't follow the rodeo circuit and see each other "on down the road" like they used to, they look forward to each get-together and just continue where they left off. They are a wonderful bunch of down-to-earth people who truly enjoy one another.

"My mule died and my wife wouldn't perform," lamented Monk Carden when asked why he quit rodeo clowning at the 1991 Cowboy Clown Reunion.

The reunion was held in Moses Lake, Washington, during the annual Round-Up in August. The festivities included a rodeo and fair, which attracted crowds from near and far. Youth from the area showed their livestock, area arts and crafts were judged, the carnival rides were kept busy well into the night, and the demoli-

1991 Clown Reunion in Moses Lake, Washington. Left to right: Wes Curtis, Monk Carden, Bill Landis, Rob Smets, Larry McKinney, Wayne Cornish, Charley Lyons, Cecil Cornish. Front row: Butch Robinson, Donny Landis, Dale Greenwood, Jack Saulls, Mac Barry, and Wright Howington.   (Photo by Gail Woerner)

Wes Curtis greets a fan before the rodeo.
(Photo by Gail Woerner)

tion derby thrilled everyone. The PRCA rodeo played to packed grandstands all three nights.

Jack Saulls, Cowboy Clown Reunion chairman, and the local rodeo committee welcomed attending rodeo clowns, families, and friends from across the country. Everyone enjoyed a welcome dinner, a street breakfast sponsored by the local Kiwanis Club, a tour of Grand Coulee Dam and barbecue each night after the rodeo performance.

Former arena funnymen dressed in their familiar costumes and greeted and signed autographs for young and old prior to each rodeo performance. They were introduced and honored during the rodeo as they assisted the hired rodeo clowns: Donny Landis, Rob Smets, and Ron Kersey.

Cowboy clowns were interviewed on radio and television as well as by local newspaper reporters. They attended the Senior Citizen Center and visited with local people. They met fans at Skeens Western Wear Store, and enjoyed watermelon with the residents of a local nursing home.

Saturday morning the clowns participated in a golf tournament at Moses Lake Country Club. Teams including some of the fearless funnymen may not have shot par, considering the number of divots seen on the course after they finished. Some clowns who had fought bulls with the precision of a brain surgeon missed that elusive white ball with great consistency. No matter, it didn't stop the laughs. Local country club members playing with each team of jokesters quickly put aside their "serious" game and joined in the hilarity.

Donny Landis, son of retired rodeo clown and bullfighter Bill Landis, has a great act featuring Mario, Donny's trained flea. "Mario comes out of his house, takes a bow, climbs to the top of an eight-foot tower, and dives into a bucket of water," so Donny describes. Mario is a bit too wee for a rodeo audience to see, but when Donny and fellow rodeo clown Rob Smets follow Mario with their eyes as he moves to the tower, then dives into the water, everyone sees the splash when he hits the water. For his final trick Mario jumps a flaming hoop, only to catch fire. It takes Donny and the entire bucket of water to save Mario. The illusion is great.

Dale Greenwood, rodeo clown of the 1944 to 1973 era, was standing on the sidelines the second night of the rodeo and was approached by his six-year-old grandson. "I can't see Mario, Grandpa," the little tyke told Dale. Dale told his grandson to come

Dale Greenwood and grandson enjoy "Mario, the Trained Flea" during the rodeo.   (Photo by Gail Woerner)

with him, and he took him into the arena during Donny's act with Mario. Dale's grandson was obviously very uneasy to be inside the arena, but his desire to see Mario from a closer vantage point out-weighed his nervousness.

As Donny proceeded with the act and as Mario climbed to the top of the tower, Dale's grandson leaned over and said, "I *can* see Mario now, Grandpa." After the act, Dale's grandson marched out of the arena well satisfied—and totally convinced he had seen Mario.

Whether they were signing autographs for youngsters, talking among themselves behind the chutes before the rodeo, or just visiting around the swimming pool at the motel, I noticed that the array of personalities among these men was amazing.

They criticize very openly the rodeo of today and the rodeo clown of today. Everyone has an opinion, no two alike. There is disgust, annoyance, anger, and then, in the wink of an eye, the mood is gone. Smiles, winks, laughs, and giggles replace the earlier emotions.

These men are as complex as the profession they pursued.

Reunion at Seniors Finals, Reno, Nevada, 1991. Left to right: Ted Billingsly, Bill Landis, Jerry Mariluch, Butch Robinson, Glenn Fritzler, Chuck Henson, Jack Rudd. Front row: Scoot LeQuieu, Larry McKinney, Wes Curtis, and Jimmy Schumacher. (Photo by Gail Woerner)

Could it be that complexity is a necessary part of the rodeo clown personality?

Attending the 1991 reunion were Dale Greenwood of Cartwright, ND; Larry McKinney, Frazier Park, CA; Bill Landis, Fresno, CA; Butch Robinson, Yerington, NV; Mac Barry, Coburg, OR; Wes Curtis, Oakland, OR; Wright Howington, Colleyville, TX; Monk Carden, Pendleton, OR; Wayne Cornish, Waukomis, OK; Charley Lyons, St. Ignatius, MT; Rob Smets, Oakland, OR; Donny Landis, Fresno, CA; and Greg Doering, Tualatin, OR.

The National Senior Pro Rodeo Finals held in Reno, Nevada, in November 1991 honored retired rodeo clowns. This was the first year for the Senior Pro Tour to honor the clowns, but plans have been made to make it an annual event.

The fearless funnymen visited local schools daily, signed autographs each day in Circus, Circus Casino and Hotel, attended all five rodeo performances, and were guests of honor at the Rodeo Clown Ball.

The first Slim Pickens Memorial Award was presented to Jimmy Schumacher. This award, originated by Jack and Nancy Keran of Santa Cruz, California, will be presented each year to a

Jimmy Schumacher received the first Slim Pickens Memorial Award presented at Reno, 1991.   (Photo by Gail Woerner)

former rodeo clown. The 1992 recipient was Wes Curtis, whose twenty-year tenure as a rodeo clown ended in 1968.

Other Occupations

Rodeo clowns didn't just grow up to be rodeo clowns. Their trails wandered through a few other occupations to reach the funnyman profession. Some of those trails went through various types of cowboying.

One example is Tin Horn Hank:

Henry C. Keenen, later known as Tin Horn Hank, was raised by his father. Two sisters and one brother were quite a handful for Mr. Keenen. The boys were wild, defiant and un-governable. Mr. Keenen bought a store and planned to put the boys to work but he found they spent a good deal of their time when they should have been delivering groceries to the women around town at the Alliance, Nebraska, corral with the mus-tangs brought in to be sent east for dog food. The kids would get the horses milling in a corral, jump on their backs from a fence, grab a handful of mane and ride—or be thrown. It was exhilarating sport for the wild ones. If they found a really tough stallion in the nondescript herds, they'd cut it into another pen, snub it down, saddle it, and mount up like the rodeo riders. Hank got pretty proficient at this, and, as a reward to himself for excellence at mustang riding, he made a pair of chaps out of an untanned goat hide. Townsfolk said you could smell him for miles.

A farmer came to town one day, leading a spoiled horse. He wanted it ridden. Hank offered his services and right away saddled the horse on Alliance's main street. When the youth stepped aboard, the horse began to pitch, bucking through the front window of a store. Hank rode the horse all the way through the store and out the back door. His father had to pay for broken windowpanes, smashed dishes, and ruined mer-chandise. The boy was 15 years old then, and his father, though dead set against such a course, knew that his son hankered to be a follower of rodeos.

A year or so later, after the father heard about Hank's deci-sion to enter a couple of upcoming rodeos, he decided to play a gambler's hand. He told his son he would loan him expense money for a trial run at professional rodeo. If he came back a winner and paid off the loan, then the father, with his blessings, would permit Hank to go off rodeoing. But if he came home broke, if his stint did not prove successful, the son was to agree he'd continue working in the family store until he was 21.

Several weeks later a touring car drove up to the Keenen store and a cowboy, wearing a big white hat and bright red shirt, got out and entered the front door. Hank told his father, "You can take this money your boy owes you and you can get yourself another storekeeper." [22 (1984)]

Hank Keenen worked Wild West shows and rodeos, including the 101, Dickey's, Hinkle, Adams, and the Cowboy Reunion at Las Vegas, New Mexico.

Homer Holcomb's trail moved in various directions: "His clowning follows life as a ranch boy, fiddler for country town dances, race horse rider with Earle Sands, cowboy, bugler with the 27th Heavy Artillery in World War days, auto racer, vaudeville performer, roper and rider, relay horse rider, chariot rider, Roman rider, and a hundred other odd jobs. In 1923 at Blackfoot, Idaho, he won the trophy as best all-around cowboy. In 1925 at Calgary, Canada, he won the world's relay riding championship." [10 (1941)]

Jasbo Fulkerson also won some in the arena: "The Judge's voice boomed through the public address system, 'High point man in the bull riding in this 1926 rodeo is Jasbo Fulkerson.' " [14] Un-

Homer Holcomb at Fontana, California, rodeo, 1938. Gordon Davis is calf roper.   (Photographer unknown; submitted by Gordon Davis)

fortunately, not all rides were that successful for Jasbo:

> "Out of chute number five, ladies and gentlemen, will come a little rider on a lotta bull, Jasbo Fulkerson of good old Cowtown." Jasbo squirmed tighter onto the Brahma's back, jammed his hat down to his ears, drew his neck down between his shoulders, and nodded to the gateman.
>
> "And there he goes," the loudspeakers cried, as the Brahma burst into the arena bawling and leaping and shaking itself like a fish trying to throw a hook. In the first seconds Jasbo sensed he was on a locoed animal; he socked both spurs into the bull's shoulders and tried to weather the storm. Unable to dislodge the rider, the bull became crazed with hate. The next moment it launched its great body into the air, twisted and crashed to the ground on its side. Jasbo saw the bull's intention too late. In desperation he tried to fling himself away from the falling brute, but the rope was wound too tightly around his hand. Jasbo disappeared under the huge black frame.
>
> The crowd gasped in unison.
>
> The Brahma staggered uncertainly to his feet and eyed Jasbo's quiet body spread-eagled on the ground, unmoving. Jasbo's clowning partner, Red Sublett, dashed in, whacked the bull smartly on the nose with his ridiculous derby hat. The bull turned and charged Red to the wall and to a nimble leap for safety. The pickup men closed in. The Brahma was driven from the arena.
>
> When Madolyn, Jasbo's wife, reached him, she turned his face up and began to brush it clean, wailing, "What did he do to you, Jas? How bad are you hurt?"
>
> The little man's eyes rolled alarmingly in their sockets before they settled on her face. He wheezed experimentally, then grinned thinly around clenched teeth. "Nothin' busted, Baby, just mashed all the air outa me."
>
> That night Jasbo quit competitive riding. [14]

In 1941 George Mills was the Rodeo Association of America World's Champion Bareback Rider. "He started his career by riding races, until he got too heavy. He's a good all round cowboy, rides saddle broncs, bareback and bulls, also bull-dogs." [10 (1943)]

An article titled "Wilbur Plaugher, Rodeo Clown, Calf Roper, Bulldogger," went on to tell: "In 1946 Wilbur went back to New York to the Madison Square Garden rodeo, and all he was able to do at that show was to win the all around title. He led in two events and lost the third, bulldogging, to Dave Campbell, by three-fifths of a second. In 1947 he went to New York again and won the bronc riding, taking $3,300 away with him. He placed second in the bronc riding finals at New York in 1948 and went on to Boston to take second place in the bulldogging finals." [10 (1949)]

Hoofs & Horns kept the reports for all: "In 1946 Scotty Bagnell won the bareback championship at Lewiston, Idaho, where Daniels and Hanna furnished some of the most hard-boiled stock of any rodeo.

"At Calgary Stampede, '47, one of the biggest and wildest and fastest shows in the world, Scotty won the North American steer decorating. A fact to 'do a man proud.' " [10 (1951)]

Hoytt Hefner also spent lots of years cowboying: "He's been in the rodeo business twenty-two years, fifteen of those years being spent as a rodeo contestant. He worked three events: calf-roping, bareback bronc and bull riding, and was usually at the pay window in all three events. In one of three he has won most of the major shows of the country including Cheyenne, two times, Denver three times, Fort Worth two times, Houston and Boston. He has made Madison Square Garden eleven times and seldom failed to money in either bull riding or bareback riding." [10 (1950)]

Ken Boen was a winner in steer wrestling: "Ken won the steer wrestling contest at Cheyenne in '46, at Houston in '47, and again at Madison Square Garden in '48. In '50 at Tulsa, Oklahoma, he threw his steer in 3 seconds. In 1948, Ken lacked 100 points of winning the World's Champion record, but due to contracts, of which he seemed to have more than usual that year, he was unable to participate in enough shows to gain the needed points."

Jack Oakey, rodeo announcer, told:

It was the final performance of the Cowboy Days Rodeo at Evanston, Wyoming, last summer Wilbur Plaugher was the next dogger. At Lehi, Utah, he had dogged a steer in 3 and 4/5th seconds, and three weeks later had thrown his steer at Spanish Ford, Utah, in 3 and 3/5th seconds. Says I to myself, "Here is a big strong boy who can really put one down. Keep your eye on him." The gate flew open, the steer crossed the six-foot line and Wilbur went after him. I turned to look at the field flagman and to my surprise saw that he was dropping the flag. I quickly looked back to Wilbur and there he was on the ground with the steer lying on his side, all four feet out. The timers gave me the time and I could not believe my ears so I said, "Wait a minute, folks, I must check this time before I announce it."

There were two official timers and both their watches showed the same thing, and two people were holding their watches on Wilbur and they all agreed, so I could no longer doubt it. "Ladies and gentlemen, believe it or not, Wilbur Plaugher just broke all records by throwing his steer in just 2 and 3/5th seconds." [10 (1951)]

An article by Hobart Normand told of Ike Tacker's cowboying: "As a contestant, Ike started riding bulls in 1931, at some of the south Texas shows where the bulls are all rough and hard to ride. As the years went by he got into the bareback riding and saddle bronc riding and then finally into the bulldogging contests. Making a top hand in all of these events, Ike went right on to within one notch of the all-round championship of the old National Rodeo Association, before it was combined with the I.R.A." [10 (1953)]

In the same issue, Joe Koller wrote: "The basis of a good clown is a good cowboy. Bennie Bender adds to clowning contract income with winnings in bareback, and Brahma bull riding, and bulldogging events. Rodeo has long recognized Bennie as a top hand and one of the most customer satisfying comics in show business." [10 (1953)]

The split-second timing a rodeo clown must perfect to stay alive and ahead of the bulls must be a help when it comes to rodeo events like calf-roping and bulldogging. Other cowboy clowns have excelled with fast time. Junior Meek was the biggest single-event money winner at St. Louis. He threw his steer in 5.4 seconds for a first-day money and won the average in a total time of 11.4 on two steers. [11 (1959)] In 1968 Wilbur Plaugher won the steer wrestling at San Antonio with 12.3 seconds on two head of stock. He left with $3,507 in winnings. [11 (1968)]

Of course, cowboying wasn't the only trail taken by arena funnymen, especially during World War II. Ma Hopkins published this letter from Howard O'Neill, who was serving in the South Pacific:

How is the rodeo world and *Hoofs & Horns?* I have been out of the picture for some time as I was called into the Army last July. Please let my friends know that I'm in the South Pacific rounding up Japs, in one of the biggest shows of them all.

We are on an island that is mostly jungle, infested with snakes, alligators and other lizards. Insects also numerous. There are no natives on this island but some came from another island and visited us. They stay in hiding most of the time because they are afraid of the Japs. The Japs stole some of their women folks, but some got away. I will never forget the first time the Jap planes came over and dropped bombs. I ran for my foxhole and hugged the bottom. There was one Jap aviator that we called Washboard Charlie. He was very slick and got away a lot of times, but we finally got him and now we are making rings and bracelets out of parts of his Zero.

One time Washboard Charlie dropped a barrel of rice for he thought the Japs were still here. The barrel landed on a jeep and broke it all to pieces, but we were thankful it wasn't a bomb. One of my buddies caught a little young parrot and is making a cage for him. He is green and red and yellow and we think he will learn to talk. We call him Washboard Charlie, too. [10 (1943)]

A year later Ma Hopkins again wrote:

Pvt. Howard O'Neill one of the O'Neill twins, spent seventeen months fighting Japs in the South Pacific. He is back in the States, suffering from malaria and shell shock. He writes a most interesting letter, parts of which we cannot print, but here is some of it. "My last campaign was in New Garagos. It's grim terrain. Among the worst in the world. We went into the jungle this way, patrols first, bulldozers next, followed by jeeps and artillery; to do seven miles took one month. Though we laid down heavy artillery barrage, the Japs crawled through it and dropped grenades in our foxholes or struck with knives in the dark. It was severe to say the least. I will be glad to hear from some of my friends." [10 (1944)]

Zeke Bowery cowboyed at an early age, then declared he'd had enough cowboying. "He went home and took up the trade of machinist. After six years he became a full fledged machinist, and also had a degree as an operating engineer. He then took a job as superintendent of a CCC camp under the Taylor Grazing Act which he held for two years. When war came he was contracted by the government as an operating engineer at one of the Los Angeles shipyards.

"In addition to their rodeo clowning Cele and Zeke play stages, parties and movies, and in the spring of 1948 made two sets of television. Zeke has played stand-in stunt parts in a number of western pictures including 'Duel in the Sun.' " [10 (1948)]

Slim Pickens was not the first rodeo great to go to Hollywood. But once he got there, he worked consistently for many years. In 1949 he signed a contract with Republic Studios. His first picture, entitled *Denver,* was shot on location thirty miles from Denver. Throughout the 1950s and '60s, rodeo periodicals kept abreast of what Slim was doing in Hollywood:

"Heard Slim is giving up the rodeos after this year's Cow Palace show and will devote his time to the picture business. He just finished a new picture, 'Story of Will Rogers.' " [10 (1952)]

"Slim Pickens, who got into pictures the hard way, has several commitments ahead, but does not intend to retire from rodeos. Some of the pictures he recently played in are 'Sun Shines Bright,' a John Ford production 'Thunderhead' with Mona Freeman, John Derek, John Barrymore, Jr.; 'Overland Trail Riders,' a Red Allen picture by Republic; and just recently released, 'South Pacific Trail,' another Rex Allen job. Slim is one cowboy who really seems to be making good in the picture game." [10 (1953)]

"Slim went back to Hollywood after the Cow Palace where he has a lot of picture commitments. He has been in pictures lately with Rex Allen and will be seen in the new Republic Picture, 'Fortune Hunters,' starring John Derek and Joan Evans." [10 (1954)]

"Slim in movie, 'The Saga of Andy Burnett,' as old Bill Williams, the trapper with his horse, Honest John, who bucks him off." [11 (1958)]

"Slim completed a picture with Victor Mature, 'Escort West,' produced by John Wayne's BatJac Co. He'll start a Walt Disney movie, 'Comanche,' about the horse that was the only living thing left of Custer's outfit after the Battle of the Little Bighorn." [11(1958)]

"Veteran clown, bull fighter, rodeo hand and now TV and movie star, Louis B. Lindley, erstwhile known as Slim Pickens, whom I once knew as a tough and durable bareback and bull rider, is soon to co-star in a new TV series, 'The Loggers,' filmed in Oregon." [12(1960)]

"Slim, former top rodeo clown and bullfighter, has recently returned from two weeks in Japan where he, along with 'The Fastest Gun,' Mark Reed; Miss Stagecoach, Carol Anderson; four Sioux Indians, David Long, Richard Red Bow, Leonard Crow Dog and Henry Crow Dog, were appearing for the World Premier of the movie, 'Stagecoach.' They were in Denver May 18th.

"Everyone who rodeoed with Slim and knew him personally when he was in his prime certainly are proud of this guy for his success in TV and movie work. For he is certainly one of the [industry's] top Western Personalities." [12 (1966)]

Rodeo periodicals also kept up with other rodeo clowns. Jimmy Schumacher had a unique second profession for a while: "Jimmy is head pastry man at the big Swander Bakery at Rapid City, S.D. Friends point out that after diving into a flour barrel day after day it keeps him in trim for the barrel dives he makes to escape the bull when he demonstrates his method of making dough in the arena." [10 (1953)]

In 1958 a group of top hands put together a weekly rodeo. The principals were Neal Gay, Jim Shoulders, Ira Akers, Harry Tompkins and D. J. Gaudin (Kajun Kid). It was actually started May 2, 1958, in Mesquite, Texas, and although the principals have changed they still have rodeos there every Friday and Saturday night. [11 (1957)]

A report from the *Rodeo Sports News* relayed: "Bill Rogers of the well-known Rogers Twins was by recently with his attractive wife on their way to the Stockton rodeo. Bill is ranching down in Fresno country now, when not rodeoing, and has three children."

Another name that continued to come up through the years was that of Homer Holcomb: "Had a nice letter from world famous veteran, Homer Holcomb, and the ex-clown and bullfighter is busy operating his resort at Moyie Springs, Idaho. Homer's brother, Elmer, also lives in Idaho and clowns several rodeos in that vicinity." [11 (1958)]

A few years later: "Homer Holcomb, famous clown and bullfighter of the '40s, has retired from his job as host of the Elks Club at Red Bluff and bought a small ranch outside of that city." [12 (1963)] And six months later: "Homer, now 65, owns and operates a Dine and Dance Club at Moyie Springs, Idaho, about 100 miles north and east of Spokane. He gets to a rodeo occasionally to visit with old friends." [12 (1963)]

Updates on supplemental careers have been numerous:

"Ted Billingsly, a former bullfighter and clown who was working Mack Barbour's rodeos a few years back, is now running a restaurant in Canby, California, and doing real good." [12 (1960)]

"Andy Womack is building contractor in Phoenix building Andy Womack Homes." [12 (1963)]

"Kajun Kid says his oil-well cleaning business will make him rich. He may even be able to afford to clown Las Vegas again." [12 (1963)]

"Uncle Charlie Shultz, retired clown and bullfighter, now has a store in Ponca City, called the Mart. He'd be happy if RCA members who are passing through would stop by for a visit." [12 (1963)]

"Melvin Fields of Burkburnett, Texas, is now in the Army, stationed at Redstone Arsenal, Huntsville, Alabama. Melvin is a clown, bullfighter and a contestant, did get off for the Chattanooga, Tennessee, rodeo and won the all-'round trophy saddle there." [12

Quail Dobbs, Kajun Kid, and friend.
(Photo by Bern Gregory; submitted by Charlie and Imogene Beals)

(1964)]

"George and Sis Mills come to Denver once a week to pick up film for their movie house located at Pine Bluff, Wyoming." [12 (1964)]

"Sherman Crane of Santa Ana, California, the rodeo clown for 20 years, has retired from the arena and has started a new career as an auctioneer. He graduated from the Missouri Auction School at Kansas City, Missouri." [12 (1964)]

"Rodeo Clown Pete Peterson and Corky Randall were down in Florida helping make the movie, 'Blindfold.' Randall trained some stock and Peterson did some stunt air-boat driving and alligator wrestling. One of the gators bit Pete. Pete's all right, though, but the other guys are claiming the 'gator died." [12 (1965)]

"Felix Cooper, long-time, well-liked, rodeo hand who rode broncs and bulls and clowned from around '35 to '52 is now running a shoe shine stand at the Planters Hotel in Brawley, California." [12 (1965)]

"Besides being a top rodeo clown, Bennie Bender is also boss of a freight crew on the Milwaukee Railroad. His rank is conductor in train service." [10]

"The first meeting of the Cowboy Chapter, Fellowship of Christian Athletes, was held in Phoenix in March, 1973. The idea came from Wilbur Plaugher. Charter members numbered seven." [12 (1975)]

More on Wilbur: "Wilbur Plaugher is an interesting cowboy and RCA contract member, an additional facet of his life makes him more interesting as a person. Wilbur also, in his own words 'spreads the word of God.' He makes no particular emphasis of it, nor does he keep it a secret. On the surface there might seem to be some incongruity between a rodeo clown also preaching sermons, but those acquainted with Wilbur accept it quite naturally. At a lot of towns over the country where he is clowning the rodeo, Wilbur will also on Sunday morning appear in the pulpits and he usually has in the audience a following of rodeo people. In a field that could be difficult Wilbur is not only liked and respected as a show-man, clown, athlete, and cowboy, but also as a man of God." [16]

"Chuck Henson, bullfighter from Tucson, and son of Marge and Heavy Henson, has been doubling in Hollywood for some of the leads in TV, films, including 'Run For Your Life.' " [12 (1966)]

Chuck Henson, present-day movie stunt man, son of early rodeo greats
Marge Greenough and Heavy Henson.   (Photo by Gail Woerner)

Two years later an article reported: "Chuck Henson has had a lot of TV and movie work lately near his home at Tucson where he worked in 'Heaven With a Gun,' also a couple of weeks in 'High Chapparal,' and starred in another picture called 'Narrow Chute' about a rodeo clown." [12 (1968)]

Other arena funnymen also had their times in front of the cameras: "Tom Lucia, funny man from Weatherford, Texas, has recently been in the movies. He filmed with Casey Tibbs, Ben Johnson, Steve McQueen and Barbara Lee. The film called 'Junior Bonner' was filmed in Prescott, Arizona." [12 (1971)]

The length of a rodeo clown's career depends on many things. One of the most important things is how the body holds up. Most often they go on to a second profession. Some push it too far and have that one accident that forces them to quit before they decide they are ready to retire. Many times it's just a bad break. (Sorry for the play on words.)

"Jasbo finished his last clowning act, as he had begun his first one—with the little mule, Eko. The 1948 season came to a close in the early fall; Eko was glad to be put out to pasture, and Jasbo was glad to get out of his baggy pants and into his shorts." [14]

Some injuries were more serious than thought to be: "Rodeo clown, Chuck Lorimer, collapsed at the Yuba City rodeo. Chuck thought he had just passed out from the dashing around the arena in the heat, but they hauled him to the hospital and found he'd had a heart attack. He'll be hospitalized in San Francisco for some time." [11 (1963)]

Homer Holcomb just kept going, despite many physical problems that kept cropping up in his later years. "Montie Montana visited Homer Holcomb near Moyie Springs, Idaho, who had just gotten out of the hospital after surgery on his legs. Doctors replaced some arteries with plastic ones—still in a wheelchair but recovering fast." [12 (1965)]

A month later it was reported Homer was hospitalized again: "One of rodeo's top clowns who rodeo'd in the '30s and '40s is having a tough winter in the Veterans Hospital, Spokane Washington, after having suffered a very severe heart attack November 22. Homer had undergone 7 hours of major surgery last June when an operation was performed which badly weakened his heart at that time.

"Mrs. Holcomb reports Homer is gaining and talks much of his old friends in rodeo. Pat believes Homer's wonderful rodeo memories are really what keeps him going. Holcomb was a really funny man and worked just about any of the big rodeos he wanted during his career as a clown when he and announcer, the late Abe Lefton, made an incomparably hilarious team." [11 (1966)]

Four years later, "Homer Holcomb is improving after Hassle with Heart" was the title of the report: "Mrs. Holcomb says he is home after a long hospital confinement. 'I wonder if Homer ever thought about the time he was locked in a trunk by a prank-minded co-worker during the Treasure Island rodeo in San Francisco, some 29 years ago to be exact?' inquired the reporter." [11 (1969)]

A report on George Mills after retirement reminisced: "George Mills was in Cheyenne. He hasn't changed a bit. He may be remembered by the fans for his bull fighting or as the World's Champion Bareback Rider of '41, but among the old rodeo hands, he's better known for having burned more hide with a cigarette than the XIT ever did with a branding iron." [11 (1966)]

"Clark Shultz was seriously injured in a Christmas Eve automobile accident, it has been learned, at the Denver headquarters.

"An auto ran a stop sign and hit his vehicle broadside. Shultz suffered fractures of all the ribs on his left side, his left hip and pelvis.

"He will be in traction for a considerable length of time and would be happy to hear from any of his rodeo friends." [12 (1971)]

Even after retirement, the injuries still come: "Retired clown Johnny Tatum, LaVeen, Arizona, has been hospitalized for massive internal bleeding of his right hip and leg, but says he'll be up and around soon. A young horse he was breaking to ride flipped over with him. He spent several days in ice packs at the hospital but says the injury isn't really serious." [12 (1973)]

And there are those who still cowboy: "Jerry Olson says he plans to devote more time to his contract act with his famed buffalo, Sam, and he also wants to put more time in as a contestant." [12 (1975)]

And there are more injuries: "Clark Shultz injured in an accident at work in Arlington, Texas—broken nose, ribs and crushed vertebrae. Hard luck is living at the Shultz house. Earlier this year wife Arline broke her hip and is in traction." [12 (1978)]

And more injuries: "PRCA clown Jim Hill got his foot broken while shoeing horses and will be out of action until the first of September." [12 (1979)]

But *some* really do retire: "Dudley J. Gaudin, the Kajun Kid, from Teague, Texas, has decided to hang up his cleats after 27 years as a professional rodeo clown. Kajun worked the Houston

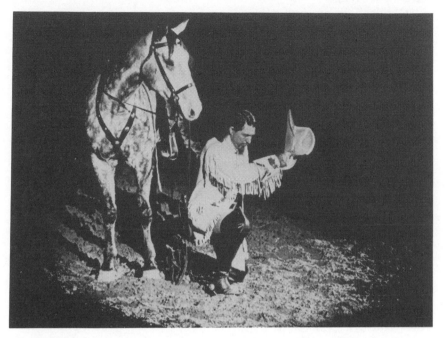

Larry McKinney plays many roles, such as Buffalo Bill, Fort Worth, 1985. (Photographer unknown; submitted by Larry McKinney)

rodeo for 25 years and at the Astrodome this year announced his retirement." [12 (1979)]

Bobby Clark sold his Oklahoma ranch, all but seventy acres, and went into the horse business, breeding and raising thoroughbreds. He has had race horses on tracks in Oklahoma, Louisiana, Arizona, New Mexico, and Wyoming. He is now area sales manager of Eastern Oklahoma for Stillwater Milling Company, selling horse and cattle feed to ranchers, sales yards, and dairies.

Larry McKinney keeps plenty busy these days as stunt man and horse wrangler in a variety of movies for television and the theater. Recent films include *Where the Hell's the Gold* and the TV mini-series *Lonesome Dove.* Larry has been Willie Nelson's stand-in the last few years and often wears the familiar Nelson trademark of beard and ponytail. Larry is short on talk. If he had his druthers he'd be living back in the nineteenth century—the 1840s, to be precise. He is presently building a typical western mining town of that era near Kalispell, Montana. It will house much of the memorabilia he has collected over the years.

Final Farewells

The end comes whether we are ready for it or not. It seems that after facing 1,800 pounds of fury again and again, then traveling miles and miles by car, truck, or whatever would run, after an exhausting performance and sometimes two a day, just barely having time to get from one rodeo to the next before the Grand Entry was ready to enter the arena, a rodeo clown does not concern himself about the Grim Reaper and when he will make his appearance. After all, what can be done about it anyway?

Jimmy Nesbitt died tragically in a house fire in 1943. Shortly afterward, in an issue of *Hoofs & Horns,* appeared a poem written by Stan of the "Roundin' Up the Paster by Stan" column that appeared in each issue. He prefaced the poem with: "When I wrote that verse I had Jimmy Nesbitt in mind—although I reckon, it would apply to most any top-hand rodeo clown in the roster of cowboy sports. I want to reprint it here as a sort of tribute to Jimmy from myself and all the other waddies who know what his work around the chutes meant to stompers in a tight spot." (The poem was originally printed in the official program of "La Fiesta de los Vaqueros," Tucson, Arizona, in 1939.)

Rodeo Clown

When the pitchin' show starts an' the folks settle down,
There's a heap of hard work for the rodeo clown.
Both the hands from the ranches an' kids from the schools
Perk right up when he enters the track with his mules.
He's the life of the party an' the zip of the show
An' both he an' his four-footed pardners shore know
All the gags an' the tricks that make spectators grin,
An' he starts to onwind from the time he gets in.

All the waddies will laugh til they purty near bust
When he clowns with them bovines an' kicks up the dust,
An' the tenderfoot dudes in the stands r'ar an' cheer
As he slides down the fence on the tail of a steer.
Between buckin' events he goes into his act
With his talented mules—they're shore peart, for a fact'
They can auger an' wrassle an' tap dance an' stalk
An' do everything else except yodel and talk.

Now some folks will allow that them clowns just have fun
An' got no chore except to amuse everyone
But when Brahmas get rough an' start proddin' about,
It is up to the clown to go straighten them out.

When a stomper get scattered an' sprawls on the ground
An' an ornery bull starts ahornin' around,
It is up to the clown to rush up to the spot
An get hooked him ownself, just as likely as not.

So between makin' waddies shake outa their hides
An' directin' his mules through their comical strides
An' then keepin' onfortunate stompers in trim,
That there clown has his routine shore cut out for him.
He don't wear cowboy riggin' an' the flashy layout
That them gals in the stands start aravin' about
But there's no one performs in a rodeo town
That deserves more peart praise than the rodeo clown.
     [10 (1944)]

Following Jasbo Fulkerson's untimely death January 11, 1949, the following article was printed in *The American Weekly:*

The maddened Brahma bull arched its back and swung its huge body like a whiplash. The rider came down hard on his right shoulder, and lay stunned in the tramped sawdust.

Directly at him charged the bull, horns lowered, murder in its angry heart. From the stands came a massed groan.

No men with guns or ropes were down there under the bright spotlights of New York's Madison Square Garden. But who was that loping wildly toward the bull?

Just a fantastic figure in a bright shirt, funny hat and floppy vest—a clown from Texas named Jasbo Fulkerson.

Across the nose of the charging beast Jasbo slapped his absurd hat. A futile gesture, thought the startled spectators. Didn't the funny little man know this was no time for a joke?

Apparently he didn't. Neither did the bull.

The agile Brahma hesitated—when two seconds more would have meant death for the helpless cowboy on the floor. Then the bull turned and chased the clown across the arena.

It was a good race. In the middle of the ring was a little barrel.

Jasbo leaped for life and landed in the barrel just as the bull's head sent it spinning.

Then other riders entered the ring, roped the bull and dragged him out. Only then did Jasbo emerge. He took a bow, somewhat wobbly but happy in the knowledge that once more he had saved a life.

As millions from Texas to Maine, Hollywood to the Garden may remember. In 19 years Jasbo had an arm broken seven times, legs broken more times than he could remember, and was gored often. But he kept coming back for more and kept the customers laughing.

Of course, it was long overdue, but Jasbo's end came the other day. Just where he would have preferred it—in Texas.

The 44 year-old clown, not on professional duty but driving a load of produce from his ranch near Watauga, overturned when his truck skidded on a slippery road.

The funny little man, who had often risked his life to save others, was dead when a highway patrolman found him.

Millions had seen him mix laughter and life-saving in the screaming arena. But not an eyewitness was present when Jasbo, who had so many times joked with death, fell victim to one of Fate's own cruel jests. [23]

The following reports announced the end of some other fearless funnymen:

"Red Sublett passed away in the Veterans Hospital in Dallas, Texas, on April 14, 1950." [10 (1954)]

Sam Stuart died December 12, 1952, of a heart attack. In the same issue of *Hoofs & Horns* that announced his death, a notice appeared: "Anyone interested in buying a good clown mule that does all sorts of tricks can contact Mrs. Lois Stuart. Lois would like for someone to get the mule who would keep her in the rodeo business." [10 (1953)]

"The whole rodeo world was shocked at the news of the sudden death of one of the foremost rodeo clowns, and grief for his untimely passing is deep in the hearts of his thousands of friends and admirers. Zeke Bowery was not only a clever clown, but a very kind and loveable person who made friends of all he contacted. He died of a heart attack at his home in Pacoima, California, Sunday, January 31, 1954." [10 (1954)]

"Elmer Holcomb, younger brother to Homer Holcomb, and also a well known rodeo clown, accidentally shot himself." [11 (1963)]

A 1966 *ProRodeo Sports News* article reported: "Bucking Ford man Roscoe Armstrong passes on at 83." [11 (1966)]

Joaquin Sanchez was killed September 13, 1966, in Tohatchapi, California: "Joaquin was going home after clowning Filer, Idaho. He pulled off the road across from a truck stop and was walking across the highway. It was said Joaquin started clowning by mistake. He was working stock for a California producer and the clown that had been hired was badly hurt. Joaquin was sent in to substitute. He did so well he was hired to clown the next week and has been doing it ever since. Pallbearers at his funeral included

Gene and Bobby Clark." [11 (1966)]

"Nocona Slim, John T. Burnett, died May, 1967. He was driving to Louisiana to see Jack Favor and was killed in a two car accident near Bowie, Texas. It seemed that Nocona's greatest delight was in making people laugh." [11 (1968)]

"Henry 'Tin Horn Hank' Keenen, noted rodeo clown of the 20s and 30s, died December 13, 1968. Seventy-three at the time of his death, he started in the rodeo world as a contestant in 1909. Burial was at Rogers, Arkansas. He is survived by a son, Henry, who lives in Aurora, Arkansas." [11 (1969)]

Ma Hopkins, the editor of the original *Hoofs & Horns* magazine from 1933 to 1954, died in her Arizona home November 3, 1969. [11] She was a "one-man" booster who had promoted rodeo when support was desperately needed. She also was a very sincere friend of the rodeo clown. There were times in the business that the arena funnyman was overlooked and ignored, but Ma always included information about the most famous, those just starting their career and those that never made it big."

"Clarence W. Gist, better known as 'Pinky Gist,' longtime rodeo clown, died mid-August, 1970, in his Phoenix home at the age of 78. He is believed to be one of the first to include trained mules in his acts." [11 (1970)]

Bennie Bender died March 31, 1973, in Tucson, Arizona, after a brief illness: "A member of the Cowboy Turtle Association, Bender was a full time contract member in the late 1940s and 1950s. He earned his gold card in 1963.

"He started in rodeo as a bareback bronc and bull rider, and later switched to clowning. He was renown[ed] for his magic broom act. Benny was born on July 26, 1914, at McClusky, N.D. He is survived by widow, Lucille, who carries a timers card in the Association, and a daughter, Billie, a former trick rider." [11 (1973)]

"Al McMillan, formerly of Blackfoot, Idaho, and member of the Turtles, passed away in September, 1972. A clown and bull-fighter Al owned the little jackass 'Stinky' which Bobbie Hill took over for his act, renaming the clever animal 'Rosebud.' " [11 (1972)]

"Jerry Hedrick, former clown, died April 15, 1973, in Wichita, Kansas, at age 61. Native of Nickerson, Kansas, and worked for years with stock contractor Walt Alsbaugh." [11 (1973)]

"Wiley McCray died November 23, 1977. Funeral at First Baptist Church, Wheeler, Texas. Survived by son Freddy of Briscoe, Texas. Wiley was born 11-1-16 and began clowning in 1939. Before then he was a contract trick rider and bull rider." [12 (1977)]

"Claude W. 'Brahma' Rogers passed away December 4, 1978. He had association card #226. Bronc rider from 1916 through 1934, then started clowning for the late Colonel Eskew. He was with him 22 years. He also created a character named 'Hardpan Hank.' Rogers is survived by his wife, Mary, sons James M., Danny J. and Will A." [12 (1979)]

"Clydel Shultz, PRCA bullfighter-clown, age 18, and three other persons were killed in an airplane crash near Ada, Oklahoma, on December 20, 1978. Clydel was following the tradition established by his late great uncle Charley Shultz, in becoming the ProRodeo clown and bullfighter." [12 (1979)]

George Mills died of cancer in 1980. Marge Greenough was with him when he died. She said he never complained.

Jeff Grigsby, age twenty-four, collapsed in the Greeley, Colorado, rodeo arena during his dog act July 1, 1992. Leon Coffee, friend and co-rodeo clown, reached him first. At the local hospital doctors determined he died of an aneurysm. Jeff was a bullfighter and had a variety of comedy routines. A polite young man who had a bright future as a rodeo clown will be missed.

Jeff Grigsby died in 1992, age twenty-four. He collapsed during his act at Greeley, Colorado, rodeo.   (Photo submitted by Jeff Grigsby)

And there are many more who have gone on to that great rodeo in the sky — they may be gone but they will never be forgotten.

Heroics and Honors

Each and every one of these fearless funnymen is a hero in the eyes of not only the cowboys they protected but their fans, young and old. It doesn't take long to realize that these men have risked life and limb to do their jobs. They don't like to talk about their heroics, nor do they want to be within earshot of others praising their abilities. But they wouldn't change places with anyone else, even if they had a chance. It is a profession that demands of those who do it to love what they do. There is no way someone could perform this life-threatening profession without the desire.

From time to time the bull-baiters have been given special awards for their outstanding abilities. Sometimes they became heroes outside the arena: "Hats off to Benny Bender who rescued a sixteen month old child from drowning in an irrigation canal north of the fair grounds at Blackfoot, Idaho. Bender, from Mobridge, S.D., still in his clown makeup and riding his clown mule, was returning from the rodeo parade. In passing the canal Bender saw two fingers of the child above the surface of the water. By the time he could leap into the water the child had sunk to the bottom but Bender brought it to the bank where it was revived. Identity of the child was not learned at the time." [10 (1946)]

The various honors and recognition that have been bestowed on the well-loved cowboy clowns through the years vary greatly: "At the end of the Madison Square Garden Rodeo in 1937 Jimmy Nesbitt was presented a silver loving cup by the contestants in appreciation of the fine job he did in protecting them from the Brahmas during the bull riding." [10 (1944)]

"Wick Peth from Bow, Washington, one of rodeo's top bullfighters in the business today has been named one of 10 finalists for the honor of being among his state's three outstanding men for 1963. Wick together with his father and brothers, Jerry, Ted and Buz, operate the family 4,500 acre farm in the heart of the rich Skagit Valley farm land." [11 (1963)]

"Rodeo clown Bobbie Hill, Missoula, Montana, has recently received an honorary invitation to be a guest of the Cub Scouts at the Centennial Ice Stampede, Calgary, Alberta, in March." [11 (1967)]

"The Joaquin Sanchez Memorial Trophy has been inaugurated at Filer, Idaho. Its permanent possession will be awarded the cowboy who wins the all round title three times at Twin Falls County Fair and Rodeo at Filer." [11 (1967)]

"Steve Sattler, of Houston, a rodeo clown since 1965 in RCA ranks, scored a repeat victory at the Red Bluff 8th Annual Cowboy Golf Tournament. He won in 67." [11 (1968)]

"Charley Davis, rodeo clown and expert archer, of Tucson, picked off a record making 17 point desert mule deer in the Tucson Mountain Park area. The deer ranked 29th as the best mule deer trophy in the Boone and Crockett Club Record Book, and is believed to be the largest trophy taken by a bow and arrow hunter." [11 (1958)]

"Felix Cooper and Wild Bill Markley fought bulls for Hank and Bobby Christianson back in the 1940s and 1950s. The Eugene, Oregon, rodeo committee got the two together during the July Round-up to accept their gold cards from RCA member Larry Mahan." [11 (1968)]

In 1970 a rodeo went to Europe: "Twenty-five cowboys, 13 cowgirls, 2 clowns, Larry Clayman and Buddy Peterson, and 8 stock handlers made the trip. They went to Italy, Switzerland, France, Holland, Germany, Belgium and Austria." [11 (1970)]

There are few things as sad as the retirement of a clown.

> Popular Jimmy Schumacher may never have had a more touching moment than at the final performance of the National Western Stock Show and Rodeo in Denver on January 24, 1971.
>
> After nearly 20 years of working the barrel at the National Western it was his last performance, and announcer Cy Taillon called attention to the many great things the veteran clown has done over the years.
>
> He was presented a plaque by National Western General Manager Willard Simms and the sellout-plus crowd gave him a standing ovation. Typically he traded his clown's hat with Simms.
>
> Jimmy will work the Rodeo of Rodeos in his home town of Phoenix in March and then will retire for good to go into business." [11 (1971)]

This report was made by Flaxie Fletcher for the Rodeo Historical Society: "Homer Holcomb, at Dean Krakel's special request, sent us the treasured mementos of his great clowning career. This was no small item. Most of his trophies were personalized with silver and gold figures of Homer waving the cape at a bull or with

Former rodeo clowns gather at a social event in Las Vegas during National Finals, 1990: Dale Wickizer, Charley Lyons, Gene Clark, Larry McKinney, and Bobby Clark. (Photo by Gail Woerner)

his little mules, Mae West and later, Parkurkarkus. One of the trophies is inscribed, 'To Homer Holcomb, from the Brahma Riders For Saving Us From Injury Many Times.' Another reads, 'Homer Holcomb from His Usher Friends, Denver Stock Show, 1939.' These are just the unusual ones." [13]

Other awards continued: "The Andy Womack award saddle at Phoenix was won in 1978 by Hawkeye Henson." [12 (1978)]

"The Clydel Shultz PRCA Memorial Scholarship Fund has been organized by citizens of Ponca City, Oklahoma." [12 (1979)]

The ProRodeo Hall of Fame in Colorado Springs held the dedication of the Hall in 1979. Those chosen as honorees are persons who have provided substantially to the development and growth of the sport of rodeo. Rodeo clowns picked as honorees have been Jasbo Fulkerson, Dudley J. Gaudin, Homer Holcomb (deceased), George Mills (deceased), Wick Peth, and Jimmy Schumacher. Wilbur Plaugher was chosen as an honoree in 1990. Jimmy Schumacher's patented walking clown barrel is on display in the Hall of Fame.

CHAPTER 5

Rodeo Clowns of Today

The Athlete

The past eighty years of rodeo clowning have developed today's arena funnymen into true athletes. Those performing today must be physically fit. As Elizabeth Atwood Lawrence explained, "A bull fighting clown is a top athlete, and must be fearless as well as agile to successfully perform the function of protecting the contestant." [20]

Greater emphasis is put on the bullfighting portion of the profession today. Corporate sponsors are funneling more money into bullfighting, and some of the earlier rules and regulations have changed.

Not only does the cowboy clown have to stay fit, he must be able to travel continually. "Leon Coffee parked his pickup at Dallas/Fort Worth International Airport in May, 1983, and got on an airplane to fly to a string of rodeos. It was August before Coffee could get back. Not only had he forgotten where his truck was parked, he also had to pay $487 to get it out of the lot. He travels about 68,000 miles a year in his pickup truck, not including air miles." [31]

Rick Chatman got into rodeoing because he needed a better grade in history. His history teacher was the rodeo team sponsor. Rick said being a bullfighter is very rewarding, especially when a cowboy comes up after his bull ride and thanks you for your efforts. During the rodeo "the adrenalin is pumping full speed," said Rick, "then it is over. When you slow down you look around—the stands are empty, trash is blowing around, everyone has cleared

Leon Coffee and sidekick "Leona" at Greeley, Colorado.
(Photo by Ed Steffes; submitted by Leon Coffee)

out and it's very depressing."

Rick said that while driving from one rodeo to the next he mentally prepares himself for the next performance. In the winter of 1986–87 Rick got lost in the mountains and suffered frostbite on his feet. Although he missed only six rodeos while recuperating, he still has problems today with his feet. Rick, Bobby Romer, and Quail Dobbs were handling the clowning, bullfighting, and barrelman chores at Cheyenne Frontier Days in 1987 when this interview took place. Rick was riding thirty to forty miles a day on his bicycle to keep his legs and feet in shape.

Mike "Smurf" Horton, of Zolfo Springs, Florida, was also interviewed at Cheyenne that year. He defined rodeo clowning as "showing off and keeping the bull riders from getting injured." Later that year Smurf won the Wrangler Bullfights at the National Finals and became Champion Bullfighter for 1987. Smurf has a small build and the agility and ability with the bulls to be tossed in the air with apparent ease. Whether it is truly easy and painless remains a mystery. However, it won the big prize for Smurf.

The Wrangler Bullfight Tour Finals held during the National

Finals in Las Vegas in December each year bring the top six bull-fighters in the country. An article in *Horse Talk News Daily Tally* during National Finals reported:

> Skipper Voss will be celebrating a special anniversary in 1987, one that most folks in the world of professional rodeo can appreciate. Voss will mark his 20th year of bullfighting this year. Now, seven knee operations later, Voss is back for another shot at big money on the Wrangler Bullfight Tour.
>
> Throughout his bullfighting career, Voss' style has been emulated by many. His precise and calculated moves carried Voss to the Wrangler Bullfight Championship in 1982, and he's been in the hunt, and in demand, ever since.
>
> Because of the weakened condition of Voss' knees, he had learned to work his bulls in his own special way—down in close, near the bull's turning radius. It's at that point that Voss does his best work, in the danger zone where bullfighting is at its finest. [32]

In an interview with Tom Feller in 1989, we talked about his being chosen the PRCA Clown of the Year in 1987. Although Tom has been the recipient of other awards (Coors Man in the Can in 1984 and 1987, and the 1981 PRCA Clown of the Year), he is most proud of the 1987 Clown of the Year award because he was chosen by the cowboys he works with and protects all year long.

Tom has a college degree in art education. In 1989 he accepted a position as executive administrative assistant with the ProRodeo Cowboys Association. His main responsibility was to serve as liaison between the PRCA sponsors and the various elements of the association in the implementation of the PRCA's sponsorship programs. After three years, Tom accepted a position with the Tony Lama Boot Company, El Paso, as director of events in the Sports Marketing Department.

Feller has seen a lot of changes in the rodeo clown profession during his career. "In the mid-to-late seventies I saw the arrival of the athlete to rodeo clowning. This was inspired by Wick Peth, Skipper Voss, Miles Hare, and Rob Smets. These men were outstanding bullfighters—but they weren't funny nor did they try to be," he said.

From the time he began his career (in 1974) until the early 1980s, rodeo clowns were only supposed to be in the arena at certain times during a PRCA rodeo performance. In fact, if they were turned in to the PRCA for being in the arena during the steer wrestling or another "off-limits" event where they had no respon-

Rex Dunn playing tag at Oklahoma City, 1979.
(Photo by Bern Gregory; submitted by Charley and Imogene Beals)

sibility, they could be fined. But cowboys would occasionally ask a clown to get in the arena and "do something" if they needed to rest their horse for a few minutes. Or the stock contractor would ask a clown to entertain while he moved stock from one arca to another, or needed to stall for time. It was a real Catch 22 situation.

"Then along came Toad Cook," said Feller. "In 1983 Toad showed Mike Cervi, rodeo producer, that a rodeo clown could be an asset to the cowboy and the contractor by being in the arena and not being a distraction. Since then a rodeo clown's responsibilities have expanded throughout the entire performance."

Rules do change from time to time. As in any profession, staying current and not becoming outdated is important.

The rodeo clown of recent times is more bullfighter than funny clown. With contests sponsored by Wrangler and Coors, and the opportunity to win more money by bullfighting, it is no wonder this imbalance occurred. The number of humorous rodeo clowns, with animals, funny cars, and such, as part of their act has diminished greatly.

One thing that hasn't changed is the tragedy of being involved

in an accident. Bullfighters still face the possibility in every performance.

Lane Frost, 1987 World Champion Bull Rider, was killed July
30, 1989, at Cheyenne Frontier Days. Frost had told friends just
minutes before his final ride that he knew he had drawn a bad bull.
He was hit from behind with one horn, then with all four feet. [33]
Bob Romer, first to get to Frost said, "I had a hold of him as he
went down I said [to] stay down to keep from creating more injury."

It was too late. Frost was dead on arrival at the local hospital.
"We're all pretty well down," said Romer afterwards. Although it
was determined neither Romer, Rick Chatman or Quail Dobbs,
who were working the event, could have done a thing, they
couldn't help feeling an emotional letdown. [34]

Rob "Kamikaze" Smets is one of today's best. He has won the
Wrangler Bullfights four times. Away from the job he's a youthful
fellow in cut-offs that likes to tease his two adoring daughters.

Rob was raised in various parts of the world, such as Thailand,
Singapore, and Australia. While in Australia Rob tried a little
rodeoing. Once back in the U.S., he met Donny Landis and Donny's
dad, Bill Landis, an active rodeo clown and bullfighter at the time.

Rob Smets "bull walking," North Platte, Nebraska, 1983.
(Photo by Bern Gregory; submitted by Charley and Imogene Beals)

When Rob expressed an interest in bullfighting, Bill was there as an expert instructor.

Rob is married to Sherri Christianson, a member of the Northwest stock contracting Christianson family. He told Sherri he would quit bullfighting when he was thirty. At thirty-two, he considers his statement to be a bit premature. He feels he has at least ten more years in the business. In fact, the more he talked the more he was convinced he could last as long as Wick Peth lasted. Rob admires Wick a great deal.

Smets said he wished the Wrangler Bullfights would return to the format they used several years ago, when the top sixteen bullfighters were chosen to participate each year. He feels that since the bullfights have been opened to all rodeo bullfighters, a lot of the competitive edge has been lost.

In front of the chutes about ready to open during the bull riding, Smets is the master. He's not afraid of the responsibility that goes with his profession. He is there to protect every bull rider, from the beginner to the seasoned champion.

It appears the profession is making the full circle and now returning to include the funny stuff. Leon Coffee said in 1991 that he was continually being contacted by rodeo producers because

Funnyman Leon Coffee at Fort Worth.
(Photo by David E. Hack; submitted by Leon Coffee)

he has the ability to be funny as well as to participate in bullfighting in front of the chutes or in the barrel. He has considered conducting rodeo clown schools to teach up-and-coming rodeo clowns the art of humor. Rodeo clown schools up until now have taught bullfighting, not comedy.

With luck we will be privileged to see the same routines our grandparents and great-grandparents enjoyed — just updated a tad.

Differences Today

Some of the changes in rodeo clowning have been obvious; others have been more subtle. But to those who participate, rules are rules.

In 1956 Gene Lamb published a book, *Rodeo, Back of the Chutes.* In that era Gene reported: "At most rodeos the clowns are in evidence from the Grand Entry through the bull riding which is the last event. They are expected to fill in any dull spots, and gloss over any delay at the chutes in getting out stock. Most of them will have separate acts, either using animals, or equipment, and which are booked and paid for in addition to the contract for the bull riding protection." [16]

Jack Long expresses his disappointment when he sees today's rodeo clowns that do not dress western when they aren't working. "They finish a performance and get out of costume," describes Jack. "They put on clothes that aren't even western, because they consider themselves athletes, not cowboys. The gas station attendant at the gas station where they fill up getting ready to go on to the next rodeo has no idea what this fellow does for a living." Jack feels they are not doing their part to help promote the sport of rodeo.

Tom Feller feels differently regarding the dress. During my interview with Tom, which was held prior to an evening rodeo performance in which Tom was clowning, Tom was dressed in a tank top, shorts, and tennis shoes. He feels that other athletes such as football players do not wear their uniforms everywhere they go, so why should the rodeo clown be expected to dress western?

Clark Shultz, rodeo clown of the 1929 to 1975 era, said, "When we went in from the Grand Entry until the last bull was rode, we were walking around talking to people, doing funny things, powdering the roped calves, roping the broncs. Now you can't touch the stock at all." He shook his head in dismay. "Can't catch or anything."

Rick Chatman sees that the biggest difference today is that the profession requires that the rodeo clown be in top physical shape. When asked about drugs in the rodeo world, Leon Coffee said, "When bulls get dope, maybe I will—but, I don't think so. A bull is eight feet long, runs 30 to 40 miles per hour and outweighs a man so much—you have got to have all your faculties."

D. J. Gaudin, better known as the Kajun Kid, said, "Clowning is a young man's game. These guys today ain't doin' nothin' more than we used to do. We used to get big bulls, and when they ran over us we knew it." Kajun shook his head and continued, "It used to be there were no horns tipped. These guys today have on so much padding and braces I don't know how a bull could get to them."

Bobby Romer, who started clowning in 1965, said, "You can't be a weekend clown anymore—some of the fun of it has been lost. Rodeo clowning today definitely requires more professionalism." When Bobby was asked what the worst part of the rodeo clown profession was, he was quick to answer: "The miles between rodeos and how desolate it is after the rodeo is over." This was heard many times over when interviewing rodeo clowns of today.

The Wrangler Bullfights at Cheyenne Frontier Days is a special event for bullfighters. In 1987 I went the second night hoping to see Skipper Voss compete. He had been injured the night before and was hurt too badly to compete the night I attended. When asked about the wreck, Skipper said, "He mashed me. Broke ribs, my chest hurts and I can't breathe and my knees hurt. Cheyenne is an unlucky rodeo for me—I got a broke shoulder last year."

About the injury the previous night, Voss said, "I had won two bullfights before Cheyenne. During my bullfight last night I knew time was passing and I knew I needed another wrap. I was standing by the barrel and I went to the bull. He got me lined out there, tripped me with his horn and when I went down he went over the top of me and stepped on me."

It was evident Skipper was in pain and even the simple effort of walking was difficult for him. Most men would have still been in a hospital bed, allowing the bruised and broken body to recover— but not a rodeo clown.

In a later interview with Voss, we talked of lifestyles of rodeo clowns today versus the lifestyles of the cowboy funnymen of yesterday. "There used to be a lot more drinking in the old days," said Voss. "It was almost required, a machismo thing. I'm not beyond taking a drink, but I never do it before a performance. But some of

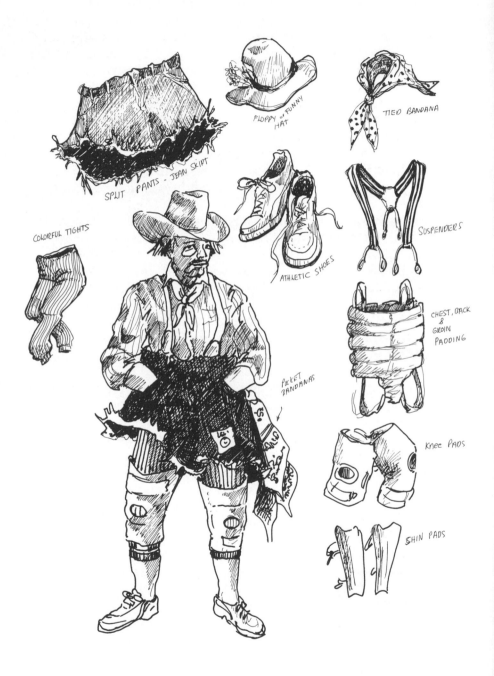

Today's rodeo clowns have more protective gear.

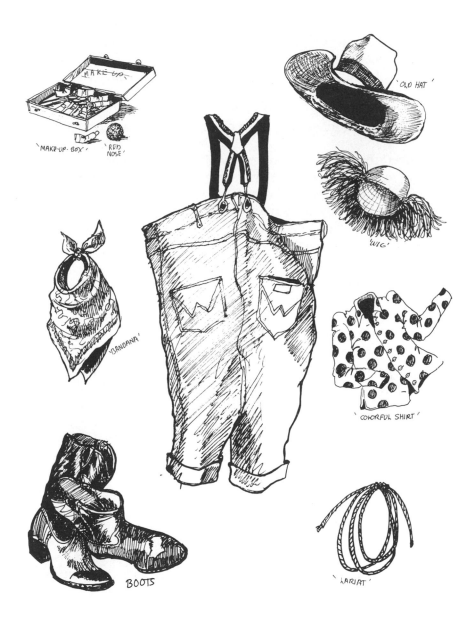

Early day rodeo clown costume.

the old-timers could do it. Listen, it didn't even affect Kajun. He's something else. He must have drunk a fifth before he got out there, but you'd never know it."

The late 1980s saw changes in the bullfighting rules. George Doak, while observing the 1988 National Finals Wrangler Bullfights, commented that today the judges award points for some of the same things that used to count against a bullfighter. His comment was made as the bull was tossing, or appearing to toss, the bullfighter in the air again and again.

After Wick Peth retired from bullfighting, he was one of the most noted judges on the Wrangler Bullfight Circuit. In 1989 Wick announced that he was no longer judging the bullfights.

As the 1990s evolve, we will see more changes take place. If they could just combine the experiences and knowledge of those hardy and humorous arena-maniacs of bygone eras and the talent and athletic ability of today's rodeo clowns, the cowboys and rodeo audiences would benefit in many ways.

Sponsors

Quail Dobbs, rodeo clown with plenty of acts, former bullfighter and barrelman, said, "In the past few years there has been a lot of growth and a lot of changes in professional rodeo. The most obvious and beneficial change has been the addition of national corporate sponsors." Quail was referring primarily to Wrangler and Coors and the sponsorships of the Wrangler Bullfights and the Coors Man in the Can program.

Sponsors are not a new idea. Early rodeo clowns also had sponsors. For example: "In 1933, when legal beer and wine came back under the Roosevelt Administration, the Calvert distillers gave Homer Holcomb, bullfighter and clown, several bullfighting capes with the word C A L V E R T in large letters. He also got a nice check for the advertising." [13]

Levi Strauss, Lee Riders, and Blue Bell Wrangler have all been major sponsors, from time to time. In the 1930s references were made to Homer Holcomb "losing his Levi's to show immaculate unmentionables." [10 (1937)]

In 1946 Blue Bell hired Rodeo Ben, a famous western-style tailor, to cut original patterns for the Blue Bell jeans. If a cowboy sent in his card number, he would receive a pair of jeans to try out. Rodeo clowns were sent $250 a quarter and their jeans. A bonus of

QUAIL DOBBS
(TEXAS)

Two unknown early cowboy clowns wear sponsor jeans-Lee Riders.
(Photo by J. A. Stryker; submitted by Bill Wittliff, courtesy of
University of Texas–Permian Basin)

a good-looking Wrangler jacket could be received if you had a bull named Old Wrangler.

Gayle Curtis, wife of retired rodeo clown Wes Curtis, said Wrangler used to send a huge box of western wear for the entire family. Daughters Drew and Punky were always dressed in fresh outfits.

Ken Boen buried his Old Grey Mare with a Blue Bell Wrangler blanket. They always advertised for Wrangler. [10 (1951)]

Sponsors throughout the years used various ways to promote their products. An article titled "Checkerboard Shirts Available to Clowns" announced: "Ed Smyth, manager of the Ralston Purina Horse Chow, advertising and sales promotion, has indicated that checkerboard clown shirts are available to any rodeo clowns or bullfighters simply by contacting Ed." [11 (1967)]

In 1979 it was announced that Nestea joined the list of corporate sponsors: ". . . another program will provide nearly 15 thousand dollars in fees to be used to purchase special insurance for PRCA clowns and bullfighters. The special insurance is over and above the insurance program included in the PRCA membership dues—extra coverage they may not be able to get themselves—a ten thousand dollar accidental death policy for clowns and bullfighters that work PRCA rodeos." [12 (1979)]

Sponsors vary from year to year. Some have one rodeo clown and some have many to advertise their product.

One national sponsor of the PRCA that includes rodeo clowns and bullfighters in their program is Bull's-Eye Barbecue Sauce. They became a national sponsor in 1989 and hold the Bull's-Eye Challenge, which pits bull riders against bulls for cash bonuses at more than twenty designated rodeos. If the contestant rides the full eight seconds, he receives the bonus. If, however, he is bucked off, the money goes to the stock contractor who owns the winning animal. Bonuses are also awarded to the announcers, barrelmen, bullfighters, and rodeo secretaries at participating rodeos.

Coors Brewing Company has been involved for the last ten years. Included in Coors' 1990 commitment is the funding of at least sixty Coors Chute-Out rodeos. They will also provide additional support through local Coors distributors at non-Chute-Out rodeos and will participate as a major sponsor of the National Finals Rodeo. In addition to giving $500 bonus checks to the winners of the five standard PRCA events and the WPA barrel racing competition, Coors also rewards the committee, stock contractor, barrelmen, and announcer at all Coors Chute-Out rodeos.

At year's end, Coors will award $45,000 in bonuses to Coors Chute-Out series winners. Coors also serves as a major NFR sponsor and awards a $3,000 bonus to the NFR contestant selected by ballot as the Coors Fans' Favorite Cowboy of the Year. In addition, Coors contributes $38,000 to the Coors "Man in the Can" Program, which recognizes the most successful PRCA barrelmen of the season. The top barrelman receives an $18,000 check. The remaining $20,000 is split among the other top five PRCA barrelmen. [35]

Justin Boots has been a National Finals sponsor since the first National Finals Rodeo was held in Dallas in 1959. In 1981 the Justin Sports Medicine Program became a reality. The boot company provides PRCA members with comprehensively equipped mobile medical centers. With the aches and pains bullfighters and barrelmen often have, they utilize the facility frequently.

In 1989 two $125,000 sport medicine mobile centers appeared at more than fifty-four rodeos, including the National Finals Rodeo and the Dodge National Circuit Finals Rodeo. The unit and its staff provide complete on-site medical attention, including advanced cardiac life support.

Permanent facilities in the center include ultrasound and whirlpool units, a traction machine, a paraffin bath, adjustable weights, a mini-trampoline, a television monitor and videocassette recorder, and a computer.

Credited with starting the program are Dr. J. Pat Evans, medical director of the Sports Medicine Clinic of North Texas in Dallas, and Don Andrews, director of Justin Sports Medicine Program and director for Mobile Sports Medicine Systems, Inc. [35]

In a conversation with Miles Hare at National Finals in 1987, he said, "Dr. Evans is one of the reasons I'm still in this program. He's drawn so much blood out of me, he's worked on me a lot. A bull drove his horn through my hip and it went through the meat of the butt. It got bad and he had to draw off blood. He's the best doctor the cowboys ever had." Miles went on to say, "I get a lot of hematomas, where you get bruised so bad it bleeds inside the bone, and you have to go in and get the blood out. If you don't have the money Evans won't make you pay. And some days in rodeo you don't have the money."

Wrangler Bullfights were started in 1979. Just as other events in rodeo developed through stages and changed, so have the bullfights.

Jim Sutton, a stock contractor from Oneida, South Dakota, drew up the format for such a contest. The first meeting to discuss the new idea included Sutton, Wick Peth, Miles Hare, and Skipper Voss.

The very first bullfight was held in Rapid City, South Dakota. Participating bullfighters were: Miles Hare, Wick Peth, Larry Clayman, Kelly LaCoste, Bob Donaldson, and Skipper Voss. Just a few bullfights were held the first year. At the National Finals, Miles Hare was the winner for the year. He also won in 1980 and 1981.

The Wrangler Jeans Bullfight Tour was started in 1981. This competition pits top-ranked rodeo bullfighters against fighting bulls in seventy-second free-style matches. Points are awarded by designated judges to bullfighters to determine the winner of each event. In 1982 twenty-three contests were held and $172,000 was paid to the bullfighters in cash awards.

By 1987 Wrangler had expanded its ProRodeo Bullfighter Tour. Four additional bullfighters were added to the tour, making a total of sixteen world-class bullfighters. They also increased the number of events by four, now totaling thirty-two events each year. The top six bullfighters qualify for the finals at the National Finals Rodeo in Las Vegas. More than $420,000 in prize money was awarded to Wrangler Bullfighters in 1987. [35]

To be considered for the tour for the following year, a bull-

George Doak at Wrangler Bullfight Contest, Rapid City, 1980. This was the first bullfight.

(Photo by Fain; submitted by Charley and Imogene Beals)

fighter must send a letter of intent to Wrangler by December 1, explained Greg Tuza, representative for Wrangler. A panel chosen by Wrangler of six rodeo clowns, four producers, four bull riders, two barrel men and two announcers then determine the top qualifiers. A new rule made in 1987 also requires that participating rodeo clowns must work at least eight rodeos a year to be eligible for the tour.

Michael "Smurf" Horton, a rookie on the tour, won the 1987 National Finals. His performance was reviewed: "Fortunately for Horton Wrangler Bullfight judges award extra points for high-risk moves and getting close to bulls. Horton's NFR performance was brilliant. In four rounds of competition he won three and took second in the fourth.

"Horton says the keys to his success as a bullfighter are 'bullsavvy' and control. He says savvy is learned; control is natural.

"Despite the fact that anyone would be tempted to take a job that paid $52,000 the first year (that is what Horton made fighting bulls in 1987, including $28,500 in NFR prize money), he says no monetary value can be placed in the dangers involved in fighting bulls for a living." [12 (1987)]

By the end of 1988, the Bullfight Tour was a popular event, as reported in the *ProRodeo Sports News:*

> Response is overwhelming—104 rodeo committees have applied for 60 open tour sites. Wrangler representative said, "Never in our wildest dreams did we think that we'd have the luxury of selecting our bullfight locations from 104 rodeos."
>
> Under the new plan, Wrangler will provide special funds for key bullfight personnel, including the stock contractor, barrelman, announcer, secretary and timers. Individual committees will be responsible for the purse which must be a guaranteed $1,200 per round for a standard three-man, three-round match.
>
> In order to meet, or supplement the purse, each rodeo committee may sell presentation rights to local Wrangler retailers. So long as each retailer is given the right of first refusal, the committee may also sell the presentation rights to local media outlets.
>
> Wrangler projects that once 60 bullfights can be efficiently managed, Wrangler would likely be agreeable to expanding the tour.
>
> Lewis Cryer of PRCA said this is a good sign for all of rodeo. "It would appear that the success of the program will benefit all the elements of rodeo. This is a very positive sign." [12 (1988)]

Just before the National Finals Rodeo it was announced that each bullfighter on the tour had fought eight Wrangler matches to determine which six would advance to the Finals. The payoff for the Finals of the Wrangler Bullfights was $102,000 alone, in 1988. Miles Hare and Rob Smets tied for first place the last night of the event and were considered Co-Champions of the 1988 World Bullfight. Each finished the year with $45,250. When the winners were announced, Miles did a back flip in the middle of the arena. Then "Hare and Smets hugged and yelled and ran around the arena together like wild men." [12 (1988)]

Mike "Smurf" Horton, the 1987 Wrangler World Bullfight Champion, suffered several broken ribs, a punctured lung, and other internal damages when he moved in to save a fallen rider January 22, 1989, at the Southwest Exposition and Livestock Show and Rodeo in Fort Worth:

"Friends and fans of injured PRCA bullfighter Mike 'Smurf'

Horton raised $35,559 to pay Horton's medical bills at a benefit bull riding, bullfight and auction, March 24 and 25, at the Northside Coliseum in Fort Worth.

"Horton's hospital bills totaled about $20,000 and were paid in full with proceeds from the benefit. The balance of the money raised will be used to create a PRCA contract acts relief fund." [12 (1989)]

ProRodeo Sports News reporter Kendra Santos summed it up in her article, "Fighters Agree, Perfect Bull Presents Catch-22":

Bullfighters on the Wrangler Jeans Pro-Rodeo Bullfighters Tour lay it on the line every time they set a cleated foot inside the arena. They know before they get there that their snorting bovine opponents would like nothing better than to stomp them into bullfighter juice.

The situation is Catch-22. To score high and win big, bullfighters need to draw bulls that want to kill them. Bullfighting thrill seekers welcome the challenge of the "baddest" bull in the herd.

But they'd also like to live long enough to see their kids grow up. Their daredevil antics in the arena don't necessarily spill over into their daily lives.

Three of the 1988 great bullfighters, Rob Smets, Smurf Horton and Jimmy Anderson, were all asked their opinions of various things concerning today's bullfighting. Which bull do you dread the most, and what traits make a fighting bull great?

Smets' answer to that was, "I like one that really comes to me and keeps coming. One that's aggressive and really bails into me. Newer, fresher bulls are better because they aren't wise to your tricks. Bulls are like fighters—the more they fight, the smarter they get. There's a reason they kill bulls in Mexico. They only fight them once with a cape."

Horton said, "A great bull will keep charging and won't set up in the corner. I don't like to climb the fence. A good one will let you stay in the middle of the arena. Fresh bulls let you really put on a show. They haven't figured you out yet."

Anderson added, "A great bull has something inside him. They say a wild cow is most important because a bull gets his fighting ability or disability from his mother. That's who raises him."

When asked which breed was their favorite fighting bull Smets said he liked the Mexican bulls, Smurf likes the brindle crossbreds if they're green and chargy, and Anderson likes the Brahma. [12]

In a 1987 interview, Miles Hare said, "Bulls are not consistent. Bull #62 last night is the bull out of the pen I wanted. He turned out to be a dirty rotten piece of junk. He had his day—bulls have headaches, too." Then he went on to say, "They can get a virus. They can sometimes do something you do not expect them to do. They are gonna try and get you. I pretty well know what I want to do with a bull, but he can pull me out of my plan if he doesn't do what I think he'll do. If you fight enough bulls you're gonna get hooked, but we are out there defying the odds, and trying to prove we won't get hooked. I've never walked in the arena and thought I was going to get hooked."

Without bulls there would be no bullfights. Therefore, although they face each other as bitter enemies, the top ten bullfighters on the tour and the eight Wrangler Jeans pro officials vote for the Wrangler Jeans Fighting Bull of the Year. In 1989 the winning bull was No. 37 of the Borba Brothers string, of Escalon, California. The Borba Brothers received a $5,000 check from Wrangler. A tie for second place between Beutler and Gaylord Rodeo's No. 48 and Cervi Championship Rodeo Company's No. 13 brought

Yeah, it's got to be more than the money! Left to right: Lecile Harris, rider Bill Conant, Harper & Morgan Bull A16, Jerry Galloway attempting to free Conant's hand, and Rudy Burns.
(Photo by Bern Gregory; submitted by Charley and Imogene Beals)

$2,500 bonus checks from Wrangler for each. [12 (1989)]

Sponsors definitely sweeten the pot for the courageous bull-baiters. Rodeo clowns of today can draw $200 to $500 a performance, but with expenses of travel, meals and lodging and the consideration of the danger involved each time they step in front of a ton of fury, are they ever paid enough? Only those who make their living as a rodeo clown, bullfighter, or barrelman can answer that. Money can't be the criteria. Maybe it's the roar of the crowd, the adrenalin that puts the athlete on a high no drug could replace, the knowledge of having saved a cowboy from a bad bull.

Yep, it's got to be more than just the money.

More Heroes of Today

Each era has those at the top of their profession, those who consistently can be counted on, and those who "also ran." They should all be commended. Each rodeo clown has his own story, just a bit different in some way from any other rodeo clown's story. Here are some worth mentioning:

Butch Lehmkuhler of North Platte, Nebraska, was named the 1989, 1990, and 1991 PRCA Clown of the Year and the 1989 Coors Man in the Can.

"Receiving the awards that I received is one of the most humbling experiences that I've ever been through," said Lehmkuhler, 35. "So many people that I worked with over the years took the time to stop and recognize me. It's moving."

Butch quit teaching woodworking in high school to be a rodeo clown full time in 1988. However, he has been a PRCA member as a rodeo clown since 1977. His trampoline act is unique, and calls on all his acrobatic skills. He was on the college gymnastic touring club while he earned his degree in physical education from Chadron State College. [12 (1990)]

Duane Reichert of New Underwood, South Dakota, has been inducted into the South Dakota Hall of Fame. He has also been awarded a two year touring grant by the South Dakota Arts Council. He will take his "Backstage With a Rodeo Clown" assembly to schools throughout the state. The 45-minute presentation serves to educate students about rodeo—he transforms himself from cowboy to a rodeo clown, from makeup to his funny clothes to his protective gear. He shares adventures from his 30 plus years as a rodeo clown, demonstrates the use of the

Senator Steve Tomac of South Dakota says there are many similarities in his senate responsibilities and being a rodeo clown.

(Photographer unknown; submitted by Steve Tomac)

barrel and concludes with comedy skits that include three dogs, a goat and a rabbit. He also shares his anti-drug and alcohol sentiments with his listeners.

"I saw a bull rider get killed because he was pilled up," he said. "I was the bullfighter and I had the bull away from him, but he was on the ground and he just couldn't react. The bull stepped on him and he died later that night." [12 (1991)]

Steve Tomac of St. Anthony, North Dakota, took office January 7, 1991, in his first four year term as a North Dakota state senator. It is his third term in the state's legislature—he previously served two terms of two years each in the North Dakota House of Representatives.

Tomac, 37, is also a barrelman and rodeo clown. A PRCA member since 1982. He draws many similarities between his two professions.

"The objective in both is to keep ahead of the bull," he said. "And the timing I use as a clown has helped me in politics, because timing is everything."

"The rewards as a senator include changing some things rather than bitching about them, and helping people understand why we do things the way we do. As a clown, the reward is in the roar of the crowd. But when you get down to the basics, you're dealing with persuasion, crowds and people in both jobs."

Steve is the second-oldest of 18 children. "Needless to say, our supper table was a riot."

Steve works 30 to 50 rodeo performances a year. North Dakota state senators meet every other year for a limit of 80 days. They also meet periodically throughout the remainder of the year, as new issues arise.

"When I started clowning in 1971, the perception of a rodeo clown where I lived was of an alcoholic who was too old to ride bulls anymore," he said. "There was no respect for them. I made a promise to myself then that if I ever had to do it with the whiskey, that I'd quit."

"Thanks to the PRCA, and things we've helped ourselves with, we've upgraded our image as clowns to professionals. We've worked hard at it. People like what we do." [12 (1991)]

In early 1991 a motion picture, *My Heroes Have Always Been Cowboys,* was released. It was filmed in 1989 at the Lazy E Arena in Guthrie, Oklahoma. Many top PRCA members took part in the movie, including rodeo bullfighters Loyd Ketchum, Greg Rumohr, Jimmy Anderson, and Leon Coffee.

In one scene Anderson was required to be hit in the back by a bull. It took ten takes before they got it right.

" 'It was one of the hardest things in my career to watch my friend go out there and offer himself to that bull,' said Leon Coffee. 'To just stand by and watch—it just went against your every instinct as a bullfighter.'

"According to Coffee, each night ended with a Polaroid photo of his costume, front and back. The next day, he would be carefully checked to make certain that his costume matched in every detail." [12 (1991)]

The movie tells of a cowboy who helped out a rodeo clown friend and was injured. He comes home to find that his elderly father has been placed in a nursing home by the cowboy's sister and brother-in-law, who say the father can no longer live by himself. His father is despondent over the thought of living anywhere but his own home. This requires the cowboy to heal, train, get his body back in shape, win a major bullriding event, and use the winnings for independence for his father and himself.

In the movie, reference was made in a pool hall scene by some antagonistic hometown fellows that the cowboy had "scraped the

Leon Coffee airborne as Mike Moore guards the barrel, Sikeston, Missouri, 1979.

(Photo by Bern Gregory; submitted by Charley and Imogene Beals)

bottom of the barrel" by rodeo clowning. Many early-day rodeo clowns did imbibe from time to time. It was not unusual to see rodeo hands take a nip before a contest. Some overdid it. The reputation had validity. But that did not mean all early-day rodeo clowns were heavy drinkers. As the profession became more precise and acute agility and speed became a must, the alcohol problem became a thing of the past.

Leon Coffee started his clowning career in 1975. He has been a bullfighter, barrelman, and rodeo clown with acts. He attended Sul Ross University and played football as well as participated in rodeos. In an interview Coffee said, "Rodeo clowning is hard on marriages. You are always away from home. It is very difficult to be a part of family life and keep the pace that is necessary to be a top rodeo clown." Coffee has been married several times and speaks from experience. Many of his peers have also suffered from the same problem.

Jerry Wayne Olson has represented the contract personnel of PRCA—announcers, photographers, rodeo clowns, bullfighters, timers, secretaries, specialty act performers, and laborers.

"When you serve on the PRCA Board of Directors your basic job is to take care of PRCA business and rodeo as a whole. As the contract personnel director, it's also my job to see that contract personnel people get a fair share of PRCA programs and money," defined Olson.

"One issue was to make sure contract personnel was paid for National Finals as well as other top rodeos. Also at National Finals audiences see everything about rodeo but specialty acts."

Olson, who has grown up in the rodeo business, has seen many changes. "I enjoy striving to make the rodeo business better. We are trying to work together as a board to make this thing work. I think one of our problems is that there are so many entities to represent that we forget the rodeo fans way too often. They pay the bills. Without them, we're nothing. If there aren't butts in the seats, we're in trouble." [12 (1991)]

Dale Woodard believes his most important responsibility is to entertain the audience. In addition to his barrelman duties he performs acts using fighting chickens, a pig (current performer is named Swinestein), and a horse. He has created his routines and is very proud of the originality.

Dale says rodeo clowning has been good to him, his wife, and

Dale Woodard clowns for his favorite fan, his wife, Reno, 1991.
(Photo taken by Gail Woerner)

Quail Dobbs has many hilarious acts.
(Photographer unknown, submitted by Quail Dobbs)

two daughters. They have a ranch at French Camp, California, a manufacturing company, and are in the process of purchasing land in Colorado—all from monies made in rodeo.

Quail Dobbs, comedy clown, bullfighter, and barrelman, has come from the front lines. "Everyone in rodeo is so much better than when I started," said Dobbs in a *ProRodeo Sports News* interview with Kendra Santos in 1989 after capturing the 1988 PRCA Clown of the Year. This was Quail's second time to be honored with this award, as he was also the 1978 recipient. [12 (1989)]

Evidenced by his many awards, including Coors Man in the Can, and numerous National Finals appearances as both barrelman and bullfighter, his occupational versatility keeps him in demand.

Passing on the profession from generation to generation seems to be no problem. However, Quail takes that responsibility one step beyond what most rodeo clowns do. He is part of a unique project in his hometown of Coahoma, Texas—"World's Original Kindergarten Rodeo." Youngsters compete on stick horses and stick bulls, some children are clowns, one is the announcer, some take the role of pickup men, and a rodeo queen presides. What a wonderful way of training tots to grow up and take their place in the rodeo world.

Just as Quail participates with the next generation of rodeo participants, many rodeo clowns and cowboys volunteer to participate in Exceptional Rodeos for mentally and physically handicapped children. The first was held February 1983. Each participant is outfitted with a cowboy hat, T-shirt, a back number, bandanna, and rope. They participate in events such as goat relay, dummy steer roping, a horseback flag race, barrel racing on stick horses, steer wrestling Cory Corriente, and an eight-second ride aboard Payday, the hand-rocked bareback horse, and Wimpy, the hand-rocked bull. All the animals used look like overstuffed animals. [12 (1989)]

Many changes have taken place in the eighty-plus years that rodeo clowns have been performing, from the earliest days when the only responsibility was to entertain and get laughs from the rodeo audience. Those who developed into the best of their day were primarily cowboys, with a desire to generate laughter. This brought about routines which included many animals, especially mules and horses. Some trained animals became almost as popular and famous as their owners. It is not unusual today to go to a rodeo

Miles Hare at work against a Borba bull, Old Blue, Bremerton, Washington, 1988. (Photo by David Jennings; submitted by Miles Hare)

and see some of the same routines that were being performed in the early days. And they still delight an audience.

When the Brahma bull was introduced, a whole new side of rodeo clowning was required. Protection of the bull rider became a high priority. As bullfighting evolved, those early "baiters" tried all sorts of tactics—some worked and some did not. Those who were considered the best continually outsmarted the bovines and kept cowboys from harm. Many variations were used, including the dummy to distract the outraged bull. The barrel, developed by Jasbo Fulkerson, uniquely gave the clown a means of safety while being right in front of the chutes. Many found the haven of the barrel, sometimes referred to as the "clown lounge," a Godsend.

As the world of rodeo came to be recognized as the sport it truly is, cowboys were recognized for their athletic abilities. Cowboys were not just heroes out of a 1950s movie or a Louis Lamour novel. They learned to solve the logistical problem of getting from one rodeo to the next. "On down the road" no longer meant driving a pickup and pulling a trailer. Some headed to the nearest airport and hopped around the country via commercial airlines, and a few even bought their own airplanes and flew themselves from performance to performance, gathering points from every possible

Allen Nelson, Jr., signing autographs for Special Olympic athletes, San Marcos, Texas, 1989.
(Photo by Gail Woerner)

corner of the nation.

This change to rodeo also affected the rodeo clown. Comic routines and animals required pickups and trailers, and time was of the essence. More and more opted to drop the acts and the hauling problems to be able to concentrate strictly on bullfighting. This was made even more enticing when Wrangler, Coors, and other corporate sponsors introduced the bullfights and other competitions, giving additional rewards to those who participated.

Bullfighters of today's era of corporate sponsorship not only face the bulls during the bullriding event ten to fifteen times a performance, but also face a fighting bull in a competitive bullfight against two to five other bullfighters eager to gather more points and unseat one another on the yearly point system. The top six bullfighters go to National Finals to compete for top money and the title of Bullfighter of the Year. [11]

Today stock contractors and producers are searching for more comic relief. The balance of rodeo clowns had become heavy in favor of the bullfighter/barrelman. A limited number of rodeo clowns are now entering the 1990s with a full complement of funny material.

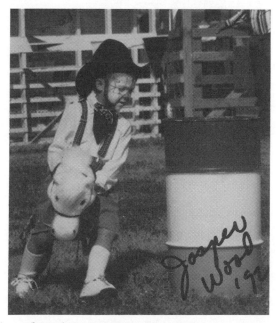

Tomorrow's rodeo clown, Jasper Wood, four-year-old grandson of Junior Meek. He already entertains at Texas Special Olympics, Denton, 1992.   (Submitted by Junior Meek)

What will tomorrow hold for the rodeo clown? Rodeos would be very somber places without the laughs and humor of the madcap funnymen. A bull rider would surely stop and consider the alternatives if he didn't have that bullfighter and barrelman out in front of him when he leaves the chute on top of eighteen hundred pounds of fighting fury.

But the audience is the real decision-maker. Does the rodeo audience come to see the rodeo clown? *You bet they do.* May the rodeo clown with his humor *and* heroics be in the arena forever.

Appendix A

COMEDY ACTS, BULLFIGHTERS AND BARRELMEN

Name	Hometown, Position*	Era	Deceased
Abbiatti, Doug	Carthage, Mo. BF	1991	
Adams, Doug	Bedford, Tx. CL, BF	1976–91	
Adcock, James	Azle, Tx. CL, BF	1986–93	
Alabama Slim	(See Fred Clancy)	1945	
Alexander, Alec		1956	
Alexander, Bryan	Castle Rock, Co. BF	1991–93	
Alexander, Doug	CL, BF		1982
Allen, Denny	Mt. Vernon, Wa. CL, BF	1964–67	
Allen, Johnny		1962	
Allen, Phillip	Cisco, Tx. BF, BM	1991	
Allen, Terry	Reno, Nv.	1953–74	
Allnutt, Casey	Galt, Mo. BF	1991	
Allred, Darl	Stockton, Ut. CL, BF	1975–89	
Anderson, Bob		1946	
Anderson, Gale	Lennox, S.D. CL, BM	1960–93	
Anderson, Jimmy	Dublin, Tx. CL, BF	1975–93	
Anderson, Overland Red	Montana CL	1920s	
Antley, Warren "Pinball"	W. Monroe, La. BF	1953–65	
Anz, Wilfred		1949	
Aplan, Jim	Fort Pierre, S.D.	1955–57	
Arave, Paul	CL, BF	1970	
Armstrong, Earl	CL	1947–50	
Armstrong, Rosco	CL	1922–47	1966
Arnew, Howard	Grass Valley, Ca. CL, BF	1950–75	
Avila, Douglas	Taft, Ca. BF	1981	
Ayer, John		1964	
Bagnell, Mickey	BF		
Bagnell, Scotty	Arlee, Mt. CL, BF	1935–53	
Barber, Monte	Fort Pierre, S.D. CL	1940s	
Barlow, Lynn	BF	1980	
Barrett, Richard W.	Sauquoit, N.Y. BF	1956–58	
Barron, Alex	San Diego, Ca. CL, BF	1945	
Barry, Mac	Coburg, Or. BF, BM	1944–87	

Barry, Rowdy	Pendleton, Or. CL, BF	1983–90	
Bascom, Earl	California CL, BF	1930s–40s	
Baumgartner, Joe	Brentwood, Ca. BF	1986–93	
Beeler, Skip	Chandler, Az. CL, BF	1928–82	
Bender, Bennie	Mobridge, S.D. CL, BF	1941–57	3-31-73
Bender, Marvin	BF	1953	
Bennefield, Benny	Elk Grove, Ca. CL	1949–57	
Bennett, Roger	Littleton, Co. CL, BF	1979–87	
Bentley, Don	Sacramento, Ca. CL, BF	1938–51	
Berry, Butch	Ronda, N.C. BF	1991	
Bevers, Terry	Azle, Tx. CL	1987–89	
"Big Butch"	Clyde Park, Mt. CL, BF	1965	
Bigham, Gary	DeQueen, Ar. CL, BF	1978	
Billingsly, Ted	Madras, Or. CL, BF	1949–57	
Bishop, Billy, Jr.	Goodyear, Az. CL, BF,BM	1989–90	
Bland, Bo	San Antonio, Tx. CL	1960s	
Bloomquist, David	Isanti, Mn. BF	1991	
Blythe, Gary	Charlotte, N.C. CL, BF	1978	
Boen, Ken	Fort Smith, Ar. CL, BF	1941–75	
Boger, Bunky	Lowell, Ar. CL, BM	1950–93	
Boger, Richard	Springdale, Ar.	1989–90	
Boger, Steve	Springdale, Ar. BM	1986–90	
Bolling, Dick		1969	
Bonaha, Anleigh	Prescott, Az. BF	1976–85	
Bond, Thomas Shepard	Purvis, Ms. BF, BM	1989–93	
Bordenave, John	Manteca, Ca. BF	1991	
Bottorf, Eric	Modesto, Ca. CL, BF	1980–91	
Bowen, Terry	Del Rio, Tx. CL, BF,BM	1964–93	
Bowery, Fred "Zeke"	Pacoima, Ca.CL, BM	1938–54	1-31-54
Bowman, Todd	Zumbrota, Mn. BF	1991	
Boyd, Tony	Fort Worth, Tx. CL, BF	1971–74	
Bradley, Robert	Pembroke Pines, Fl. BF, BM	1979–93	
Brannon, Lin	Mason City, Ia.	1989	
Braswell, Terry	White House, Tn. BF, BM	1991	
Brauer, Jeff	Elmwood, Ne. CL, BF	1987	
Brinkerhooff, Robbie	BF	1983	
Britt, Ford	Red Oak, Tx. CL, BF	1979–93	
Bronson, Spike	Fort Pierre, S.D. CL, BF	1949–60	
Brooks, Johnny			
Brown, John	Baker, La. CL, BF	1979	
Brown, Robert G.	Dade City, Fl. CL, BF	1981–93	
Brown, Vernon	Pecos, Tx.	1961	
Bruce, Bobby	Wichita, Ks.CL, BF, BM	1963–64	
Bruegman, Colt	Cheyenne, Wy.	1989	
Brumbley, E. A.		1954	
Burke, Russell III	Brandon, Ms. BF	1989–93	
Burnett, John T. (Nocona Slim)			5-67
Burney, Kirby	Pasadena, Tx. CL, BF	1967–91	
Burnham, David	San Saba, Tx. CL, BF	1976–93	

Burns, Bobby	Ardmore, Ok. BF, BM	1991	
Burns, Rudolph	Smithdale, Ms. BF, BM	1977-93	
Burris, John	Okmulgee, Ok. CL, BM	1979-82	
Busick, Pinky	Abbyville, Ks. CL, BF	1964-66	
Butcher, Ivan	Grand Prairie, Tx. BF	1984-89	
Byrd, Bob G.	Roff, Ok. BF, BM	1991	
Byrne, Ryan	Prince Albert, Can. BF	1982-93	
Cabral, Louie		1956	
Calkins, Randy	Del Valle, Tx. BF	1990-93	
Callihan, Mark	Gainesville, Tx. BF	1987-89	
Cameron, G. Scott	Golden, Co. CL, BF	1989-93	
Campbell, Dave	Denver, Co. CL	1930	
Campos, Kilos	Selma, Al. CL, BF	1967	
Caraway, Eddy	Williamsport, Tn. BF,BM	1991	
Carden, A. O. "Monk"	Pendleton, Or. CL	1928-38	
Carlton, Goldie	Lovington, N.M. CL, BM	1956-63	5-22-65
Carruthers, John	South Carolina		
Carter, Kenneth	Woodstown, N.J. CL, BF	1988-93	
Cervi, Mike	Sterling, Co. CL, BF	1955-60	
Chance, Cotton	Fort Worth, Tx.	1956-58	
Chancellor, Snuffy	Fort Worth, Tx. CL, BF, BM	1963-93	
Chandler, Jerry	Ellensburg, Wa. CL	1955	
Chapman, Dave	LaGrande, Or. CL, BF	1973-75	
Chatman, Rick	Rio Vista, Tx. CL, BF	1975-93	
Chausse, Wayne	Maschouch, Can. BF	1984-89	
Cheatham, Denny	Bakersfield, Ca.CL, BM	1984-93	
Childers, Rick	Gilroy, Ca.	1974-75	
Chism, Carl Dee	Tulsa, Ok. BF, BM	1991	
Chitwood, Frank	Sanish, N.D.	1949	7-28-50
Church, Fred	CL, BF	1962	
Cisco, Shorty		1940	
Clancy, Fred (Alabama Slim)	Largo, Fl.	1946	
Clark, Bobby	Warner, Ok.CL, BF, BM	1948-79	
Clark, David Eugene	Redmond, Or. CL, BF	1947-79	
Clayman, Larry	Hylandville, Mo. CL, BF	1963-75	
Cline, Clyde	Baggs, Ok. CL	1930s-40s	
Coffee, Luke "Leon"	Austin, Tx. CL, BF, BM	1975-93	
Cogburn, D. C.	Guthrie, Ok. CL	1974-77	
Coleman, Ted	Ignacio, Co. BF	1987-93	
Conley, Larry	S. Coffeyville, Ok. BM	1991	
Connelle, Bud		1962	
Connors, Bob		1955	
Conrad, Gary	Xhurubusco, In. BF, BM	1991	
Conrad, Jerry Lee	Park City, Ut. BF	1985-89	
Cook, Bobby "Toad"	Big Rapids, Mi. CL, BM	1981-93	
Cooper, Felix	Pelican, La. CL, BF	1940-54	
Cooper, Marty	Wister, Ok. BF	1991	
Copher, David	Manchaca, Tx. CL	1974-87	
Cornish, Wayne	Waukomis, Ok. CL, BM	1950-72	

Coulter, Danny	Cherokee, Ok. BF	1991	
Courtney, Bob	Independence, Ks. BF, BM	1979–89	
Cowley, Alan	Roff, Ok. BM	1990–93	
Cox, Danny	Altoona, Ks. CL, BF	1969–89	
Cox, Rodie	Ramona, Ca. CL, BF	1982–93	
Crane, D. R.	Cazenavia, Wi. CL, BF	1969	
Crane, Sherman	San Juan Capistrano, Ca.		
	CL, BF	1946–65	8-80
Craver, Ronald	Ottumwa, Ia. BF	1986–93	
Crethers, John	CL		
Crist, Skeeter	Tucson, Az. CL	1940–41	
Cromwell, Ted	Baton Rouge, La. CL, BF	1979	
Crouch, J. G.	Montague, Tx. CL, BM	1977–91	
Cunningham, Moses	Bartlesville, Ok. CL	1946	
Curry, Frank		1960–63	
Curtis, Gene	Okanogan, Wa. BF	1937–56	
Curtis, Wes	Oakland, Or. CL, BF	1948–68	
Cypher, T. J.	Willard, Mo. CL, BF, BM	1981–89	
Dahl, Douglas	Baker, Mt. CL, BF, BM	1977–93	
Damuth, G. C. Bo	Magnolia, Tx. CL, BF	1947–59	
Darling, Happy Jack	CL	1947	
Davis, Bert	Copperopolis, Ca.CL, BF, BM	1974–93	
Davis, Charley & Gene	Tucson, Az. CL, BF	1955–60	
Davis, Kevin C.	Battiest, Ok. CL	1990–93	
Dechow, Scott	Conroe, Tx. CL, BF	1982–93	
Dent, Danny	New York CL	1963–70	1974
Diamond D. Dewey	CL	1939	
Dickson, Jimmy	Riverside, Ca. CL	1945–49	
Dix, Dan	CL	1911–27	
Dixon, Harold		1956	
Doak, George	Irving, Tx. CL, BF	1953–81	
Dobbins, Kenny	Tulsa, Ok. BF	1991	
Dobbs, Quail	Coahoma, Tx. CL, BF, BM	1963–93	
Doering, Greg	Tualatin, Or. CL, BF	1975–93	
Doering, Karl	Roseburg, Or. CL, BF	1948–76	10-19-83
Donaldson, Bob	Wellington, Co. CL, BF	1974–93	
Doody, Dan	CL	1952	
Douglas, Tommy	Burbank, Ca. CL	1913–28	
Doulton, Seth	Santa Ynez, Ca. BF	1971–93	
Drake, Dean	Denver, Co.	1963	
Driver, Charlie	CL, BF	1962–63	
Dryden, Stephen	Marianna, Fl. BF	1981–93	
Dunn, Hans	Montgomery, Al. BF	1981–93	
Dunn, John		1975	
Dunn, Rex	Hastings, Ok. CL, BF	1970–93	
Dutruch, Robert	Poplarville, Ms.CL, BF, BM	1985–93	
Dwyer, Ted	Hastings, Ok. CL, BF	1982	
Earls, DoDo	El Centro, Ca. CL	1955–57	
Eaton, Duane	Lamont, Ca. BF	1983–87	
Eby, Benjamin	Hiawatha, Ia. BF, BM	1983–93	

Eddy, Ed	CL	1914–16	
Edmiston, Keith	Benton, Ks.	1958	
Edwards, Donk	Fort Collins, Co.	1972–74	
Edwards, Harold T.	Prairieville, La. BF	1988–93	
Elick, Martin (Oklahoma Slim)			
Ellick, Greek	Dexter, Ks. CL, BF	1978	
Ellick, Greek, Jr.	Anderson, Al. BF, BM	1991	
Ellis, Cecil		1955	
Ellis, Frank	Athol, Id. CL, BF	1955–76	
Erhardt, Shane	Mandan, N.D.	1990–93	
Ezell, Ed	Highland, N.Y. BF	1991	
Farley, Stacy	Osseo, Wi. BF	1985–90	
Feller, Jim Bob	Granbury, Tx. CL, BF, BM	1971–93	
Feller, Tom	Colorado Spgs, Co.CL, BM	1973–89	
Ferguson, Jim		1960	
Fields, Melvin	Coffeyville, Ks. CL, BF	1958–73	
Flechsig, Dick	E. St. Louis, Il. BM	1961–63	
Fontenot, Keith	Ethel, La. BF	1981–87	
Ford, Frank		1957	
Forell, Guy	Alva, Ok. CL, BF	1986–93	
Forrest, Jim Bo	McLean, Il. BF	1974–75	
Forzani, Doug J.	Carmel Valley, Ca. BF	1989–93	
Foster, Bueno	Tucson, Az.	1940s–50s	
Foster, J. S.		1963	
Foster, Wayne	Tucson, Az.	1978	
Fowler, Don	Cheriden, Az. CL, BF, BM	1978	
Francis, Nick		1947	
Franco, Ernesto A.	N. Lauderdale, Fl. CL	1990–93	
Franks, Jess C.	Flora Vista, N.M. CL, BF, BM	1979–93	
French, Bill	Fort Pierre, S.D. CL		
French, Don	Kansas City, Ks. BF	1991	
Freouf, Don G.	Yuba City, Ca. BF	1987–93	
Fritzler, Glenn	Lodge Grass, Mt.CL	1948–65	
Fulkerson, Jasbo	Watauga, Tx.CL, BM	1927–48	1-11-49
Fulkerson, Shorty	CL	1953	
Fuller, Swede		1957–58	
Galloway, Jerry Don	Keller, Tx. CL, BF	1982–93	
Garsee, Bill	Moscow, Tx.	1957–68	4-85
Garten, Stanley "Shorty"	Pawhuska, Ok. BF	1978–93	
Gaudin, D. J."Kajun Kid"	Teague, Tx. CL, BF	1952–79	
Gayle, Dickie	Baton Rouge, La.	1979	
Gayle, Johnnie	San Antonio, Tx. CL, BF	1975–85	
Gibbs, Timothy	Paola, Ks. BF, BM	1991	
Gillett, Terry A.	Terrell, Tx. BF	1989–93	
Gilstrap, John	Burns, Tn. BF, BM	1991	
Gist, Clarence "Pinky"	Phoenix, Az. CL	1946–50	8-70
Glover, Joe W.	Florence, Tx. BF	1989–93	
Goodman, Raymond	Manitoba, Can.		
Goodrum, Joe E.	Bryan, Tx.	1990	
Gorrell, Marvin	Clovis, N.M. BF	1990–93	

Graham, Jinx	Alva, Ok.	1956–57	
Graham, Skip		1959–68	
Grande, Beau			
Gratney, Rich	Olathe, Ks. CL, BM	1988–93	
Graves, Chas., Jr.	Toccoa, Ga. BM	1991	
Graves, Lefty	Arlington, Az.	1991	
Green, Charlie	Green Forest, Ar. BF	1991	
Green, Donny	Battleground, Wa.		
	CL, BF, BM	1973–93	
Greenwood, Dale	Cartwright, N.D. CL, BF	1944–73	
Griffin, Faron	Cache, Ok. BF	1991	
Griffin, Raymond	Cache, Ok. BF	1991	
Griffith, Curly	Fort Worth, Tx. CL	1917	
Grigsby, Jeff W.	Saginaw, Tx. CL, BF	1987–92	7-1-92
Groene, Ted F.	Clayton, Ca. BF	1984–93	
Grugan, Shorty		1938	
Guimond, George	Ignacio, Co. CL, BF	1990–93	
Guldenbecker, Kenny	Bellmont, Id.	1964	
Gulick, Oklahoma Slim	Rich Hill, Mo. CL, BF	1930–40s	1980
Guy, Kirk	Paradise, Tx. BF	1991	
Gwinn, Frank	Walla Walla, Wa. CL		
Hackney, Woody	Tellico Plains, Tx.	1963–69	
Hale, Jason W.	Bassano, Can., BF	1991–93	
Hale, Wayne	Bassano, Can.	1969	
Hall, Kenny	Nampa, Id. BF	1991–93	
Hall, Kevin "Bunky"	CL	1980s	
Ham, Carl III	Andrews, Tx. BF	1978–87	
Ham, Stan S. III	Andrews, Tx. BF	1989–90	10-1-90
Hamm, Joe		1966	
Hammett, Jackie	Gaffney, S.C. CL, BM	1963–93	
Hankins, Barry	Saginaw, Tx. CL. BF	1990–92	
Hano, Elaish "Huck"	Holden, La. CL, BM	1979–93	
Hansen, Swede		1955–56	
Hanzlik, Boyd	Durango, Co. BM, CL	1990–93	
Haralson, Sean	Coalinga, Ca. BF	1990–93	
Harbison, Brahma Bill		1938–40	
Hare, Miles	Ringling, Ok. BF	1968–93	
Hare, Tommy	Moore Haven, Fl. BF	1990–93	
Hargo, Dwayne	Placerville, Ca. CL, BF	1984–93	
Harris, Andy		1975	
Harris, Cliff	Waco, Tx. BF, BM	1991	
Harris, Homer	Antlers, Ok. CL	1946–50	
Harris, Jason	Allsworth, Ne.	1990	
Harris, Lecile	Collierville, Tn. CL, BF	1960s–93	
Hart, Lynn "Smokey"	Denver, Co. BF	1988–93	
Hartsell, Sherry	Gilmer, Tx.	1989	
Hartup, Carl		1963	
Hatfield, Eddie	Haslet, Tx., CL, BF	1976–91	
Hatfield, Perry		1959	
Havely, Jeff	Joplin, Mo. BF	1991	

Hawkins, Terry Joe	Morgantown, W.V. BM	1976-93	
Hayden, John	Eureka, Mo. BM	1985-87	
Hayes, Leland Shorty	Cottondale, Fl. CL, BF	1978-90	
Hayes, Rodney R.	Humble, Tx. CL, BF	1991-93	
Hayner, Earl	Mont. CL	1920s	
Headrick, Jerry	Nickerson, Ks. CL		4-15-73
Heaton, Buddy	Ullyses, Ks. CL, BF	1944-73	
Hebert, Joey	Sulphur, La. BF	1986-93	
Hedeman, Gary Roach	Bowie, Tx. CL, BF	1977-93	
Hefner, Hoytt	Bethany, Ok. CL, BF	1942-63	6-16-77
Hefner, Ross	Wichita Falls, Tx.	1956-58	
Hempstead, Pat	Loveland, Co.	1990	
Henry, Brian	San Antonio, Tx.	1989-90	
Henson, Chuck	Tucson, Az. CL, BF	1940-93	
Herket, Al		1940s	
Herman, Jake		1920s	
Higley, Kevin	Hooper, Ut. CL, BF, BM	1984-93	
Hill, Bobbie	Paradise, Mt. CL	1920-67	5-85
Hill, Jim	Enid, Ok. CL, BF, BM	1959-93	
Hill, Travis	Wichita Falls, Tx. CL, BF	1991-93	
Hinkle, Milt	Kissimmee, Fl. CL	1919	1972
Hogan, Earnest "Turk"	Tulsa, Ok. CL		1985
Hogsett, Karl	Fort Worth, Tx. BF	1986-87	
Holcomb, Elmer	CL, BF	1941-58	1963
Holcomb, Homer	Lewiston, Id. CL, BF	1919-49	11-15-71
Hold, Bob		1947	
Holland, Bob	McLean, Il. BF	1970-75	
Hollander, Happy Jack	CL	1922	
Holliday, Pistol	Bryan, Tx. CL, BF	1950-67	
Holloway, Rebel	CL	1950	
Honeycutt, Scott	Arlington, Az. CL, BF	1989-93	
Hopkins, Andy	Logan, Ut. CL, BF	1988-93	
Hopkins, James	Bells, Tn. BF, BM	1991	
Horton, Mike "Smurf"	Zolfo Springs, Fl. CL, BF	1978-93	
Hostetler, Shorty		1957	
Howington, Wright	Colleyville, Tx. CL, BF, BM	1955-93	
Hudson, Royce	Bryan, Tx.	1956-58	
Hughes, James	Ash Flat, Ar. BF	1991	
Hughston, Denver	McBain, Mi. BF, BM	1991	
Hunsaker, Curley	Ogden, Ut. BF	1974-75	
Hunt, Tom	CL	1937-45	
Hyland, Bill	Carson City, Nv.	1967	
Isley, Keith	Reidsville, N.C. BF, BM	1991	
Ivey, Frank	Mesquite, Tx. CL, BF, BM	1963	
Jacobs, Slats	Valentine, Ne. CL	1928-30s	
Jaynes, Ted	League City, Tx. CL, BF		
Jenkens, Bert	CL, BF	1955	
Jobloneski, R. W.		1960	
Johnson, Barry	Lamar, Ne. CL, BM	1990-93	
Johnson, Jessie Ray		1955	

Johnson, Mike	Poplar Bluff, Mo. CL, BF	1987–93	
Johnson, Ronald	Piggott, Ar. CL, BF	1990–93	
Johnson, Slivers	Waupun, Wi.	1935–57	
Johnson, Snowball	CL	1914	
Johnson, Swede			
Johnson, Tony	Berino, N.M. CL, BF, BM	1986–90	
Jones, Deacon Lee	Portales, N.M. BF	1984–93	
Jones, Gary W.	Pasadena, Tx. BF	1989–93	
Jones, Pete		1955–62	
Jones, Steve	Millersville, Md. BF	1985–90	
Jones, Ward		1963	
Joyce, Jack	CL	1939	
Keen, Billy	Kissimmee, Fl. CL, BM	1927–65	12-28-81
Keenen, Tin Horn Hank	Rogers, Ar. CL, BF	1912–51	12-13-68
Kehler, Billy	Alberta, Can.	1989	
Kell, Jess	CL	1937–45	3-5-54
Kennedy, T. K.	Hamilton, Oh. BF	1991	
Kersey, Ronald	Moses Lake, Wa. BF	1985–93	
Kersten, Michael	Cody, Wy. BF, BM	1986–93	
Kersten, Rooster	Cody, Wy. CL, BM	1989–93	
Ketchum, Loyd	Miles City, Mt. BF	1987–93	
Kimsey, Bruce	Chelan, Wa. BF	1987–93	
Kimzey, Ted	Strong City,Ok.CL, BF, BM	1974–93	
King, Billy	Anton, Tx. CL	1960	
King, Don	Gainesville, Tx.	1955–56	
Kinney, Chuck	Sulphur, La. CL, BF	1981–90	
Kite, Charles J.	Montfort, Wi. CL	1991–93	
Klein, George	Goldendale, Wa.	1971	
Kline, Marvin		1972–87	
Klives, Clyde			5-65
Knapp, Jack PeeWee	Hollywood, Ca. CL, BF	1944–51	
Kobza, Jeff	Claypool, Az. BF	1980–93	
Korkow, Jim	BF	1963	
Krause, Gene	CL		
Kuehn, Richard	Durant, Ia. BF	1986–89	
LaCoste, Kelley	Medicine Hat, Can.		
	CL, BF, BM	1978–93	
Lancaster, Larry	Aurora, Co. BF	1982	
Land, Eddy	Montrose, Co. CL, BF	1979–82	
Landis, Bill	Fresno, Ca. CL, BF	1948–70	
Landis, Donny	Fresno, Ca. CL, BF, BM	1973–93	
Lane, Bill	Riverbank, Ca. CL, BF	1956–90	
Large, Randy	Steamboat Springs, Co.		
	BM, CL	1990–93	
Larson, Perle		1964	
Latham, Tim		1979	
Lebouef, Dwain	Raceland, La. CL, BM	1986–93	
LeClair, Willis	Riverton, Wy.	1978	
Lee, Coy	CL	1947	
Lefton, Abe	San Francisco, Ca. CL	1920s	2-24-58

LeGrand, Buck	Sedan, Ks. BF	1949–75	
LeGrand, Tom	Braman, Ok. CL, BF, BM		
Lehmkuhler, Butch	North Platte, Ne. CL, BF, BM	1977–93	
Lepard, Tim	New Albany, Ms. BF, BM	1991	
Lewis, Dwayne	Tulsa, Ok.	1989–90	
Lewis, Joe	CL	1913–32	
Lindell, Curtis	Medina, Tx. CL, BF	1973–91	
Lindley, Louis "Slim Pickens"	Canoga Park, Ca. CL, BF	1944–54	12-8-83
Lindsey, John	Wichita Falls, Tx. CL, BF	1927–63	2-28-74
Linn, Jack	Seminole, Ok. BM	1957–64	
Liskey, Bill			1960
Long, Dee	Osage City, Ks. BF, BM	1991	
Long, Jack	San Antonio, Tx. CL	1949–61	
Longren, Sidney			1957
Loose, Dave			1959
Lorette	CL	1911–18	
Lorimer, Chuck	Napa, Ca. CL, BF, BM	1941–58	
Lornes, Willie "Smokey"	Texas CL	1943–57	
Lucia, Tommy G.	Weatherford, Tx. CL, BF, BM	1965–93	
Lucia, Tommy Joe	Weatherford, Tx. CL, BM	1972–93	
Ludlow, Jay	Spring Valley, Ca. BF, BM	1977–90	
Lulim, Tommy		1960s	
Lyons, Charlie	St. Ignatius, Mt. CL, BF	1955–81	
McAfee, Bobby	Henryetta, Ok. CL, BF	1974–75	
McBride, Joseph, Jr.	Middleton, N.Y. BM	1991	
McClain, Scott D.	Torrington, Wy. CL	1989–93	
McCracken, Dale	Wheaton, Mo. BM	1991	
McCray, Wiley	Briscoe, Tx. CL, BF, BM	1939–54	1-23-77
McEnaney, Bill	Rossville, Tn. CL, BF, BM	1951–91	
McFarland, Sid	Montgomery, Al. CL, BF	1975	
McGrann, Eddie		1967	
McGuire, Floyd	Clarksville, Tx.	1991–93	
McIlvain, Wm. Frank	Balch Springs, Tx. CL, BF, BM	1957–93	
McIlvain, Frank, Jr.	Mesquite, Tx. CL	1974–90	
McIntosh, Byron	Davie, Fl. BF	1991	
McKinney, Larry	Frazier Park, Ca. BF	1955–77	
McLain, Jim D., Jr.	Duncan, Ok. CL, BF	1981–93	
McMann, Jerry	Phoenix, Az. CL, BF	1970–75	
McMillan, Al	Blackfoot, Id. BF, CL	1942	9-72
Mahlum, Duane		1979	
Malotte, Kato	Vinita, Ok. BF	1991	
Mann, Joe	Weatherford, Tx. CL, BF	1980–87	
Mann, Orval "Stillwell Shorty"	Stillwell, Ok. CL, BF	1949–56	
Manns, Ed		1955	
Marchio, Lou	Golden, Co. CL	1964	
Mariluch, Jerry	Wells, Nv. CL, BF	1970–93	
Markley, Bill	Eugene, Or. CL, BF	1939–54	
Marshall, Lyle	Binilla, S.D. CL		

Martin, Bryan	Dallas, Tx. CL, BF	1986–87	
Martin, Buddy	BF	1970s	
Martin, Dave	Gettysburg, Pa. BM	1991	
Martin, Don	Smartsville, Ca. BF	1991	
Martin, Dutch		1956	
Martin, Red	Owasso, Ok. CL, BF	1947	
Martin, Ronald F.	Ballston Spa, N.Y. BF	1954–93	
Mascardo, Casey	Riverton, Ut. CL	1984–87	
Mawson, Roger	Fort Smith, Ar. CL, BM	1956–93	
Maxwell, Phil	Monrovia, Ca. CL, BM	1962–93	
Mayberry, Kiss	CL, BM	1959–64	
Mead, Thomas	Loveland, Co. BF	1983–89	
Meadows, Shorty	Lisbon, Il. CL	1963–64	
Meek, Junior	Godley, Tx. BF	1954–74	
Meeks, Rory	DeWitt, Ia. BF	1985–89	
Miller, Darrel	Arizona	1966	
Miller, Johnnie		1948	
Mills, George	Phoenix, Az. CL, BF	1934–56	9-21-80
Mills, Hank	Grand Junction, Co. CL, BF ,	1943	
Minchey, Larry	CL	1974	
Milter, Dow		1955	
Moens, George	Pendleton, Or. CL	1928–38	4-27-83
Money, Owen	Roseburg, Or. CL	1978	
Monismith, Monty		1955	
Mooney, Tex		1945	
Moore, Mike	Austin, Tx. BF	1979	
Moore, Roger "Apache"		1960	
Moore, Sid "Beeswax"	Tucson, Az. CL	1946–57	
Morgan, Larry D.	Comanche, Tx. CL, BF, BM	1989–93	
Morgan, Scott	Haughton, La.	1989	
Morris, PeeWee	Custer, S.D. CL	1948	
Morrison, Raymond	Tahlequah, Ok. BF	1991	
Moser, Ray Moe	Ogden, Ut. CL, BF, BM	1965–93	
Mosley, Dixie Reger	Amarillo, Tx. CL, BF	1948	
Mowery, Steve	Presho, S.D. BF	1980–89	
Mulhair, Chuck	CL, BF	1945–49	
Munns, Randee	Garland, Ut. CL, BF	1971–93	
Murray, Harold	Poplar Bluff, Mo. CL	1987–93	
Myers, Paul	Denison, Tx. CL, BM	1989–93	
Nabb, Don	Fayetteville, Ar. CL, BF	1978	
Nash, Budge	Arlington, Tx. CL, BF	1987	
Nash, Marvin	Victoria, Tx. CL, BF, BM	1978	
Neal, Yod	Cody, Wy.	1991–93	
Neff, Lee	Hickory, Pa.	1970	
Nelson, Allen S., Jr.	Morrilton, Ar. CL, BF, BM	1982–93	
Nelson, James	Monroe, La. BF	1989–93	
Nesbitt, Jimmy	Oklahoma CL, BF	1925–43	11-13-43
Newman, Gene		1951	
Nichols, Vernon		1962	
Nix, Dan & Donk	Fort Collins, Co. CL, BF, BM	1970–75	

Nord, Dann		1956	
Nordell, Codt	Johnstown, Co. CL, BF	1979	
Norton, Jerry	Mitchell, S.D. CL, BF	1990-93	
Novotny, John Lee	Helena, Mt. CL, BF	1982-93	
Oberry, Edward, Jr.	Altoona, Fl. BF	1991	
O'Connor, Craig	Porterville, Ca. BF	1982-93	
O'Keefe, Jim	Missoula, Mt. CL, BF	1964	
Olson, Alan Wayne	White River, N.D. CL, BF	1985-93	
Olson, Harry		1968	
Olson, Jerry L.	Fruitdale, S.D. CL	1954-75	
Olson, Jerry Wayne	Belle Fourche, S.D. CL, BM	1974-93	
Olson, Larry		1956	
Olson, Larue	CL	1967	
O'Neill, Harold	Air Oaks, Ca. CL	1925-46	
O'Neill, Howard	Fair Oaks, Ca. CL	1925-46	
Ohstad, Chris	Irving, Tx. BF, BM	1991	
Otis, Si & Fanny	El Cerrito, Ca. CL	1937-46	
Owen, Jack	Wills Point, Tx. CL, BF	1943	
Oyler, Tim	Pocatello, Id. CL, BF	1968-75	
Pairsh, Jimmy	Bonham, Tx. CL, BF, BM	1971	
Panhandle Pete	(see Buddy Reger)	1941	
Papon, Bruce	Hardtner, Ha. CL, BF, BM	1977-78	
Parli, Gary	Morrison, Ok. CL, BF, BM	1966-93	
Parli, Shane	Morrison, Ok. BM	1991	
Parsons, Dave	S. Red Deer, Can. CL, BF	1968-69	
Patch, James "Scrapiron"	Miles City, Mt. CL	1928-48	12-2-85
Paul, Bobby	Galax, Va.	1991	
Paulsen, J. Scott	Ontario, Or. BF	1989-90	
Pedrett, Terry	Kimball, Ne.CL, BF	1961-64	
Pence, Bobby	Edinburg, In. CL	1947	
Perkins, Cy	CL		
Perriman, Jim		1953	
Peters, Jim		1964	
Peterson, Buddy		1970	
Peterson, Pete	Silver Springs, Fl. CL, BF	1947-85	
Peterson, Swede	Lenore, Id. CL, BF, BM	1978-93	
Peth, Wick	Bow, Wa. BF	1949-85	
Pickens, Slim (see Louis Lindley)			
Plaugher, Wilbur	Sanger, Ca. CL, BF	1945-93	
Pierce, James M.	Thibodeaux, La. CL, BF	1988-93	
Pierce, Munk	El Centro, Ca. CL, BF	1957-63	
Pope, Timothy	Brighton, Co. CL, BF	1990-93	
Portwood, Jerry		1957	
Pring, Johnny	Haden Lake, Id. CL	1927	
Procell, Bruce "Woodie"	Fort Collins, Co. CL, BF, BM	1978-90	
Purcell, Kirk	Houston, Tx. CL, BF	1969-71	
Quait, Elmer	CL, BF	1939	
Quebedeaux, Mike	Lake Charles, La. CL, BF, BM	1977-78	
Quinn, Ray L.	Rapid City, S.D. CL, BF	1990-93	
Ragland, Butch	Gilmer, Tx. CL, BM	1966	

Raleigh, Gene		1956	
Randall, Glenn	California CL	1925	
Ray, Keith	S. Ogden, Ut.	1969-70	
Redmon, Larry	Nacogdoches, Tx.	1989	
Reger, Buddy	Lubbock, Tx. CL, BF	1938-52	3-28-84
Reichert, Duane	New Underwood, S.D.		
	CL, BF, BM	1961-93	
Reinert, Rich	North Platte, Ne. CL, BF, BM	1977-93	
Reynolds, Fess	Buckeye, Az. CL, BF	1945-67	
Reynolds, Max	North Platte, Ne. CL	1993	
Reynosa, Sammy	Redwood City, Ca. CL, BM	1943-58	
Rhoades, Frank	Deport, Tx. CL, BF, BM	1966-77	
Rice, Larry G., Jr.	Madisonville, Tx. CL, BF, BM	1978	
Rich, Kevin	Windsor, Co. CL	1981-93	
Richardson, Spud	Natchitoches, La. CL, BF	1949	
Ridgely, William "Chip"	Glenwood, Md. CL, BM	1989-93	
Rivers, Wm. C.	Winchester, Ca. CL	1979-93	
Robbins, Walter			
Roberts, Jerry		1960	
Roberts, Mark	Marion, Ia. BF, BM	1991	
Robinson, Buck	Oklahoma City, Ok.CL, BF	1940s-55	
Robinson, Butch	Yerington, Nv. CL, BF	1963-79	
Robinson, Wayne, Jr.	LaMesa, Ca. CL, BF	1968	
Roe, Charlie	Tucson, Az. CL, BF	1968-75	
Rogers, Claude			
(Brahma Twins)	Tyler, Tx. CL	1937-49	12-4-78
Rogers, Clyde			
(Brahma Twins)	Tyler, Tx. CL	1937-49	
Rogers, Damon	San Saba, Tx. CL, BF	1990-93	
Rogers, Stan	Yuma, Co. CL, BF	1979-82	
Rollman, Roger	Wichita, Ks. BF, BM	1991	
Romer, Bob	Hurley, N.M. CL, BF	1965-91	
Rose, Kenneth E.	Idabel, Ok. CL, BF, BM	1955-85	
Routh, John	Fort Worth, Tx. BF	1956-72	
Rudd, Jack	Salt Lake City, Ut. CL	1956-71	
Rudsell, Rusty	Davis Junction, Il. BF, BM,	1991	
Rumohr, Gregory W.	Cleburne, Tx. CL, BF	1986-93	
Rutherford, David	Brawley, Ca.	1974-91	
Sanchez, Joaquin	Bakersfield, Ca. CL, BF	1952-66	9-13-66
Sandell, Sandy	Littleton, Co. CL	1957	
Sanford, Sylvester	Pasco, Wa. BF, BM	1983-93	
Satterfield, Carl	Tucson, Az. CL, BF	1946-55	
Sattler, Steve	Houston, Tx. CL, BF	1965-75	
Saunders, Arthur B.	Missouri, BF		1981
Savage, Art	CL, BF	1949-51	
Sayre, Jim		1955	
Schriner, Paul		1968	
Schumacher, Jimmy	Prescott, Az. CL, BM	1949-72	
Scott, Ken		1957	
Sells, Albert	Wynnewood, Ok. CL	1940-78	

Serpa, Tuffy		1955	
Seward, Roy		1951	
Shannon, Steve	CL, BM	1936–45	
Sharp, Buck		1962	
Shaw, Bill	Nacogdoches, Tx. CL, BF	1978–82	
Sheffield, Tommy	Rankin, Tx. CL, BF	1969–77	
Sheppard, J. A.	Springfield, Il. BF, BM	1991	
Shiller, Don		1962	
Shultz, Charley	Marland, Ok. CL, BF	1914–52	1985
Shultz, Clark	Arlington, Tx. CL, BF	1929–75	
Shultz, Clydel	Marland, Ok. CL	1978	12-20-78
Shultz, Leroy "Sonny"	Ponca City, Ok. CL, BM	1955	
Siens, John	Owasso, Ok. CL, BF	1943–47	
Sikula, Ray	Elgin, Il. BF	1991	
Sloan, Jimmy	Arizona CL, BM	1945–55	
Sloan, John	Springfield, Il. CL, BF	1967	
Smets, Rob "Kamikazi"	Oakland, Or. BF	1976–93	
Smith, Claud	Fort Worth, Tx. CL	1949	
Smith, Doug		1974	
Smith, Glenn	Roswell, N.M. CL, BM	1955–93	
Smith, Mark	Conway, Ar.	1970	
Smith, Rod		1960	
Smith, Todd	Kansas, Ok. BF, BM	1991	
Snow, Anthony	Holly Springs, Ms. BF	1991	
Sparks, Donny	Texarkana, Tx. BF	1988–93	
Sparks, Ronny	Texarkana, Tx. BF	1988–93	
Spencer, Mike	Coal Creek, Co. CL, BF, BM	1965–89	
Spencer, Michael	Porterville, Ca. BM	1962–90	
Spruell, Johnny	Pueblo, Co. CL, BM		6-15-79
Sikula, Ray	Elgin, Il. BF	1991	
Stahlman, Darrell	Alta Vista, Va. M	1991	
Stapp, Virgil	Houston, Tx.	1937–45	
Stayton, Harold Punk	Wann, Ok. CL, BM	1975–89	
Steed, Dean	Ogden, Ut. CL	1979	
Steed, Harold	Ogden, Ut. CL	1979–89	
Steele, Bill	Montana, CL		1939
Stensland, Jack	Wolf Point, Mt. CL, BF	1976–90	
Stephens, Duane	Troup, Tx. BF	1952–67	
Stephens, Larry "Jake"	Weiser, Id. BF	1973–93	
Stewart, Joey	Mesquite, Tx. CL, BF	1977–78	
Stober, Earl	Oklahoma		5-10-40
Stokes, John	Golden, Co. BF	1964	
Stokes, Paul		1945	
Strout, Frank	Arcadia, Fl. CL	1972–93	
Strout, Hank	Reeltown, Al.	1964	
Stuart, Sam	Fort Worth, Tx. CL, BF	1938–49	12-12-52
Sublett, Red	Fort Worth, Tx. CL, BF	1919–50	4-14-50
Sullivan, James C.	Cheyenne, Wy.	1962–90	
Sumerville, Bob "Slim"	Eugene, Or. BF	1953	
Sweet, Frank	Blackshear, Ga. CL, BF	1971–93	

Tacker, Ike	Rosebud, Tx. CL, BF	1945–58	
Tacker, J. T.	Sealy, Tx.	1940–50	
Tagg, Lloyd	Broomfield, Co.	1957	
Talimentez, Ray	BF	1991	
Tatham, Tom	Laramie, Wy. CL, BM	1964	
Tatum, John	Laveene, Az. BF	1960–80	
Tatum, Timothy E.	Wayross, Ga. CL	1991–93	
Taylor, George	Cleburne, Tx. CL, BF, BM	1956–83	
Taylor, Hubert "Brother"	Wimberley, Tx. CL, BM	1966–93	
Taylor, Jon "Chipmunk"	Agar, S.D. CL, BM	1970–93	
Taylor, Ronnie	Crandall, Ga. BF	1978–89	
Taylor, T. O.	Fort Worth, Tx. CL, BF	1968–75	
Temple, Jon	Joshua, Tx. CL, BF	1956–69	
Thompson, Billy	Wichita, Ks. CL	1934–37	
Thompson, Danny		1957	
Thompson, Squatty	Katy, Tx. CL, BF	1989–90	
Thorpe, Bill	Arcadia, Fl. BF, BM	1991	
Thrift, Wilmer	Cantonment, Fl. BF	1986–87	
Tinsley, Spike	Waverly, N.Y. BM	1940–41	
Tomac, Steven	St. Anthony, N.D.CL, BM	1970–93	
Travis, Jerry	Ankeny, Ia. CL, BF, BM	1974–93	
Travis, Martin	Polk City, Ia.	1986–89	
Tyler, George	Gainesville, Tx. CL, BF	1940s	5-31-83
Ulmer, Mike	Mt. Vernon, Mo. BM	1991	
Underwood, Lee	Wilburton, Ok. BF, BM	1991	
Urban, Glen		1976	
Urquides, Robert D.	Wickenburg, Az. CL	1991–93	
Van Alfen, John	Hooper, Ut. CL, BF	1970	
Vaughan, Gary	Madisonville, Tx. CL, BF	1988–90	
Veach, Ben	Missouri, CL	1940s	
Verbois, Jack		1964	
Vernon, Oke		1948	
Viers, Eric	Nevada, Ia. CL, BF	1979–87	
Villa, Pancho			
(George Ritchie)	BF	1937–51	
Vine, Ken	Magnolia, Ms. BF	1990–93	
Voss, Skipper	Grand Prairie, Tx. BF	1967–89	
Waddell, Tom	Brewster, Wa. CL, BF	1964–65	
Walden, Jeff	Cheyenne, Wy. BF	1980s	
Walker, Casey	Center Hill, Fl. CL	1988–93	
Walker, Marcel	Buckholtz, Tx.	1953	
Walls, Rusty	Muskogee, Ok. CL, BF	1978	
Waltz, Freddie	Joshua Tree, Ca. CL, BF, BM	1983–93	
Washborn, B. C.	California	1945	
Watson, Kenneth	Maryville, Ca. BF	1983–93	
Webb, L. Scott	Hickory, N.C. BF	1991	
Webb, Ronnie		1957	
Welch, Mike	Guy, Tx. BF, BM	1991	
West, Charlie "Too Tall"	Loomis, Ca. CL, BM	1982–93	
Wettach, Ed	Geyser, Mt. CL, BF	1974–75	

Wetterman, Tom	Hinkley, Ca. CL, BF	1984-90	
Wheaton, Lee		1960	
Whetsel, Joe	CL, BF	1948	
White, Bill		1979	
Wickizer, Dale	Tempe, Az. BM	1960-72	
Wiggins, Cactus	Phoenix, Az. CL	1955-70	
Wiggins, Sticker	Leona, Tx. CL, BF	1982-93	
Wiley, Raymond A.	Greenwood, La. CL, BF	1990-93	
Willett, David	Indianapolis, In. BF	1991	
Williams, Bonnie Eloise	Las Vegas, Nv. BM	1960-62	
Williams, H. R.	St. Grabriel, La. BF	1958-72	
Williams, Jess	Modesto, Ca. CL, BF	1963	
Williams, Paul	Owasso, Ok. BF, BM	1991	
Williams, Steve	Durant, Ok.	1978	
Williamson, Robert	Tyler, Tx. BF	1983-89	
Willis, Dan	Aquilla, Tx. BF	1972-80	
Willoughby, Gene		1956	
Wilson, John	Gustine, Ca. BF	1971	
Wise, Jim	Loveland, Co. CL, BF	1955-66	
Wizwell, Ernie	CL	1945	
Wofford, Earl		1960	
Womack, Andy	Phoenix, Az. BM	1947-91	1-15-92
Womack, Tim	Phoenix, Az. CL, BF	1966-70	
Wood, Dave	Chelsea, Ok. CL, BF	1956-57	
Woodard, Dale J.	French Camp, Ca. CL, BF, BM	1966-93	
Wright, Ed	Valley Center, Ca. CL	1918-25	3-31-75
Wylie, Doug	Fort Worth, Tx. BF	1980-87	
Yates, Don A.	Phoenix, Az. CL, BF	1991-93	
Young, Rick	Independence, La. CL, BF, BM	1974-93	
Zimmerman, Happy Herb	El Subrante, Ca.	1961-?	
Zundel, Bruce	Garland, Ut. BF	1980-87	

* CL – Clown
  BF – Bullfighter
  BM – Barrelman

Appendix B

PRCA NATIONAL FINALS CLOWNS AND ALTERNATES

YEAR		CLOWNS	AGE
1992		Loyd Ketchum, Miles City, Mt.	
		Joe Baumgartner, Brentwood, Ca.	
		*Dale Woodward, French Camp, Ca.	
1991		Rob Smets, Oakland, Or.	32
		Miles Hare, Ringling, Ok.	36
		*Leon Coffee, Austin, Tx.	37
1990		Rob Smets, Oakland, Or.	31
		Miles Hare, Oscar, Ok.	35
		*Butch Lehmkuhler, North Platte, Ne.	36
1989		Miles Hare, Oscar, Ok.	34
		Rob Smets, Oakland, Or.	30
		*Jess Franks, Farmington, N.M.	39
	alt.	Dwayne Hargo, Placerville, Ca.	28
	alt.	*Dale Woodard, French Camp, Ca.	43
1988		Miles Hare, Oscar, Ok.	33
		Mike Horton, Zolfo Springs, Fl.	26
		*Quail Dobbs, Coahoma, Tx.	47
	alt.	Rick Chatman, Rio Vista, Tx.	32
	alt.	*Jess Franks, Farmington, N.M.	38
1987		Rob Smets, Oakland, Or.	28
		Mike Horton, Zolfo Springs, Fl.	25
		*Ted Kimzey, Strong City, Ok.	35
	alt.	*Ryan Byrne, Prince Albert, Man.	24
1986		Rex Dunn, Hastings, Ok.	30
		Ryan Byrne, Prince Albert, Man.	23
		*J. G. Crouch, Killeen, Tx.	33
	alt.	Rob Smets, Roseburg, Or.	27
	alt.	*Ted Kimzey, Strong City, Ok.	34
1985		Miles Hare, Fort Worth, Tx.	30
		Rex Dunn, Hastings, Ok.	29
		*Quail Dobbs, Coahoma, Tx.	44
	alt.	Jimmie Anderson, Everman, Tx.	32
		*Tom Feller, Everman, Tx.	37
1984		Rick Chatman, Burleson, Tx.	28

		Leon Coffee, Austin, Tx.	30
		*Bobb, "Toad" Cook, Big Rapids, Mi.	42
	alt.	Miles Hare, Fort Worth, Tx.	29
1983		Rob Smets, Roseburg, Or.	24
		Rex Dunn, Hastings, Ok.	27
		*Jon Taylor, Crowley, Tx.	42
1982		Jimmy Anderson, Everman, Tx.	29
		David Burnham, Round Rock, Tx.	27
		*J. G, Crouch, Austin, Tx.	29
	alt.	Rick Chatman, Fort Worth, Tx.	26
	alt.	*Tom Feller, Everman, Tx.	34
1981		Rick Chatman, Fort Worth, Tx.	25
		Bill Shaw, Nacogdoches, Tx.	31
		*Tom Feller, Everman, Tx.	33
	alt.	Rob Smets, San Martin, Ca.	22
	alt.	*Jon Taylor, Crowley, Tx.	40
1980		Mike Moore, Austin, Tx.	24
		Rick Chatman, Fort Worth, Tx.	24
		*Ted Kimzey, Strong City, Ok.	28
	alt.	Rob Smets, San Martin, Ca.	21
	alt.	*Jon Taylor, Crowley, Tx.	39
1979		Leon Coffee, Austin, Tx.	25
		Wick Peth, Bow, Wa.	48
		*Jon Taylor, Crowley, Tx.	38
	alt.	*Tom Lucia, Weatherford, Tx.	38
	alt.	Mike Moore, Austin, Tx.	23
1978		*Quail Dobbs, Coahoma, Tx.	37
		Bob Donaldson, Golden, Co.	26
		Skipper Voss, Crosby, Tx.	34
1977		*Frank Rhoades, Deport, Tx.	55
		George Doak, Aledo, Tx.	40
		Miles Hare, Gordon, Ne.	22
	alt.	Tommy Sheffield, Rankin, Tx.	30
1976		Bob Romer, Canyon, Tx.	31
		Johnny Tatum, Laveen, Az.	33
		*Gary Parli, Caney, Ks.	31
	alt.	Jerry Mariluch, Elko, Ne.	23
	alt.	*Tom Feller, Everman, Tx.	27
1975		Wick Peth, Bow, Wa.	45
		Bobby McAfee, Henryetta, Ok.	24
		*Bunky Boger, Fayettville, Ar.	45
	alt.	Bob Romer, Canyon, Tx.	30
	alt.	*Gary Parli, Caney, Ks.	30
1974		Rick Young, Independence, La.	40
		Skipper Voss, Crosby, Tx.	30
		*Jon Taylor, Burbank, Ca.	33
	alt.	Wick Peth, Bow, Wa.	44
	alt.	*Gary Parli, Caney, Ks.	29
1973		Larry Clayman, Hylandville, Mo.	
		Jerry Olson, Belle Fourche, S.C.	38

		*Tom Lucia, Weatherford, Tx.	32
	alt.	Wick Peth, Bow, Wa.	43
	alt.	*Bunky Boger, Fayetteville, Ar.	43
1972		Quail Dobbs, Coahoma, Tx.	31
		Wilbur Plaugher, Fresno, Ca.	50
		*Wiley McCray, Brisco, Tx.	55
	alt.	Wick Peth, Bow, Wa.	42
	alt.	*Tom Lucia, Weatherford, Tx.	31
1971		George Doak, Fort Worth, Tx.	34
		Chuck Henson, Tucson, Az.	40
		*Frank Rhoades, Arlington, Tx.	49
	alt.	Karl Doering, Roseburg, Or.	41
	alt.	*Roger Mawson, Fort Smith, Ar.	37
1970		Bobby Clark, Warner, Ok.	40
		D. J. Gaudin, Teague, Tx.	41
		*Wright Howington, Colleyville, Tx.	30
1969		*Jimmy Schumacher, Phoenix, Az.	48
		*Frank Rhoades (replaced injured Schumacher)	
		Wick Peth, Bow, Wa.	39
		H. R. Williams, St. Gabriel, La.	29
1968		*Jimmy Schumacher, Phoenix, Az.	47
		Buck LeGrand, Morrison, Ok.	36
		Larry McKinney, Tucson, Az.	30
1967		*Jimmy Schumacher, Phoenix, Az.	46
		Buck LeGrand, Morrison, Ok.	35
		Chuck Henson, Tucson, Az.	36
1966		Wick Peth, Bow, Wa.	36
		*Jimmy Schumacher, Phoenix, Az.	45
1965		Buck LeGrand, Morrison, Ok.	34
		*Jimmy Schumacher, Phoenix, Az.	44
1964		Wick Peth, Bow, Wa.	34
		*Jimmy Schumacher, Billings, Mt.	43
1963		Wick Peth, Bow, Wa.	33
		*Jimmy Schumacher, Billings, Mt.	42
1962		Wick Peth, Bow, Wa.	32
		*Jimmy Schumacher, Billings, Mt.	41
1961		Wick Peth, Bow, Wa.	31
		*Wiley McCray, Vernon, Tx.	45
1960		D. J. Gaudin, Baton Rouge, La.	31
		Buck LeGrand, Ponca City, Ok.	29
		*Jimmy Schumacher, Billings, Mt.	39
1959		D. J. Gaudin, Baton Rouge, La.	30
		*Buck LeGrand, Ponca City, Ok.	28
		Gene Clark, Bakersfield, Ca.	33

*Barrelmen

Appendix C

PRCA CLOWN OF THE YEAR

YEAR	CLOWN
1992	Lecile Harris
1991	Butch Lehmkuhler
1990	Butch Lehmkuhler
1989	Butch Lehmkuhler
1988	Quail Dobbs
1987	Tom Feller
1986	Ted Kimzey
1985	Rex Dunn
1984	Rick Chatman
1983	Leon Coffee
1982	Wilbur Plaugher
1981	Tom Feller
1980	Rick Young
1979	Jon Taylor
1978	Quail Dobbs
1977	Chuck Henson

This award is presented to the PRCA bullfighter, barrelman, or clown who best exemplifies the image of the professional rodeo clown.

Appendix D

WRANGLER WORLD CHAMPION BULLFIGHTER

YEAR	CLOWN
1992	Ronny Sparks
1991	Loyd Ketchum
1990	Greg Rumohr
1989	Dwayne Hargo
1988	Rob Smets
	Miles Hare (tie)
1987	Mike Horton
1986	Rob Smets
1985	Rob Smets
1984	Rick Chatman
1983	Rob Smets
1982	Skipper Voss
1981	Miles Hare

This honor is won by collecting the most points in the Wrangler Bullfights throughout the year.

Appendix E

COORS "MAN IN THE CAN"

YEAR	CLOWN
1992	Butch Lehmkuhler
1991	Rick Young
1990	Quail Dobbs
1989	Butch Lehmkuhler
1988	J. G. Crouch
1987	Tom Feller
1986	Quail Dobbs
1985	Quail Dobbs
1984	Tom Feller

Initiated in 1984, this award is presented to the PRCA barrelman who scores highest in five different categories of professionalism, as judged by the twelve Wrangler Bullfight Tour participants, pro-rodeo announcers, and top bull riders.

Resource Material

[Reference numbers within text refer to this list.]

1. *Black Cowboys,* by Paul W. Stewart and Wallace Yvonne Ponce. Phillips Publishing, 1986.

2. *The Wild West,* by Don Russell. Amon Carter Museum, 1970.

3. *American Rodeo: From Buffalo Bill to Big Business,* by Kristine Fredriksson. Texas A&M University Press, 1985.

4. *My Fifty Years in Rodeo,* by Foghorn Clancy. The Naylor Co., 1948.

5. *Daddy of 'Em All: The Story of Cheyenne Frontier Days,* by Robert D. (Bob) Hanesworth. Flintrock Publishing, 1967.

6. *Rodeo Road: My Life as a Pioneer Cowgirl,* by Vera McGinnis. Hastings House, 1974.

7. *Rodeo Trails,* by Bill King. Jelm Mountain Press (Laramie), 1982.

8. *Western Horseman,* article by Jerry Armstrong. May 1965.

9. *Cheyenne Frontier Days, A Marker from Which to Reckon All Events,* by Milt Riske. Frontier Printing, 1984.

10. *Hoofs & Horns,* various issues, Ethel A. Hopkins, editor. Hoofs & Horns Publishing Co.

11. *Rodeo Sports News,* various issues. Published by the Rodeo Cowboys Association. 1974.

12. *ProRodeo Sports News,* various issues. Published by PRCA Properties, Inc.

13. *The Ketch Pen,* official publication of the Rodeo Historical Society.

14. *Jasbo,* by Wayne Ingram and Jane Pattie. The Naylor Co., 1959.

15. *Man, Beast, Dust: The Study of Rodeo,* by Clifford P. Westermeier. University of Nebraska Press, 1947.

16. *Rodeo: Back of the Chutes,* by Gene Lamb. 1956.

17. *Those Magnificent Cowgirls,* by Milt Riske. Wyoming Publishing, 1983.

18. *Who's Who in Rodeo,* by Willard Porter. Powder River Book Co.

19. *Rodeo—Cowboys, Bulls & Broncos,* by Sam Savitt. Doubleday, 1963.

20. *Rodeo: An Anthropologist Looks at the Wild and the Tame,* by Elizabeth Atwood Lawrence. University of Chicago Press, 1982.

21. *On Down the Road: The World of the Rodeo Cowboy,* by Bob St. John. Eakin Press, 1983.

22. *The Western Horseman,* "A Clown from Another Time" by Willard H. Porter. May 1984.

23. *The American Weekly,* May 1, 1949.

24. *The Daily Oklahoman* newspaper, "It's Time to Send in the Clowns," by Willard H. Porter.

25. *Let 'er Buck: A Story of the Passing of the Old West,* by Charles Wellington Furlong. G. P. Putnam's Sons, 1921.

26. *The Rodeo of John Addison Stryker,* by Ron Tyler. Encino Press, 1977.

27. *The Tulsa Daily World* newspaper.

28. *Book of Knowledge,* editor-in-chief Hollan D. Thompson. College of City of New York, 1938 edition.

29. *Life Magazine,* "Behind the Funny Act, A Life and Death Job—Rodeo Clown," by Colin Lofting. July 19, 1963.

30. *The Evening News* newspaper (Harrisburg, Pennsylvania). 1957.

31. *Austin American–Statesman* newspaper (Austin, Texas). April 15, 1989.

32. *Horse Talk News Daily Tally* newspaper (Las Vegas, Nevada), December 11, 1987.

33. *Austin American–Statesman* newspaper (Austin, Texas), August 1, 1989.

34. *Rocky Mountain News* newspaper (Denver, Colorado), August 1, 1989.

35. *Official Professional Rodeo Media Guide,* Professional Rodeo Cowboys Association, 1987, 1988, 1989, 1990.

36. *The Representative Old Cowboy Ed Wright,* by Edgar Wright. 1954.

37. *Recorder* newspaper (San Francisco, California).

38. *Tipperary: Diary of a Bucking Horse, 1905–1932,* Paul Hennessey. Sand Creek Printing, 1989.

39. *The Wild Bunch,* official publication of The Rodeo Hall of Fame, National Cowboy Hall of Fame and Western Heritage Center, Oklahoma City, Oklahoma.

Index